THE APOCALYPTIC VISION OF
MIKHAIL BULGAKOV'S
THE MASTER AND MARGARITA

THE APOCALYPTIC VISION OF MIKHAIL BULGAKOV'S *THE MASTER AND MARGARITA*

Edward E. Ericson, Jr.

Studies in Slavic Language and Literature
Volume 6

The Edwin Mellen Press
Lewiston/Queenston/Lampeter

Library of Congress Cataloging-in-Publication Data

This book has been registered with the Library of Congress.

This is volume 6 in the continuing series
Studies in Slavic Language and Literature
Volume 6   ISBN 0-7734-9766-8
SSLL Series   ISBN 0-88946-290-9

A CIP catalog record for this book
is available from the British Library.

The Edwin Mellen Press
Box 450
Lewiston, New York
USA 14092

The Edwin Mellen Press
Box 67
Queenston, Ontario
CANADA L0S 1L0

The Edwin Mellen Press, Ltd.
Lampeter, Dyfed, Wales
UNITED KINGDOM SA48 7DY

Printed in the United States of America

For Ed and Julie and Bill

TABLE OF CONTENTS

ACKNOWLEDGMENTS

This book has been some two decades in the making. In more than the usual way, it is a labor of love. Although during this period my normal duties were comprised of teaching undergraduate English courses, with all too many administrative assignments added in, I kept returning to *The Master and Margarita*, my favorite novel. I taught it to students at Northwestern College (Iowa) and Calvin College. I sought out persons who had read it, including some who had written about it. I combed bibliographies for works about it. I jotted down my own observations. In this long process I have accumulated more debts than I can fully acknowledge, and I beg the indulgence of those who know that they have helped me but whose names do not appear here.

My greatest debt is owed to Calvin College, a true academic community (tensions included) and therefore an excellent place to work. I pay special tribute to my colleagues in the English Department. Authentic, unforced, warm collegiality prevails. The department is an oasis of humaneness in the all-too-often inhumane world of the humanities. Also, I thank the college for its generous financial support. For my work on this book, I received a sabbatical, a substantial Calvin Research Fellowship, and a small grant for faculty research from the Alumni Association. My main editorial adviser on this project was our redoubtable colleague Richard R. Tiemersma, now Professor Emeritus of English. Departmental secretaries Alma Walhout and Barbara De Vos did their usual careful typing and retyping of the manuscript. Also, I received valuable aid from student assistants too numerous to recite. And Robert Alderink, the college's Manager of Publishing Services, demonstrated, in the preparation of the manuscript, the cooperativeness and competence which characterize this institution.

Many beyond the confines of Calvin also helped me on this work. Chief among them are Vladislav G. Krasnov, of the Monterey Institute of International Studies; Laura D. Weeks, of the College of the Holy Cross; and Paul D. Steeves, of Stetson University. These Slavic scholars helped me on things Russian, especially matters of language, and their encouragement saw me through times of self-doubt. Milorad Drachkovitch, of the Hoover Institution at Stanford University, gave a vital boost at an early stage to my layman's study of modern Russian writers, especially Solzhenitsyn and Bulgakov. Solzhenitsyn himself, when I described to him my thesis about *The Master and Margarita*, offered words of encouragement which I have much valued.

I have received financial support for this book from three outside agencies. The Earhart Foundation, of Ann Arbor, Michigan, and the Marguerite Eyer Wilbur Foundation, of Santa Barbara, California, gave me timely grants. And I was the recipient of a small grant for research from the University of Chicago, through the Occasional Fellowship Program of its Midwest Faculty Seminar.

Always there is my family to thank. My wife Jan is ever serenely indulgent of my quirks and works. My sons Ed and Bill have shown more interest in what I do as they themselves move in young adulthood toward academic careers. My daughter-in-law Julie adds sparkle to our family life.

Finally, I wish to pay my respects to Bulgakov critics, into whose company I have insinuated myself. Although my understanding of "our" novel is distinctive, generally they have framed the right questions, I think, and often they have pointed me in good directions. Although I cite many of them, and profusely, I have read many others whose works are not cited here. Among the uncited, Andrew Barratt deserves special mention. His book *Between Two Worlds: A Critical Introduction to the Master and Margarita* (Oxford) reached me too late in my composing process to be included, for I would have had to interact with it at many points. It may be that others will find our often competing interpretations stimulating.

When I am indebted to so many, it is especially important to say that the errors of understanding and expression in this volume are mine alone.

*   *   *

Grateful acknowledgment is given to the following for permission to quote from their publications.

Excerpts from *The Master and Margarita* translated by Michael Glenny.
    Copyright English translation ©1967 by the Harvill Press and Harper & Row, Publishers, Inc. Reprinted by permission of HarperCollins Publishers Inc.
Ernst Benz, *The Eastern Orthodox Church* (Chicago: Aldine Publishing Co., 1963). Reprinted in arrangement with Sanford J. Greenburger Associates, New York, NY.
Austin M. Farrer, *The Revelation of St. John the Divine* (Oxford: Clarendon Press, 1964). By permission of Oxford University Press.
Lesley Milne, *The Master and Margarita: A Comedy of Victory* (Birmingham, England: Birmingham Slavonic Monographs, 1977). By permission of Lesley Milne.
Ellendea Proffer, *Bulgakov: Life and Work* (Ann Arbor: Ardis, 1984). Copyright ©Ardis. By permission of Ardis.
From *The Method and Message of Jewish Apocalyptic*, by D. S. Russell. Published in the U.S.A. by the Westminster Press, 1964. Copyright ©SCM Press, Ltd., 1964. Used by permission of Westminster/John Knox Press.

Calvin College
Grand Rapids, Michigan
February 1, 1991

Chapter One

Introduction

❖ ❖

Two factors readily justify devoting full book-length treatment to *The Master and Margarita*. One is its high literary quality. On this point the testimony of the critics of the novel is virtually unanimous. The other is its complexity. This point every reader of the novel will immediately understand. It has been my experience that first-time readers of *The Master and Margarita* are fascinated and even enthralled by it. Yet they are well aware, as also are sophisticated literary critics, that there is much in the novel which they are missing. They sense that this is a novel which will reward, as few can, repeated reading and rereading. It contains, indeed, an "at times bewildering mass of detail."[1]

Mikhail Afanasyevich Bulgakov composed an extensive body of work. He wrote many plays, quite a few short stories, some novels, and innumerable *feuilletons*. A good number of these works are of very high quality and will probably be read for a long time to come. Even so, this one novel, *The Master and Margarita*, is worth more than all of his other works combined. In A. Colin Wright's words, "Although I would not agree with the not infrequently expressed view that Bulgakov produced only one important work, it is immediately evident that in *The Master and Margarita* his reflections upon life reach their deepest level."[2] At the least, there is a full agreement among Bulgakov critics that this novel is the author's greatest work.

There is solid evidence from the author's career that he viewed the novel as his masterpiece. Born in 1891, trained as a medical doctor, Bulgakov, who died in 1940, spent the last two decades of his life writing. Most of his works he composed relatively swiftly; he did not labor over each of them for years. But *The Master and Margarita* he labored over for more than a decade, sending it through eight separate revisions.[3] As he approached the end of his life, he abandoned all other projects (except for a few which he was under obligation to do) and focused his attention on this one. He was still putting finishing touches on it almost up to the time when he died.

It was more than a quarter of a century after Bulgakov's death that *The Master and Margarita* was published, appearing initially in the literary magazine *Moskva* (*Moscow*) in November 1966 and January 1967. Almost at once, it was translated into various languages, with two versions appearing in English. Unfortunately, the translation generally considered the better one, Mirra Ginsburg's, was of what turned out to be the censored version, as it appeared in *Moskva*. Therefore, the citations in the following chapters will come from the complete English text as translated by Michael Glenny.[4]

From the very beginning, reviewers of the novel almost uniformly recognized it as a great work of art and lavished praise upon it. According to Ernest J. Simmons, it "is probably destined to take its place among the few superb novels with universal appeal that have appeared in the USSR in the last fifty years."[5] Patricia Blake said, "Had *The Master and Margarita* appeared when it was completed...it would surely have long been considered a classic of 20th-century fiction."[6] Michael Glenny asserted that it "may well come to be regarded as the glory of twentieth-century Russian literature."[7] Helen Muchnic hailed it as "a major work of the twentieth century."[8] Donald Fanger declared that it "may well be one of the major novels of the Russian 20th century."[9]

Two decades have passed since the novel was greeted with those initial encomia. A quite large body of criticism has developed around it. Indeed, one critic notes that *The Master and Margarita* "has become one of the most studied of all twentieth-century Russian novels, surpassing in recent years even *Doctor Zhivago* in terms of Western and Soviet scholarly industry."[10] Another observes, "The number of critical articles since the book's appearance is staggering: for indeed *The Master and Margarita* seems to demand interpretation."[11]

The later critics are as insistent as the early reviewers in their high view of the work. Wright, author of the first book-length general study of Bulgakov published in the West, calls Bulgakov "one of the major Soviet writers" and ranks *The Master and Margarita* among the greatest works of the Soviet period.[12] T. R. N. Edwards considers *The Master and Margarita* "a novel which ranks among the most important of this century and a worthy inheritor of the great nineteenth-century tradition it so often recalls."[13] Edythe Haber declares, "From the first the novel was recognized both for its literary merit and for its enigmatic quality, and numerous literary scholars and critics took upon themselves the demanding yet exhilarating task of wending their way through the maze of plot and subplot, literary, religious, and socio-historical allusions."[14] Providing a summary statement applicable to these and many other similar comments, Nadine Natov notes that Bulgakov, "since the late 1960s, has been considered one of the most outstanding writers of the twentieth century."[15]

Thus, it should come as no surprise that already Bulgakov has been the subject of several books, many dissertations, scores of articles, two special issues of scholarly journals, and separate sectional meetings at professional conventions. The lion's share of the attention has gone to *The Master and Margarita*.

Nearly as widespread as the early reviewers' high praise for the literary quality of *The Master and Margarita* was their acknowledgment that the novel is laden with spiritual significance. Theodore Solotaroff, for instance, said, "...a satire on the vices and follies of Bolshevik materialism is enclosed within a supernatural setting and framed by Christian values.... Bulgakov was a modernist and a moralist through whom flowed the deep religious current of Russian culture."[16] Similarly, Muchnic observed, "Interested in...man as believer rather than doer, he always began with the actualities of Soviet Russia, but saw them in the context of a larger philosophical scheme...."[17] Howe stated, "Bulgakov's version of the Christ story approximates the spirit of primitive Christianity...."[18]

Once again, the later critics have generally followed suit. Val Bolen finds the novel to be "rich in philosophical implications."[19] Lesley Milne speaks of "the ultimate supremacy of the spiritual over the material" in the novel.[20] Beatie and Powell call the conclusion "a religious epiphany."[21] D. G. B. Piper notes, "Bulgakov himself remained a Christian throughout his life...."[22] Wright observes, "The values he admired are essentially those of the Christian intellectual middle class...."[23] Donald Fiene specifies, "Yet for all of Bulgakov's cheerful irreverence, a truly Christian theme emerges in his work."[24]

I do not mean to suggest that the particular theological reading offered in this book is supported by these and other critics who remark on the presence in Bulgakov's novel of religious categories. Indeed, to name one, Piper's interpretation could hardly be further from mine than it is; he insists upon "the unorthodox nature of his [Bulgakov's] beliefs,"[25] and this view seems to be the majority opinion, in one variant or another. I mean to suggest only that it is not unreasonable to look to Christian theology to see what clues it might provide for the unraveling of the meaning of this book. And I believe that such an approach yields fruitful results—indeed, results far more fruitful than have yet been realized. No one can miss the almost ubiquitous biblical and religious allusions. The challenge is to find the pattern of meaning underlying Bulgakov's use of them.

We have available some external evidence that Bulgakov considered himself a spiritual writer. In a now famous letter to the Soviet government, he described himself as a "mystical writer."[26] None of his works fits so well this cryptic self-description as does *The Master and Margarita*, and it is the case that by the time of the letter he was at work on this novel. To cite the words of Lesley Milne, "There is some evidence that Bulgakov himself regarded *The Master and Margarita* as a 'philosophical novel' and it therefore merits consideration as such."[27] Bulgakov's third wife, Elena Sergeevna, in a letter to her mother, described the novel as "a very original thing and philosophical."[28] Since she was intimately involved in the composition of the novel, it seems correct to remark, "...it is likely she was expressing Bulgakov's own conception of the novel."[29]

Although not every critic has homed in on the spiritual and cosmic themes of the novel, the reviewers and critics cited above, as well as others not cited, have pointed the reader in the correct direction. Still, to borrow the phrasings of the early reviewers, what is the larger philosophical scheme? What are the universal implications? What are the grave matters of eternal importance? What are the Christian values? What is the theology? What is Bulgakov's relationship to the religious current of Russian culture? Their exceptional haziness in providing even the bare outlines for explicating the novel is mute testimony to its extreme complexity.

The critics who followed the initial reviewers have endeavored to solve the problem. Some have settled, quite consciously, for chipping off pieces of the novel's meaning—a worthy task, to be sure. Others have sought to go further and to provide a paradigm for the understanding of the novel as a whole. The fact remains, however, that none of these analyses has said quite what I believe needs saying if we are to penetrate the heart of *The Master and Margarita*.

That is to say, we are faced even now with the issue which Irving Howe raised early and accurately:

> *The Master and Margarita* is a very difficult book. Those reviews I have seen mostly skirt the critical problem it raises: the reviewers declare it a splendid novel and a work of spiritual force, all of which is true, but they do not offer a coherent account of plot, character, and theme. That such an account can be offered after a first reading I doubt; whether it would be possible after several readings I am not sure..... It is as if all the pieces of the puzzle were there, but the pattern had not yet become visible.[30]

Michael Glenny early sounded a similar note:

> As a philosophical disquisition in a fictional vehicle it is extra-ordinarily stimulating, yet it leaves a sense that there is still something missing; there is a feeling that Bulgakov just failed to place the keystone on his philosophical construct.[31]

Quite interestingly, despite the considerable work done in the meantime, the same note of puzzlement continues to be voiced. For instance, Judy Ullman, in her 1976 doctoral dissertation on the novel, says that "...despite some fine efforts, a convincing detailed interpretation of the entire book needs to be written."[32] In her dissertation of the same year, Shirley Gutry calls the novel "a complex and even baffling book."[33] Glenny says, "Bulgakov loved mystification. His use of it was intentional...."[34] David Bethea goes so far as to assert, "Let it be said that there is no single interpretation, no single blade to sever the Gordian knot of *The Master and Margarita*."[35] Haber summarizes well: the criticism of *The Master and Margarita* has "not thus far produced a consensus either as to its structural principles or its meaning."[36]

The central critical problem posed by the novel itself is the presence within it of three very different strands of plot which become intricately intertwined as the novel advances, so that "many levels"[37] and "baffling correspondences"[38] appear among the characters and events in the separate plots. Later critics agree with early reviewers on this point as well. However, the critics, unlike the reviewers,[39] have been, in general, quite emphatic that *The Master and Margarita* is an essentially complete work.

Any writer of a book knows that a book is never really finished. Always, more could be said. But we can summarize the case for the finished status of this book by citing representative remarks from critics. Lakshin notes that "not everything in it has been polished evenly and finally...."[40] Milne notes that "death overtook Bulgakov before he had time to complete the correction of his manuscript." But she immediately adds, "The misplaced pieces, however, are details which do not affect the main lines of the novel's structure."[41] Ellendea Proffer declares that the novel was finished and even bound.[42] Citing details of dates, Beatie and Powell conclude, "The novel was complete."[43] Bolen suggests that the presence of "thematic coherence" in the novel is evidence of its essential completeness.[44]

Marietta Chudakova has given us the details that we need in order to rest confident in the essential completeness of the novel. She tells us, for instance, that in 1938 Bulgakov's wife wrote in a letter that "he wants to do the final corrections on his novel, which he finished this summer...."[45] In 1940, shortly before Bulgakov died, his wife was reading to her now blind husband the passage about Berlioz's funeral. He stopped her and said, "So, it is enough."[46] The work could go as it was. Chudakova is correct in concluding, "The extensiveness of the insertions and corrections in the first part and the beginning of the second indicates that at least as much work was envisioned for the remaining parts, but the author did not succeed in finishing it."[47] Final polishing was not completed; the novel itself was.

Given the above, we must return to Howe's early question: can there be a coherent account of this novel? Did Bulgakov "place the keystone on his philosophical construct"?

The purpose of this book is to answer Howe's question affirmatively by giving a specific reading of the novel. Further, this book proposes to amass evidence for that reading—evidence which, if it is to be persuasive, must depend on its cumulative weight. The novel is as complex and puzzling as Howe and many later commentators have said that it is. No single study, even one of book length, can explain all of the details in it. This study is designed to open the main door of the mansion, to open many of the rooms inside, to peek into others, and to indicate some of the doors which remain closed.

But let it be said at this point that the simplest sample of the difficulty which this novel poses, especially for first-time readers, is that the key to understanding it comes only in the final chapters.

The exceptionally complex interweaving of the three plots makes difficult a clear organization of the explication of *The Master and Margarita*. The approach of this study is to begin with an extended summary of the argument with a minimum of documentation from the novel itself, plus a chapter on theological background, to be followed by a detailed discussion, with expansive documentation, of the three plots; the study concludes with an examination of the final section of the novel, the place in which Bulgakov gives us the keys to his artistic kingdom. That is to say, one can know this general interpretation by reading the second chapter, "Overview." But the case for the interpretation will not be complete apart from the rest of the volume.

However, before proceeding to the body of this work, I must address two additional matters. The first, and the lesser of the two, has to do with my handling of the evidence from the novel. The serious student of the novel quickly becomes aware, as other published studies have demonstrated, that Bulgakov often gives important clues in little details. So it is difficult to avoid the bane of earnest literary critics, that of over-interpreting. At the same time, one who senses Bulgakov's playfulness is left with the uneasy feeling that he is not sure when Bulgakov is pulling his leg and when he is dropping serious clues. The lack of final polishing of Book Two adds to the interpreter's sense of unease. My own approach is to take the risk of occasionally looking silly about certain details, secure in the belief that most of the time I am doing an appropriate task. Bulgakov was a very learned man, and so I have chosen to take the risk of erring occasionally on the side of over-interpreting.

The second matter has to do with religion. It is my settled conviction, after more than twenty readings of this novel, that *The Master and Margarita* is Mikhail Bulgakov's spiritual—specifically, Christian—testament. Although he kept trying, during his career, to write things which the authorities would find acceptable, this one time he would write what he really felt and believed—let the devil be damned.

There are obvious external facts validating the search for Christian significance in Mikhail Bulgakov's work. His father was a professor of theology. His father's cousin, thus Mikhail's second cousin, was the famous theologian Sergius Bulgakov. It is beyond question that Mikhail Bulgakov, whatever his view of the institutional church, had a thorough knowledge of Christian, and particularly Russian Orthodox, theology. So perhaps we should not be surprised when we read that Valentin Kataev, a writer of note and a sometime friend of Bulgakov, said of him, "His moral code contained all the preachings of the Old and New Testaments, as if they were unconditional."[48]

Then, there is that most intriguing statement by the author himself about having written a work stimulated by his mother and wanting to write one stimulated by his theologian father. The author said, "If my mother served as a stimulus for the creation of the novel *The White Guard*, then according to my plans the figure of my father is to be the starting point for another work that I have in mind."[49] Milne comments:

> If Bulgakov actually carried out this creative plan, then a strong case can be made for *The Master and Margarita* as the work in question; there is no other of his works so likely to have been inspired by the memory of a Professor of Theology.[50]

Of course, external evidence, even if it were more extensive than it is in this case, is inconclusive in and of itself. For purposes of this book, it is significant only if the ensuing presentation of evidence internal to the novel is convincing. But, I repeat, I believe that Christian theology is the key which unlocks the main door to the magnificent edifice which is *The Master and Margarita*.

If my approach turns out to be correct, I would suggest that Bulgakov's intention, and a clearly considered one at that, was to write primarily for those who have eyes to see and ears to hear. Specifically, he wanted, according to this supposition, to sneak past the censors something which they would forbid if they understood what it said. Eventually, so the hypothesis continues, the truth would out, but by then it would be too late to withdraw the book. Persons without sympathy for the outlook of the author, the censors in particular, would not see the import of the work until it was too late.

Some small evidence of the justness of my approach is that the Soviet officials who initially censored the novel for *Moskva* did so on a basis which makes little, if any, sense. True, their chopping predictably took out certain satirical passages having to do with nudity, social problems such as the housing shortage, and occasional passages referring to Jesus Christ. However, the censors allowed equally offensive passages to remain. There seems, in retrospect, little rhyme or reason to these cuts. The censors did not know what Bulgakov was up to. It may even be the case, since most of the cuts were toward the end of the novel, that their primary concern was to fit the text into an assigned space limit. Of course, for a novel in which meaning comes into clear focus only toward the end, such cuts are deeply damaging.

Despite the pluralism which prevails in literary criticism today, religion remains a delicate subject, because deep beliefs are at stake, beliefs which frequently govern one's self-definition. Recent literary theory has paid considerable attention to the responses of readers to the text under consideration. Though this study is old-fashioned in the sense that it keeps its focus tightly on the text itself, it is well understood today that readers bring to a text their life experiences and outlooks, even if sometimes unconsciously; that is, no one is a neutral, value-free observer. If my view is correct that Christian theology is not only helpful but necessary to a full and proper appreciation of *The Master and Margarita*, then each reader's attitude toward religion and theology comes into play. It is good for this matter to be one of conscious awareness.

To find in Christian theology a key to understanding a writer is not at all to ascribe to that person a practiced commitment to an organized church. John Milton, in his later years, is a prime case in point. Many similar cases abound in which persons who do not participate in the exercises of organized religion are still deeply committed to theological convictions which ordinarily have their external manifestations in churchmanship. Mikhail Bulgakov did not need to be a churchman himself to experience, at the deepest level of his being, a strong tug toward the beliefs of his theologian-and-churchman father. It is theology, not personal religious practice, which is involved in this study.

Whether or not this theological reading of *The Master and Margarita* bears up under scrutiny, readers might simply to try to imagine what a Christian author would do with the elements of this novel if he were to start with the idea of writing a fictional version of his Christian vision—and decided to do so by means of the ultimate parody of having Satan represent God and having Satan as the inspirer of the Gospel story. Granted that much, what would a

Christian author living in the Soviet Union have done differently from what Bulgakov did? Granted that much, is there anything in *The Master and Margarita* which clearly cannot be interpreted consistently and coherently according to the pattern which the following chapters unfold?

Yet, even so, and as intriguing as such speculative questions may be, the focus of this book is not biography but textual interpretation. In this study, with its hypothesis of coherence of meaning, it is the internal evidence which counts.

Chapter Two

Overview

❖ ❖

The premise of this book is that the key clue to discerning the pattern which runs through *The Master and Margarita* is orthodox Christian doctrine, particularly as it is expressed by Eastern (specifically, Russian) Orthodoxy. That theological context will be discussed in Chapter Three. This chapter sticks to the novel. However, for all of their apparent differences, these two chapters fit together as a unit and should be read as such.

It must be understood that all of orthodox Christian theology, whether Western (Catholic and Protestant) or Eastern, agrees on central doctrines. The Apostles' Creed is a fair summary applying to both. Both belong to the Occident, not to the Orient—that is, to Europe and its Christianity, not to Asia and its distinctive religions (Buddhism, Hinduism, and others). But it must also be understood that there are some not insignificant variations between the branches of Christendom. When these differences surface, it is to the Eastern, not to the Western, part of Christendom that we must look for light on *The Master and Margarita*. Thus, one who is reared on Western Christian theology or has studied it may easily misread Bulgakov's theological references and borrowings.

The above distinction may be seen most pointedly in that area of theology which is of special interest to the Eastern Christian Church: eschatology, the doctrine of last things leading to the consummation of human history. The Eastern Church pays more attention than the Western one does to the apocalyptic vision of judgment and resurrection. This doctrinal matter, as we shall see, figures substantially in *The Master and Margarita*.

But, first, let us observe simply that all of the essential elements of the Christian world view are to be found in the novel: the creation of man in the image of God, human depravity, a moral universe in which beliefs and actions have their inevitable consequences, divine providence, a personal God who intervenes in human history, a personal Devil who does likewise, the intimate relation between the supernatural and the natural realms, the centrality of the Incarnation (God taking on human form), the vicarious atonement by Christ through his death and resurrection, Christ's descent into hell, Christ's intercession for sinful man, the forgiveness of sin, the judgment of evil, the resurrection of the body, the life everlasting, heaven and hell. This list is virtually a summary of the venerable Apostles' Creed, which antedates the split between the Eastern and the Western Churches.

Beyond this list of Christian teachings, we have internal evidence from the novel of Bulgakov's familiarity with and interest in religious matters, some of them abstruse. In the very opening chapter Bulgakov mentions Philo, Josephus Flavius, and Tacitus; the Egyptian god Osiris, the Phoenician Tammuz and Adonis, the Babylonian Marduk, the Aztec Vitli-Putzli, the Phrygian Attis, the Persian Mithras; and the religious thought of Kant, Schiller, and Strauss.[1] And, of course, four chapters of this novel are devoted to a retelling of the story of Jesus Christ and Pontius Pilate.

Almost all critics who have commented on *The Master and Margarita* have recognized Bulgakov's interest in matters religious. The question is what to make of it. Probably the most common general approach is to say that Bulgakov makes free use of these materials, especially the biblical ones, for purposes of allusion but that any religious viewpoint which he may be expressing is pointedly not one which could be called orthodox. Maybe it is some heretical strain like Gnosticism or Manichaeism; but it is not orthodox Christian. To this issue we shall return at various times.

We can begin to penetrate this complex novel by breaking it down into its three distinct strands of plot—though they are intertwined and not kept separate. The first plot to surface is the appearance in Moscow of the Devil and his retinue. The second plot is the story of Pilate and Jesus, focusing on the latter's trial, death, and burial. The third is about two Muscovites: a man without a name, who is called simply the Master and who is writing a novel about Jesus and Pilate, and a woman who loves him, named Margarita. These two characters interact with the supernatural characters of the other two plots, and it is their story, the title plot, which pulls all three plots together. The result is an artful orchestration of the three plots which imposes a unity upon the extremely divergent basic materials.

Thus, the natural and the supernatural realms are inextricably bound together. And this is surely the main theme of the novel, the one which comprehends all others. God and man are bound together. Reality cannot be circumscribed by nature alone. Any outlook which denies the ontological reality of the supernatural—classical Marxism, for instance, or any variant of it operative in the Soviet Union—is therefore pathetically inadequate to explain the reality of the human condition.

The novel both opens and closes with an emphatic insistence on the facticity and historicity of the events and personages described therein. When in the opening pages Satan appears to two writers who are good Soviet atheists, their immediate reaction is, "It can't be!" (p. 4). Indeed, it cannot be—according to their view of reality. Bulgakov's comment, *in propria persona*, is, "But alas it was..." (p. 4).

Or was that Bulgakov speaking? Or a narrator separate from the author? It is a critical commonplace to draw a sharp distinction between an author and his narrator; this approach often yields fruitful results and is sometimes positively necessary. Critics have brought up the matter with regard to this novel.[2] Whereas the question of who tells the Pilate chapters is a difficult one, which will be discussed later in this chapter, the issue at hand is the narrator of the Moscow chapters, which comprise the bulk of the novel. As interesting as the discussions of the narrative voice(s) are, no earth-shaking conclusions come out of them. The narrator's voice does seem sometimes ironic and knowing, sometimes naive, and so on. But Bulgakov loves to play tricks and can change his tone and mood to fit the occasion and his whim. So it seems fair to blur the distinction between Bulgakov and his narrator, treating the two as the same.

In any case, there can be no question that, when in the opening chapter the two writers try to persuade Satan that Jesus Christ never existed (the official Soviet line), the Devil imperiously controverts them: "Jesus did exist, you know.... It's not a question of having an attitude.... He existed, that's all there is to it" (p. 14).

The end of the novel, the Epilogue, returns to the theme of facticity. After all of the cavortings of Satan and company are concluded, the "educated and cultured people" (p. 383) reject the incontrovertible evidence that supernatural powers had visited their city. "A reason was found for everything, and one must admit that the explanations were undeniably sensible" (p. 385). (Surely, here the narrator is ironic and knowing, not naive.) The problem, though, is that the events were supra-sensible; they were beyond the range of normal empirical investigation, so that, at best, "*nearly* everything was explained away" (p. 387, emphasis added). The naturalistic explanations are clearly unsatisfactory and incredible—long-distance hypnotism, mass hypnotism, astounding feats of ventriloquism, and the like. Readers easily sense that Bulgakov wants them to see that these "plausible" reasons are the truly implausible ones.

Thus, early and late, Bulgakov separates himself from those who hold a naturalistic, materialist world view, and in the Epilogue he even mocks them:

> But facts, as they say, are facts, and they could not be brushed aside without some explanation: someone had come to Moscow. The few charred cinders which were all that was left of Griboyedov, and much more besides, were eloquent proof of it. (p. 383)

In this envelope structure of anti-naturalism is a plain warning by Bulgakov about how his novel is *not* to be read. Therefore, it is ironic, though obviously anticipated by the author, that a good number of the published readings of the novel have fallen victim to precisely the error which the author was at pains to warn against.

Closely related to this theme of natural-supernatural interaction (Orthodoxy makes the point most emphatically) is the insistence on divine providence, another subject which appears near the beginning and the ending of the book.

God controls the world which he has made, and he intervenes in the affairs of men and women, those beings whom he created in his own image. Satan early drops broad hints about providence when he queries the two atheistic writers: "But this is the question that disturbs me—if there is no God, then who, one wonders, rules the life of man and keeps the world in order?" (p. 10). This being, superior to humans, must chortle inwardly as he receives the reply, "Man rules himself" (p. 10). He remarks the folly of such a view, since "to rule, one must have a precise plan worked out for some reasonable period into the future" (p. 10), which mankind clearly does not have. Satan then ominously suggests that a sudden death can end a man's life when he least expects it, and he goes on to prophesy the imminent death of one of them, the literary authority Berlioz. And, shortly thereafter, the death occurs, just as Satan had foretold. Satan knows of the reality of the supernatural realm which Berlioz and his fellow naturalists deny.

Not only so, but Satan knows more: that it is God and not Satan who ultimately rules. He announces his own limitations (p. 283). His department may be large; but it is only one department, and it has limits. The point is made very sharply in an earlier version, the rough draft dated 1934. In it the last conversation between Woland and the Master goes as follows:

> "I have received instructions concerning you. Very favorable ones. In general I can congratulate you—you have succeeded. I was ordered..."
> "Can they really order you?"
> "Oh, yes. I was ordered to take you...."[3]

It is the Devil himself who assures the heroine, Margarita, of the operation of a benevolent divine providence: "All will be as it should; that is how the world is made" (p. 379).

If it is correct that Bulgakov wished to highlight the theme of the intermixture of the natural and the supernatural, how in terms of fictive technique could he go about doing so? He chose as his primary vehicle the deployment of fantasy—fantasy always mingled with realistic accounts. Bulgakov had demonstrated in works prior to *The Master and Margarita* a taste for a Gogolian strain of fantasy. But in this culminating work he puts this device to the service of a larger, cosmic purpose than it serves elsewhere.

Late in the novel Bulgakov says that "tiny grains of truth were embellished with a luxuriant growth of fantasy" (p. 338), and therein he provides a clue not only to how the novel is to be read but also to the difficulty in discerning the novelist's intent. One must see through the camouflaging effect of the luxuriant fantasy. (Sometimes critics get lost in it.) Bulgakov's vision of life is presented subtly, suggestively, allusively; but it is there, to be discovered by the persevering reader.

The context of the clause quoted in the preceding paragraph is significant. Unbelieving Muscovites pass along wild rumors about the strange events which they and their fellow citizens have experienced. But even in their inaccurate accounts there is present the element of abiding truth, though they do not have eyes properly trained to see it.

Not only is the fantasy an obstacle to immediate perception of Bulgakov's purpose, but the author compounds the reader's problem by his ongoing but eccentric use of symbolism. Much of this study is, therefore, of necessity devoted to explicating this intricate symbolism. The novel is loaded with details which have no apparent significance, apart from a symbolic reading. It is precisely because of the symbolism that Bulgakov is able to insist on calling his fantastic tale "a true story" (p. 212), a "truthful account" (p. 390). It is worth noting that these two assertions are placed strategically at the ends of Book I and Book II, respectively. The story is true because what is represented symbolically in the novel is the story of human life in all of its richness and complexity.

Of all of Bulgakov's devices for intentional obfuscation, perhaps the most perplexing one is that the symbols do not hold steady throughout the novel but keep shifting. The best image is that of a kaleidoscope. The task is to sort out the kaleidoscopic melange of multi-layered and overlapping levels of meaning.

The use of parallels is a familiar device in Bulgakov's works. For example, in his play *A Cabal of Hypocrites* Bulgakov draws parallels between King Louis XIV and Stalin, theistic religion and atheistic Communism, priests and the literary establishment, the Cabal of the Holy Writ and the Union of Soviet Writers, and Molière and himself.[4] But these parallels hold steady in a way that the symbols in *The Master and Margarita* do not. A work which relies on parallelism to convey its meaning sometimes seems to cry out for an allegorical interpretation, that is, one in which the correspondences hold steady throughout. But *The Master and Margarita* does not yield itself to that kind of neat schematization; its correspondences do not hold in a constant one-to-one relationship throughout.

Thus, at one time the Master is a disciple of Yeshua Ha-Notsri (Jesus of Nazareth), and at other times the Master is followed by Margarita and Bezdomny. At yet other times he represents variously the Creator, Everyman, and Bulgakov himself. (We shall examine in Chapter Six the autobiographical component in the novel.) Pilate at times represents oppressive state authority, presumably including Stalin, and at other times he is a follower (or a quasi-follower, a searcher) after Jesus. He has his own faithful disciple, the dog Banga. Margarita sometimes represents mankind, sometimes the Virgin Mary, sometimes the Church, sometimes the female principle, sometimes Bulgakov's wife Elena. Satan (Woland) is sometimes his literal self, sometimes Stalin; at other times, through parody (the ultimate parody), he represents God. A further complication is that a character may play more than one role at the same time.

The symbolism in the novel is not at all limited to the correspondences adhering to the characters. However, the symbolism attaching to the sun, the moon, roses, colors, and so on does not share in the shifting nature of that involving persons.

Although these correspondences may seem fanciful or even untenable when presented as bald assertions, they will become credible as the explication of later chapters proceeds. For now, though, let us ask why Bulgakov developed this elaborate kaleidoscope of symbolic correspondences. The answer, I believe, is to be found in Christian theology—again, particularly, Eastern Orthodox theology. Life, for Bulgakov, cannot be explained neatly, mechanistically. It always contains the element of mystery, and mystery is at the heart of Christian theology. The supernatural realm is beyond man's exhaustive knowledge; man can approach it only through metaphors, analogies, symbols—as parts of the next chapter will explain.

As though things were not difficult enough by now, there is an additional major complication. The correspondences in the novel are not only shifting ones; they are also generally oblique, often even skewed and distorted. For instance, Yeshua Ha-Notsri has only one disciple, Matthew, intead of the biblical twelve. There is only one account of Jesus' life, Matthew's, instead of the canonical four. Then, Matthew takes on the role of other individual disciples, as well. Bulgakov transfers Peter's denial of Christ to Matthew; he has Matthew, not Nathaniel, sitting under the fig tree. The four devils who accompany Satan to Moscow represent all of the fallen angels, though they do so asymmetrically. Similarly, the Master and Margarita represent mankind only in a fragmentary and asymmetrical form.

The obliqueness of the symbolic correspondences allows Bulgakov a kind of economy. He can use just a few details to stand for much. He needs to use only enough to suggest the parallel.

The reason why Bulgakov's correspondences can be called oblique and yet be considered legitimate is that the author relies heavily on parody. Indeed, the principle of parody is well-nigh omnipresent in the novel—almost as all-pervasive as the moon. And there is a direct relationship between these two. Most of the events happen "by the light of the moon, deceptive as it always is" (p. 460). The moon has no light of its own but merely reflects and in a sense imitates, or parodies, the light of the sun. Thus, in *The Master and Margarita* it is quite often the case that events and characters are not seen in their true aspect but only through the filter of the dim and inevitably distorting light of the moon. Moonlight is Bulgakov's device for presenting St. Paul's dictum, "Now we see through a glass, darkly" (I Corinthians 13:12). It is easy to misapprehend that which is seen only by moonlight.

The sun-moon antinomy serves two other purposes in the novel. One is that these heavenly bodies serve as natural symbols for the Kingdom of Light and the Kingdom of Darkness. When the moon is shining, men and events are under the influence of Satan. Satan's Ball occurs at midnight. In contrast, good events, such as Margarita's daily visits to the Master at noon, occur by sunlight. Jesus' death, an event which all believers in him consider the supreme good, occurred during daytime hours, with the moon absent.

A second purpose of the sun-moon antinomy is that it serves as an imagistic device to help unify the disparate elements. A Soviet critic has observed, regarding "the master's beloved Moscow and Pontius Pilate's hated, barbarous Jerusalem," that it is the presence of the sun and the moon that "artfully links the episodes so remote in space and time.... The two heavenly luminaries, alternately shedding their light on earth, almost become partici-pants in the events, active forces in the novel."[5]

Similar to the sun-moon imagery and directly related to it is the substance-shadow juxtaposition. As usual, Bulgakov waits until late in the novel to offer the following explanation, spoken by Satan to Matthew when the latter is sent on a mission to earth by his now glorified Master, Yeshua:

> You spoke your words as though you denied the very existence of shadows or of evil. Think, now: where would your good be if there were no evil and what would the world look like without shadow? Shadows are thrown by people and things. There's the shadow of my sword, for instance. But shadows are also cast by trees and living beings. Do you want to strip the whole globe by removing every tree and every creature to satisfy your fantasy of a bare world? You're stupid (p. 357).

As evil is the shadow of good, so Satan is offered as the shadow of God. However, shadows do not have an independent existence of their own; they depend upon the substance for their very existence. Bulgakov is no Manichaean, who posits eternally warring and equally powerful Forces of Good and Evil in the universe. As has been noted earlier, Bulgakov's Satan is the very one who acknowledges that he operates just one department and is not omnipotent (p. 283). He never declares his independence from God. Just the opposite is true. Woland is well aware that he is an instrument whom God uses to carry out his purposes on earth, regardless of Satan's preferences.

It was St. Augustine, himself at an early time in his life a Manichaean, who formulated the classic Christian statement on the subordinate and dependent status of evil in relation to good. Two brief citations suffice for our purposes: "...evil has no positive nature; what we call evil is merely the lack of something that is good"; and "...absolutely no natural reality is evil and the only meaning of the word 'evil' is the privation of good."[6] The general context for these passages includes, interestingly, a discussion of angels, particularly fallen angels, in which Augustine makes precisely the point that God uses the Devil's wickedness for his, God's, own good purposes. In the same general passage, while discussing good and evil, fallen and unfallen angels, Augustine also discusses light and darkness, sun and moon. It is not necessary to demonstrate that Bulgakov drew directly from Augustine on these matters, though he was so learned that he almost surely knew this eminent Church Father first-hand. The point is that this conjunction of ideas and images is natural and fitting for use by an orthodox Christian.

It is in this context that we must understand the epigraph to the novel:

> Say at last—who art thou?
> That Power I serve
> Which wills forever evil
> yet does forever good.

This epigraph is borrowed from Goethe's *Faust*. Critics have expended considerable energy exploring the relationship between *The Master and Margarita* and *Faust*. An early and often-cited article on this subject is Elisabeth Stenbock-Fermor's.[7] Details in later chapters will demonstrate that, however important *Faust* was in the early stages of the writing of the novel—and it certainly played a major role then—it has only a tangential relationship to the final version of *The Master and Margarita*. There are just too many divergences on crucial matters, and it is not very fruitful to extend to Woland the treatment of Mephistopheles by Goethe. Also, the Master turns out to be most unlike Faust. The only human being who somewhat resembles Faust is Margarita. But, then, what happens to any ostensible connection between her and Gretchen? Frieda, a minor character, comes closer to a linkage with Gretchen than Margarita does. In short, it seems that Bulgakov Christianizes the epigraph which he takes from *Faust*. It is not Goethe but Orthodox theology which serves to illuminate the heart of Bulgakov's novel.

It must be noted that a number of critics have chosen to label Bulgakov a Manichee. Ellendea Proffer, for one, asserts that "there can be little doubt" that Bulgakov "was influenced" by the Manichaean "way of explaining the world."[8] (Her vagueness here is not unusual for critics on this subject.) Glenny sees Bulgakov as "very close to a Manichaean position...."[9] (Again, note the vagueness. How close is *very close*?) T. R. N. Edwards says, "Hatred of worldly things and joy in destruction point towards a definite Manichaeism in *The Master and Margarita*...."[10] Both Glenny and Edwards go on to note that early in the novel there appears a reference to Herbert Aurilachs, described as a ninth-century necromancer.

A full article, by Laszlo Tikos, has been devoted to this single reference.[11] Insisting that the proper spelling is Gerbert Aurillac (an insistence which Proffer dismisses, along with the article in general)[12] and that he belongs to the tenth century, Tikos makes the case that "Bulgakov incorporated a mass of information about Gerbert into the major philosophical outlook of the novel."[13] The Tikos article is one of several efforts to support the notion that Bulgakov adheres to one or another heretical offshoot from Christianity. However, the evidence from the novel, which will be marshaled in later chapters, suggests that Mikhail Bulgakov would agree with Sergius Bulgakov that "world-denying Manichaeanism...separates God from the world by an impassable gulf and thus makes the existence of God-manhood out of the question."[14] Mikhail is no more a Manichee than Sergius is.

Regarding the passage in which Herbert Aurilachs is mentioned, we may simply make the point that, in the novel, some of his manuscripts have been unearthed by the National Library in Moscow and that Professor Woland, as the only specialist in black magic, has been invited to decipher them. This is flimsy evidence upon which to develop an interpretation of the whole novel. On this evidence alone, one could as easily, or more easily, argue that Bulgakov's view was diabolism. Even in a Christian interpretation, Satan (Woland) would be the perfect choice to decipher the works of a black magician. All of these monkeyshines should be understood quite readily as Satan's twitting explanation to the atheists about why he is in Moscow; the matter is never again mentioned in the novel.

Related to the idea that *The Master and Margarita* is Manichaean is the idea that it is Gnostic. Wright's influential book posits this view (actually, one variant of it, since the variants are many). And his definition of Gnosticism is close to that of Manichaeism. The distinction, for what it is worth, is that standard Manichaeism sees two forces, those of Good and Evil, as eternal and equal in power, ever warring against each other for control of the universe, whereas Wright's brand of Gnosticism has the forces of good and evil struggling against each other but still under a reigning God. So Wright asserts, "Bulgakov, it would seem, aligns Woland with darkness or evil, Ieshua with light or good, leaving both of them as subordinate to the only God, in whom good and evil are one."[15] Elsewhere, Wright comments,

> Healthy gnosticism, a total acceptance of good and evil as necessary for mankind, is seen as a positive force, as opposed to doctrinaire narrow-mindedness; one only need have faith that "everything will turn out right." There can be little doubt that this reflects Bulgakov's own religious attitude, for he has no time for orthodoxy in any area of life: it is the thinking, struggling man whom he admires, and this book is ultimately an expression of his whole life.[16]

All who succeed Wright in commenting on *The Master and Margarita* will be in debt to him. But his viewpoint strikes me as quite wrong, though at least he does look to religious categories to explain the novel. Is it self-evident, on the face of things, that orthodox Christian doctrine is narrow-minded? Wright announces, "It will be obvious that Bulgakov's whole conception is broader than that of Christianity."[17] But is it readily apparent that a failed old sectarian notion is to be considered broad, broader than a Christianity which has survived intact for two thousand years? Wright's first piece of evidence is that the Yeshua of the novel differs from the Jesus Christ of the New Testament—as if Yeshua were Bulgakov's creation and not the Master's, as if Yeshua were Bulgakov's own picture of the historical Jesus Christ. (More on these matters shortly.) And one does wonder to what kind of God Bulgakov was praying at the end of his life in his final words, "Forgive me, receive me!"—which matter Wright mentions.[18]

Wright forthrightly acknowledges, "I have several times been taken to task for claiming that Bulgakov had a 'gnostic' view"; and he adds modestly, "...indeed the question is a confusing one."[19] Wright admits even, though a bit cryptically, that "...in *The Master and Margarita* we cannot follow gnosticism to its extremes."[20] Further, he notes, regarding the common Gnostic notion of crediting the Devil with creating the world, "No such implication is present in Bulgakov."[21] But his point remains, in terms of this novel, "not that good will overcome evil but that both are equally right and necessary within God's creation."[22]

Wright is not alone is ascribing Gnosticism to Bulgakov. Edwards seems to have drunk at Wright's well. Beatie and Powell also seem to suggest that Gnosticism is at the root of Bulgakov's vision.[23] The main observation to be made here is that basic to Wright's view is that Bulgakov was a religious writer. The question is to which religious view of life and the world he adhered.

We have seen earlier that Bulgakov's Satan insists both upon the reality of the supernatural realm (how could he not, being of it?) and also upon his own limitedness and the ruling power of God. We turn now to the role of the Devil in Bulgakov's use of the principle of parody in this novel. The Devil has always had a strong appeal to the Russian imagination; literary depictions of him by Dostoevsky, Lermontov, and Andreyev, among many others, come readily to mind. Similarly (and probably related), the Russian Orthodox Church has been readier than Western branches of Christendom to give the Devil his due. In his other writings Bulgakov frequently depicted the Devil. He entitled an early story "Diaboliad." In *Black Snow: A Theatrical Novel* an editor, Rudolfi, appears to Maxudov, the writer-hero, in the guise of the Devil, Mephistopheles. In the same novel Maxudov is spared from suicide through the indirect influence of the Devil, as the hero delays action at the crucial point in order to hear Mephistopheles' lines in a recording of an operatic version of *Faust*.

However, in *The Master and Margarita* Bulgakov puts his long-standing fascination with the Devil to a special use, one in which parody is paramount. In a novel dominated by the symbolism of moon and sun, it should not be surprising that the Devil figures prominently. One of the main things to understand about Bulgakov's treatment of him is that he comes to embody the supreme parody: Satan standing in the place of God. Sometimes, as we have noted, he acknowledges his subordination to God; in those cases, he conforms to the role assigned to him by traditional Christian teaching. At other times, and more often, his dealings with men are a parody of God's dealings with humans as understood by orthodox Christianity.

Satan, who traditionally was able to assume any disguise, even that of an angel of light (II Corinthians 11:14), comes to Moscow in the form of a man, directly paralleling the Incarnation of Christ. His disguise is that of a professor, not a carpenter or meek servant. In the Satanic incarnation Bulgakov's character comes to Soviet Moscow: the capital of atheism, as it were. But atheists do not believe in the Devil any more than they do in God. To accept his reality would be to break out of the naturalistic mode of thinking, just as much as if one were to accept God's reality. Hence, they reject him, and they deny to his face—and despite overwhelming evidence, some of it solidly empirical—the reality of his existence. As Jesus "came unto his own but his own received him not" (John 1:11-12), so Satan comes unto his own, but they know him not.

At the same time, Satan's appearance as a parody of God does not eliminate, according to Bulgakov's treatment of him, the reality of his status as the Devil according to traditional Christian understanding. He remains, in some of his manifestations in the novel, the Prince of Darkness in his own right. His power over God-rejecting humanity is apparent throughout. His confident assertion that "nothing is hard for me to do, as you well know" (p. 349) coincides remarkably well with St. John's observation that "the whole world lies in the power of the evil one" (I John 5:19, New English Bible). He has successfully persuaded men to exchange the truth of God for a lie (Romans 1:25).

Still, some aspects of the traditional Devil are more prominent in this novel than others. Specifically, there is little, if anything, here of the tempter. (One thinks, by way of contrast, of the tempting of Eve and Adam or the testing of Job.) No character in *The Master and Margarita* sins because of Satan's initiative. Certainly, the reality of the Devil is never used to excuse a human being from responsibility for his own wrongdoing. What does occur is that Satan dispenses a painful justice to those who deserve it. They are the ones who fall into his department of cosmic responsibility. Never are the punishments inflicted by Satan meted out arbitrarily.

In both of his major aspects, his appearance in his own right and his presence as a parodistic parallel to God—actually, in the combination of these two aspects—Satan's existence is "The Seventh Proof," which is central to the novel and our understanding of it. Bulgakov gives this title to one of his chapters. It is surprising how little this subject of the seventh proof has been treated by Bulgakov's critics. Piper is one who does refer to it, but his calling it "the seventh proof of the existence of good and evil and of the inadequacy of reason"[24] is not at all satisfying.

In his opening conversation with the two Soviet literary men, Berlioz and Bezdomny, Satan speaks of the traditional five proofs of medieval scholasticism for the existence of God and of Immanuel Kant's refutation of them. But, offers Woland, Kant then outdid himself: "...he completely demolished all five proofs and then, as though to deride his own efforts, he formulated a sixth proof of his own" (p. 9)—the moral argument.

The mention of the five proofs is apparently a reference to the Five Ways of St. Thomas Aquinas. However, Thomas's Ways do not correspond directly with what Kant sought to disprove. In fact, one of Thomas's Five Ways is very close to Kant's own moral argument, and some of Kant's attacks were directed against proofs developed by other medieval scholastics. Actually, scores of proofs for the existence of God were offered in the Middle Ages. The facts of the history of philosophy need not detain readers of a novel in which all sorts of things are askew. We must recognize, though, that these proofs have to do with the subject of the existence of God, not merely with the existence of good and evil and certainly not with "the inadequacy of reason."

Bulgakov goes Kant one better and offers a seventh proof for the existence of God. That proof is the existence of the Devil. As the existence of the shadow proves the existence of that which casts the shadow and as the existence of moonlight presupposes the existence of sunlight, so Satan's existence bears witness to God's existence. And how, Bulgakov wants to say, can man, even atheistic Soviet man, deny the existence of Satan? Evil is too palpable and personal to allow such a denial. In terms of the novel itself, those who deny to the end cannot be credited and shall not be saved. Only those who do not believe in the reality of the Devil are punished by the Devil.

Bulgakov's concentration on the reality of Satan is his method of indirection for propounding the reality of God. Bulgakov knows that it is no more difficult to believe in the reality of God than to believe in the reality of the Devil—and really no easier. The watershed issue is the reality of the supernatural realm. Once that fact is granted—in whatever form, however fragmentary or badly distorted, so goes the burden of the novel—the rest of the Christian world view follows with comparative ease.

Viewing Satan both as a parody of God and as an agent of divine providence vitiates an error made by some critics that Satan is a sentimentalist with a good—and soft—heart. Raymond Rosenthal, for example, entitled his early review "Bulgakov's Sentimental Devil."[25] Ewa Thompson writes at some length of "the sympathetic light" in which Bulgakov presents Woland and of "the devil's generosity." She links Bulgakov's character with the Romantic fascination with Satan, the kind of heroic character with "a redeeming aura about him," whose "greatness makes him unfit for condemnation, so to speak."[26]

However, Satan is not a sentimentalist who violates his own devotion to evil for the sake of the appealing Margarita and her Master, nor is he a "good guy" incognito. It is true that he does what would generally be called good deeds. But he does not do them out of compassion or weakness of will. His "kind" acts are those willed by God, not by himself. Far from being a sentimentalist, he executes an impartial justice. He punishes those whose actions have brought their own bad consequences upon themselves. He spares those who belong to the realm of light and not to his realm of darkness; he is not allowed to touch such persons. The God who knows the number of hairs on one's head will not allow the Devil to bring harm to the heaven-bound. In sum, there is nothing in Bulgakov's depiction of Woland which violates orthodox theology.

The time setting offers *prima facie* corroboration for the idea that Satan's incarnation in modern Soviet Russia is a parody of Christ's Incarnation in ancient Palestine. In both cases the time is the second half of Holy Week, the climax of the Incarnation, which provides it with its ultimate meaning and which ushers in the joy of Easter Sunday. The story of Yeshua opens in sunlight, on the morning of Good Friday. There is a reference back to Jesus' dinner with Judas on Wednesday night. Christ's resurrection is not told in the novel, for a reason which will soon become clear. However, by the end of the novel, when we see the risen Lord, it is logical to accept that resurrection and to assign it to the traditional time of Easter Sunday morning. It is significant that Bulgakov carefully keeps Satan and his retinue from sharing in the joy of that day.

Woland comes to Moscow on Wednesday—significantly, at sunset. His magic show at the Variety Theater occurs on Thursday (night, of course). Satan's Ball, or Rout, is held on Friday night, the night when God, in the person of Jesus, is said to have descended into hell following his death on the cross. Temporarily, it seems that the forces of evil have triumphed. At sunset of Saturday, Satan and his host must leave: the Russian Orthodox retained for their ecclesiastical calendar the Jewish system of starting a new day at 6:00 p.m. and not midnight. Thus, Sunday, Resurrection Day, the day of Christ's victory over death and hell, formally began at 6:00 p.m. Saturday. (It is true that in certain places Bulgakov makes use of the fact that the Easter service of the Orthodox Church focuses on midnight.) The Master and Margarita are reunited on Good Friday night, the firstfruits of Christ's victory through his death and resurrection. The novel ends with the transfiguration of the pair (more about transfiguration in the next chapter) and the disappearance of Satan and his henchmen into the abyss—at dawn of Sunday. No natural, earthly events take place on Sunday; it is a day of the supernatural, the eternal day.

An understanding of moon and shadow imagery and of Satan as a parody of God will also clear away what seems so far to have been the major stumbling-block to a correct reading of The Master and Margarita: the unorthodox, apocryphal picture of Jesus. Yeshua is guilty of a cringing weakness which ill suits the Son of God, and he holds notions which are at odds with the teachings of the Jesus of the New Testament. (The character of Yeshua will be treated in detail in Chapter Five.) How, it might well be asked, can one argue for an orthodox Christian interpretation of the novel when the picture of Jesus is obviously far removed from that given in the Gospels? It is not surprising at all that many critics, while recognizing clearly Bulgakov's deployment of traditional Christian materials, conclude that his message lies outside the mainstream of Christian thought—let it be Manichaean, Gnostic, some version of secular, or whatever.

The key issue here is one of technical narrative point of view. Who is it who tells the story of Pilate and Yeshua? Whereas the issue is somewhat cloudy, one thing must become crystal clear: Bulgakov does not tell it. The Jesus depicted is not Bulgakov's but someone else's.

There are three sections (four chapters in all) of the Pilate-Yeshua account. One is presented orally by Woland. Another is drawn from the poem by Bezdomny (whom the Master calls his disciple and whose name Mirra Ginsburg translates literally as "Homeless"). The third is a direct recording of part of the Master's novel. Since the Devil says, late in the book, that he has read the Master's novel, it could be that in his chapter he is quoting from it. It is less easy to transfer the Master's words to Bezdomny. One must not rule out the possibility that Bulgakov's strategy is again one of deliberate obfuscation.

What is important to see here is that all three fragments cohere. Further, the style is consistent from one fragment to another, and it is a style different from anything in the Moscow chapters. So a good case can be made for single authorship of all three fragments. If so, the choice of author would have to be the Master. (The possibility that Bezdomny is the author will be discussed in the chapter about him.) If this ascription of authorship is correct, one must keep in mind the troubled nature of the Master's personality and therefore make a very sharp distinction between that fictional character and his creator, the novelist Bulgakov.

At the same time, whether the Pilate-Yeshua accounts come from three minds or one ultimately matters little. What is necessary to understand is that all three fragments have a sublunary origin. Their consistent distortion of the New Testament account arises because reality is now being perceived through the filter of diabolical influence, that is, perceived in the distorting light of the moon. Prominent among Bulgakov's early purposes for his novel was to write "The Gospel according to the Devil."[27] That early purpose would still be served in the final version if the author of the "Gospel" were to be under the influence of the Devil.

Eastern Orthodox theology emphasizes that fallen man is enslaved by the Devil and that he cannot see the truth whole apart from divine revelation and the illumination of the Holy Spirit. Although the Master sometimes corresponds to author Bulgakov, the correspondences are constantly shifting. Both do write about Jesus Christ, but they do not write the same things. It would be as serious a mistake to identify this author and his main character as it would be to fuse (and thus confuse) Swift and Gulliver. If Bulgakov has the Master writing under the influence of the Devil, then we are to perceive the Master's account, however stimulating and revealing, as ultimately untrustworthy, as not Bulgakov's own view.

Whereas Bulgakov's use of parody is seen nowhere so clearly as in the character of Woland, this same principle is present in the story of Pilate and Yeshua. The Master's novel is the moon-inspired parody of the story of the Sun of Righteousness. As God inspired the stories of the four Gospel writers, so Satan inspires the story of the Master. Thus, as the orthodox accept the Bible as God's Word while not denying human authorship, so we are to accept the Pilate-Yeshua chapters as both the Master's novel and the Gospel according to the Devil. The Master wants to see the truth, but he cannot escape the control of that Power who holds all men in thrall.

Once the symbolic correspondences are sorted out and once the veil of parody is penetrated, we see that Jesus is as surely God's minister of mercy, love, and grace as Satan is God's minister for justice, power, and retribution. The Master perceives some of this reality about Jesus. He has an abiding fascination with him. But his perception is fragmentary and distorted. He cannot see the truth clearly.

It is interesting to note which details Bulgakov singles out for inclusion in the Master's novel. They are not arbitrarily selected. Yeshua's apocryphal lines about cowardice as one of the worst sins, however they are to be explained in theological terms (see Chapter Five), certainly highlight Bulgakov's intermittent satire of Soviet society. His assertion that all people are good, while perhaps jarring to Western ears, fits rather well with the Eastern Orthodox concept of the ultimate deification of humans (see Chapter Three).

What is really interesting, though, is that, regardless of details which diverge from the biblical accounts, enough canonical details are included, whether exactly or inexactly, for every reader to recognize Jesus in Yeshua. Pertinent here is St. James' observation that "the devils also believe, and tremble" (James 2:19). At the very opening of the novel, Bezdomny's poem is being criticized by editor Berlioz because it depicts Jesus not as pure myth and superstitious invention but as "...well, completely alive, a Jesus who had really existed, although admittedly a Jesus who had every possible fault" (p. 5). Here is a clear clue about how to read the not-always-flattering account of Yeshua which will appear in the Master's novel-within-the-novel. The Master's Jesus is filtered through a diabolical distortion. Even so, this distorted Jesus is a Jesus who is both alive and recognizable. In theological terms, we would say that even persons under diabolical influence remain, by virtue of creation, image-bearers of God and therefore have some perception, however dim, of the truth. Again, parody is the operative principle.

Bulgakov, then, is not the immediate author of the three fragments of the Pilate-Yeshua story. However, he—and not one of his characters—is the direct source of one depiction of Jesus Christ. That is, Jesus appears in *The Master and Margarita* outside of the novel-within-the-novel. Specifically, he reappears at the end of Bulgakov's (not the Master's) novel, when the eternal fates of the main characters are being decided. In this reappearance he does not exhibit any of the faults which were evident in the apocryphal, sublunary account(s). He is now the risen and glorified Lord. Technically, he does not appear, not *in propria persona*. But he sends Matthew on a mission, carrying orders to Woland. What we learn of him through Matthew's reportage of his statements is quite different from the flawed Yeshua of the earlier chapters. He is now emphatically the voice of final authority. Similarly, Pilate reappears in the final chapters, that is, outside the novel-within-the-novel. As both representative man and an individual, he is real and has an eternal destiny and cannot therefore be relegated to the status of apocrypha, any more than this late-appearing Christ can.

This larger life of Jesus helps us understand why Bulgakov chose for the Master's hero the Aramaic name of Yeshua Ha-Notsri: Jesus of Nazareth, not Jesus the Christ, or the Messiah. The Master's depiction gives us only the humanity of Jesus, not his divinity. A further purpose served by the Master's skewed account is that we receive a fresh view on an old topic about which all have their judgments and pre-judgments. Thus, Bulgakov removes the story of Jesus from the dustbin of stale doctrinal formulations. Whereas Bulgakov's final picture of Yeshua is as the resurrected Lord, the Master's depiction of Yeshua emphasizes and underlines the literal reality of the Incarnation. The fault of the Soviet atheists, Bulgakov surely knows, is to deny the literal reality, the historicity, of Jesus. Jesus really did exist, Bulgakov's Satan said. The common fault among Christian believers, despite their theology, is to think of Christ as God but not to be able to visualize Jesus as man. Bulgakov seems at pains to avoid both erroneous extremes and thus to present the theologically orthodox view of the God-man. Also in keeping with orthodox theology, the final vision of Jesus is of one who conquered death and still exists.

The Master and Margarita is a one-of-a-kind work, *sui generis*. Thus, the hunt for a genre or sub-genre to which to assign this novel, interesting though such a search might be to specialists, does not offer much to the illumination of the work. At the same time, it is clear to the student of all of Bulgakov's works that this novel grows out of the same artistic imagination that the others do. As Ullman says, "*The Master and Margarita*, Bulgakov's best and most ambitious work, is, in a sense, a companion to all the others."[28] Because other commentators have done excellent work in pointing out the parallels, both formal and thematic, between *The Master and Margarita* and those other works,[29] I shall forego an extensive treatment of these parallels, though I shall mention in the final chapter some interesting parallels with *The White Guard*.

But there is one matter of parallelism which it is useful to note at this point. The conscious distortion of the facts of the Pilate-Yeshua story is analogous to distortions of historical materials in others of Bulgakov's works. Perhaps the clearest example is the treatment of Molière. Bulgakov had written a factual biography of Molière, but in his play *A Cabal of Hypocrites* he deliberately distorted those very facts. Ellendea Proffer has commented:

> Bulgakov, who had done extensive research on Molière, both for the play and for the biography, certainly knew his facts. In the play, however, names of real persons are changed, and fictitious characters and events are added. Actual events described one way in the biography are

given a completely different coloration so that the ban [of *Tartuffe*] occurs near Molière's death, when in actuality it occurred long before....[30]

She adds that, despite the historical inaccuracies, "Bulgakov tried to convey accurately the atmosphere of France under Louis XIV."[31] The resemblance to the handling of the Pilate-Jesus story is obvious. This parallelism of distortion helps render untenable the view that Bulgakov gives us in Yeshua his actual personal view of the Jesus of the Gospels.

A similar device of indirection may be seen in Bulgakov's treatment of the Whites in such works as *The Days of the Turbins, The White Guard,* and *Flight.* Although he ostensibly condemns the Whites as decadent, he subtly shows his sympathy for the Whites by his failure to glorify the Reds of the Revolution. This left-handed praise of the Whites, the only kind possible in the political atmosphere of the time, seems analogous to the depiction of a Jesus with all possible faults, yet a Jesus who truly lived.

The stratagem employed in these instances is best explained by Bulgakov himself in his *Molière*:

> Molière decided to resort to another method of bringing his play back to life. This method has long been familiar to playwrights: under powerful pressure, the author deliberately mutilates his work. It is an extreme method! Thus a lizard, caught by the tail, breaks off the tail and escapes. For every lizard realizes that it is better to live without a tail than to lose its life altogether.[32]

The task of the reader, then, is to discern the principles upon which Bulgakov does his work of "mutilation" in *The Master and Margarita.* This chapter contains one understanding of what those principles are. Sooner or later, Bulgakov believed, his work would live. The task of discernment is no easy task, and it is evident why there is as yet no consensus on how to read the novel.

Chapter Three

The Orthodox Setting

❖ ❖

This chapter will investigate the setting of Eastern Orthodox theology for Bulgakov's *The Master and Margarita*, focusing on those elements which seem to offer insight into the novel, with special attention given to those which are not shared by the Western Church. The elements which need to be rehearsed are more than just a few. Often the differences between East and West lie not in the general doctrines themselves but in the emphases given within the general doctrines. The citations will come from Orthodox sources, mostly theologians.

It will quickly be apparent that this chapter takes more from Sergius Bulgakov than from any other authority. It is of course convenient that Mikhail's elder second cousin[1] was one of Russia's great theologians. There is no external evidence that Mikhail relied directly on Sergius' writings. However, as it turns out, the theological writer whose expressions most closely parallel and most helpfully illuminate *The Master and Margarita* is Sergius Bulgakov. There can be no question that Mikhail knew Sergius' works, and he must have known Sergius personally in his (Mikhail's) young years when both were located in Kiev. We recall, also, that Mikhail's father was himself a theological scholar of some note. Although a chapter on theology may be difficult reading for the theologically uninterested, an understanding of the theological basis of *The Master and Margarita* is essential to an accurate interpretation of the work.

Whereas Western Christianity and Eastern Christianity share the central mysteries of the faith and both accept the basic dogmatic formulations spelled out in the Apostles' Creed and by the early church councils, there are substantial differences between the two. Perhaps the overriding difference, one of general approach to the Christian faith, lies in the balance between rationality and mysticism. Nicolas Zernov, always a sage guide to Eastern Orthodox thought and one of its best interpreters to a Western audience, has written:

> Western man has always been more confident than his Eastern counterpart in the power of human reason to penetrate into the mystery of life, and to define with precision the relations between Creator and creation.... The entire theology of the West is more rational, more abstract and more authoritarian than that of the East.[2]

Of course, the difference here is one of emphasis; rationality and mysticism are present in both branches of Christendom, though in differing degrees. But just this difference allows Zernov to proceed to make a statement about Eastern Orthodoxy which no spokesman would make, at least not in the same vocabulary, on behalf of Western theology:

> The East stresses the transformation of the whole human being, of his restoration to the original prototype and the enlightenment of mind and heart which accompanies man's rebirth in Christ through the action of the Holy Spirit. This transfiguration brings men into new and more personal fellowship with the Triune God, but however intimate their communion, the divine essence remains impenetrable to the human mind, since the Eastern emphasis on apophatic or negative theology insists that we can only say that God is beyond all our definitions and speculations.[3]

One of the results of the mysticism of Orthodoxy which affects the doing of theology is that the East "mistrusts over-elaborate definitions" because it "treats religion more as a life than a doctrine."[4] In a similar vein, Sergius Bulgakov insists that the Orthodox Church needs and has only "a small number of dogmatic definitions."[5] He also remarks, "In general the tendency of Orthodox doctrine is not to increase the number of dogmas beyond the limits of the purely indispensable. In the realm of dogma, Orthodoxy rather makes her own the rule, 'not to govern or dogmatize too much.'"[6] He considers that this minimum has been stated in the Nicene-Constantinopolitan Creed; but, beyond those essentials, "the rest has not been so formulated as to become obligatory dogma for all."[7] In other words, there is considerably greater latitude for Eastern theologians than for Western theologians, whether professional (Sergius) or amateur (Mikhail?).

There is useful imagery to highlight this difference between East and West. Imagine that Western theology is a set of books on a shelf which begins with the person of God; proceeds through such doctrinal categories as creation, angelology, anthropology, hamartiology, soteriology, ecclesiology, and eschatology; and results in a *system* of rational consideration of all Christian dogmas. Then imagine that Eastern theology is like an onion (think of the onion-shaped domes on Orthodox churches) which is to be unpeeled layer by layer as the theologians seek to penetrate closer and closer to the core—to the heart of the mystery.

The heavily mystical quality of Orthodoxy offers a perfect context for Bulgakov's series of allusive symbolic correspondences. As R. M. French has written, "Orthodoxy is meeting, the meeting of two worlds, the contact of the material and the spiritual and even the penetration of the material by the spiritual."[8] Zernov has described Orthodoxy as "an all-embracing type of Christianity which did not accept division between secular and sacred, which believed that the whole earth must be transformed through man into the temple of the Holy Spirit."[9] Orthodoxy is heavily liturgical, and the liturgy is consistently designed to reflect the correspondences between the supernatural and the natural. As Sergius Bulgakov has commented, "The Liturgy is Heaven on earth."[10]

It is the doctrine of the Incarnation—of God's taking on human flesh—which validates the parallelisms between the supernatural and the natural that are so prominent in Orthodoxy. Zernov has observed,

> Christianity is the religion of the Incarnation, of union between heaven and earth, time and eternity, God and man. Its main affirmation is that the divine and human can be made one without losing their identity. This is achieved, not because God and the world are the same, but because God is the creator, the world is His creation, and the Creator is the absolute Master of His own work.[11]

Sergius Bulgakov concurs: "And at the very heart of things there stands, as of old, the basic Christian dogma of the Incarnation, of the Word made flesh."[12]

It is on the foundation of this doctrine that Sergius Bulgakov made mysticism and its concomitant symbolic correspondences the very heart of his extensive theological endeavors:

> The life invisible of the Church, the life of Faith, is indissolubly connected with the concrete forms of earthly life. "The invisible" exists in the visible, is included in it; together they form a symbol. The word "symbol" denotes a thing which belongs to this world, which is closely allied to it, but which has nevertheless a content in existence before all ages. It is the unity of the transcendent and the immanent, a bridge between heaven and earth, a unity of God and man, of God and the creature. In this sense the life of the Church is symbolic; it is a mysterious life, hidden under visible signs.[13]

The sacraments, central as they are in Orthodox life and worship, are precisely demonstrations of this mystical symbolism, according to Sergius Bulgakov:

> The essence of the sacraments is a union of things visible and invisible, of an exterior form with an interior content. The very nature of the

Church is here reflected, of that Church which is the invisible in the visible, and the visible in the invisible.[14]

The mysticism embodied in the sacraments brings back to mind Mikhail Bulgakov's self-description, cited earlier, that he is a "mystical" writer. Again, Sergius Bulgakov sheds light on the topic. He says, "For mysticism to be possible, man must have a special capacity for immediate and superrational and supersensual conception, the capacity for intuitive perception which we rightly call 'mystic.'"[15] This mystical insight goes far beyond what is generally meant by the irrational. Sergius Bulgakov continues as our guide: "We must distinguish between this and the state of mind which borders on the subjective-psychological condition. Mystic experience has an objective character; it is founded on a departure from one's own narrow limitations and a resultant spiritual contact or encounter."[16] Obviously, the ascription of such insight to the novelist demands a reasonably full explication of the novel. The rest of this book will document that these perceptions, and most pointedly the following one, apply to Mikhail Bulgakov in *The Master and Margarita*:

All the life of Orthodoxy is full of heavenly visions. This is what is essential to Orthodoxy, something which its travelling companions do not see, and thus they do not see its inner meaning.... The whole life of Orthodoxy is bound up with vision of the other world. Without that vision Orthodoxy would not exist.[17]

Sergius Bulgakov's discussion of mystical typology is a major part of his effort to explain *sobornost*, an untranslatable word which Sergius calls "the soul of Orthodoxy."[18] He devotes several pages to trying to define the term, in which he offers as a synonym the French word *conciliarité* and then *harmony* and *unanimity* as the closest English synonyms available. At one point in the passage, he calls *sobornost* "the state of being together."[19] In another work he calls it "the communality of the body of the Church."[20] What this concept stands mainly in contradistinction to is the notion of individualized salvation, which is especially prominent in Protestantism. So, to be specific, a person like the Master is not to be judged by Western criteria but by Eastern ones, as vague as they often are.

What all of the preceding has to do with *The Master and Margarita* should be apparent. Mikhail Bulgakov's method comprises the same kind of correspondence, parallelism, and typology explained by Sergius Bulgakov and other Orthodox spokesmen and to which Orthodoxy naturally and congenially gives rise. Not only so, but the primary symbols in the novel coincide remarkably closely with those prominent in Orthodoxy. Further, the doctrines upon which these symbols touch comprise something like an irreducible core of Orthodox belief. Even the free handling of traditional Christian materials finds a justification in the Orthodox attitude toward the whole process of theologizing. We need only to add the element of parody, of seeing imperfectly and obliquely, to complete a summary statement of the novelist's method.

Perhaps the discussion thus far can be highlighted and succinctly concluded by a recounting of certain statements by Sergius Bulgakov on the subject of icons. One can hardly overstate the importance of icons to the Orthodox imagination. They are both artistic and theological—exactly the blend which is to be found in *The Master and Margarita*. Sergius Bulgakov starts with the artist: "The making of icons...is, in its original purity, a work of religious creation."[21] He continues, in terms as appropriate to novels as to paintings, "The icon, then, is religious contemplation reclothed in images, colours and forms. It is a revelation under artistic form; it is not abstract idea, but concrete form."[22] Icons must always be seen primarily not as art works in their own right but as symbols: "To know and to preserve the symbolic meaning of the icon—this is the tradition of iconographic painting...."[23]

One readily thinks of the Master's novel when he reads the following words from Sergius Bulgakov about how icons can vary from their prototypes:

> ...there exists a certain canon for the painting of each icon, the 'original' which indicates how a given Saint or event should be represented. This canon dates from the earliest times. To be sure, it has only a general, directive value. It not only leaves room for personal inspiration and for the creative spirit (which insensibly modifies it), but even presupposes such creativeness.[24]

So Sergius Bulgakov concludes this section, most appropriately, by conjoining artist and theologian:

> Icons are born of art and should remain in the realm of art.... That art is not the slave of the canon as an exterior law, but freely accepts it as a vision of ancient and interior truth. The painting of icons is a branch of symbolic art, but more than that, it is a vision of God, a knowledge of God, a testimony given in the realm of art.
> Truly to attain to this art of the icon, an artist and a contemplative theologian must be united in the same person. Art alone cannot create an icon, nor can theology alone.[25]

One way of reading this novel is to view it as an icon in fictional prose. Everything that has been said thus far of Orthodox theology, including these paragraphs on icons, can be applied to *The Master and Margarita*.

Incorporated in these general concerns of Orthodoxy are certain specific concerns which bear on *The Master and Margarita*, including the Fall of Adam as rendering man the slave of the Devil, the Eucharist as a re-enactment of the central issues of the Christian faith, the highlighting of Christ's descent into hell between his death and resurrection, the distinctive teaching of the Virgin's visit to hell, the emphasis on corporate rather than individual aspects of redemption, the overwhelming importance of Easter among the holy days of the Church calendar, the significance placed on the intervention of the fallen angels in human affairs, the doctrine of the ultimate deification of man, and the weight given to the apocalyptic vision of the divine consummation of human history.

All branches of Christendom, despite certain dissimilarities of doctrinal formulation, share the view that Adam's initial transgression plunged the whole of mankind into a state of sin, that is, with a natural proclivity toward evil. There are, however, significant differences between theological anthropologies East and West.

> Whereas the Western mind defines sins as a violation of the divinely established legal relationship between God and man, the Eastern mind—influenced by Greek philosophy—defines it as a diminution of essence, a loss of substance, a wound or infection of the original image of God....[26]

In brief, Western theology perceives the Fall of man in juridical terms; there has been a disobedience which brings with it as its consequence a punishment. Rather than speaking of the guilt of Adam and also the guilt of his descendants, which language is common in Western theology, the Eastern Fathers, more simply, "preferred to interpret the state of affairs inherited from Adam as slavery to the Devil, who exercises a usurped, unjust and deadly tyranny over mankind since the sin of man's Progenitor."[27] Furthermore, "The East regards sin as only a temporary malady which hurts man but does not annihilate his God-like image."[28]

Thus, if the West thinks of God as the Judge and of sinful man as the guilty defendant, the East thinks of man as a slave to the Devil and therefore held away from God's province. And what does one do for a slave? Ransom him. The word *ransom* appears regularly among Orthodox theologians, as it does not among Western theologians.[29]

We shall see soon what happens, in terms of theological anthropology, as the effect of redemption. For now, though, we observe how Sergius Bulgakov speaks of sin, particularly as it affects mankind. Echoing the point of St. Augustine cited in the preceding chapter, he offers an image about evil—and one which coincides virtually exactly with that adduced in *The Master and Margarita*—when he writes, "Evil is a parasite, possessing no substantive title to existence, but subsisting by means of the *confusion* of good and evil, as shadows, and darkness itself, are only apparent by contrast with the light."[30]

One very important outgrowth of the emphasis on the retaining of the divine image is that, as God the Creator is the great Artist, so man is a derivative artist, despite the Fall. As God is the Master of all creation, so man is the master of his own creation. Although a Western Christian could proclaim the same, once again the emphasis in the East (think again of icons) offers a special piquancy. Zernov clarifies:

> A Roman Catholic may be described as a disciplined member of a universal society, a Protestant as a man who has committed himself to the religion contained in the Bible. An Orthodox worships God as an artist, for he brings to the throne of his Lord and Master the works of his

creative imagination.... The Church in its sacraments taught that the physical world is good and real and that man has been appointed by the Creator to be its responsible master.[31]

As God controls the world of his creation, so Mikhail Bulgakov's Master controls the world of his creation, namely, the Pilate-Yeshua story.

It is perhaps needless to document fully the central place given to the Eucharist in Orthodoxy; all commentators on Orthodoxy acknowledge it. To cite just one, "Orthodox theology can be summed up in these two significant happenings—Easter and Eucharist—which are so integrally bound together in Orthodox worship."[32] All of Bulgakov's treatment of Yeshua is of course a version of the original which the Eucharist re-enacts. Also, as we shall see, Satan's Ball, or Rout, is, on one level, a parody of the Eucharist.

The teaching of Christ's descent into hell between his death and his resurrection is not familiar to all Western Christians. Some Protestant traditions do not accept it as literal; others do, as also do Roman Catholics. But nowhere in the West does it play as large a role as it does in the Orthodox imagination and its iconography. There is certainly a logic in Orthodoxy's featuring of this concept: it fits with the idea that sinful man is enslaved to the Devil and must be ransomed through the death of Christ, as the following reference demonstrates:

> The Christ of Easter is Christ victorious over the hostile powers which held man in thrall, the triumphant warrior carrying off mankind as the prize of victory, the liberator of Adam and of all the righteous men of old whom he sought out in the depths, Christ the victor, who brings light and life: "Now the light-bearing torch, Christ's flesh, is hidden beneath the earth as under a bushel, and it drives away the darkness of hell" (Stasis of Psalm 118).[33]

Orthodox iconography offers vivid detail on the harrowing of hell.

> ...he [Christ] is shown storming the innermost fortress of Satan, or breaking the bars of the gate to the underworld, or lifting the gates of Hades from their hinges. On one such "Resurrection icon" Christ is shown standing upon the gates of hell which he has lifted from their hinges and arranged in the form of a cross; from the interior emerged the souls of the devout of ancient times, led by Adam and Eve, who having been first to fall are the first to be liberated from Hades. Behind the first parents come the just patriarchs, kings and pious fathers of the Old Testament, who have been waiting all this time for their redemption. These icons are the counterparts of the Easter hymns of the Eastern Church, which take Christ's journey to Hades as their subject.[34]

In addition to Christ's visit to hell to harrow it (to cleanse it, that is, to take out of it those redeemed Old Testament souls waiting for the shedding of the blood of the Son of God for remission of sins), there is another visit to hell which is totally foreign to Western Christendom. It is the visit of the Virgin Mary, which comes down from Russian medieval legend. [35]

"The Descent of the Virgin into Hell" is a rather confused piece of late apocryphal literature. The Virgin asks to see the suffering ones in hell, then weeps over them. Their various punishments, graphically portrayed, are reminiscent of those suffered by the damned in Dante's *Inferno*. Although her mediation does not free any souls from the prison of hell, God does allow Christ to grant Mother Mary's intercession to this extent: that those in hell can have from Holy Thursday to Pentecost to rest and to praise the Trinity.[36] The focus of the piece is on the compassion of Mary, rather than on the fates of the damned.

Bulgakov reworks the idea of the visits to hell in two ways. First, the Master and Margarita are freed from thralldom to the Devil, they having previously appeared in more than one of Bulgakov's parodied versions of hell. Second, Margarita's presence at Satan's Ball seems to be a parody of Mary's visit to hell. Margarita appears in Apartment 50, one of Bulgakov's versions of hell, and she intercedes for sinners. The apocryphal story does not loom large in Orthodoxy, but Bulgakov seems to have it in mind as the background for this very important chapter of the novel. Thus, we have here a striking example of the extensiveness of Bulgakov's knowledge of theology and Orthodox tradition.

Another theological matter, and one of considerable importance for our purposes, is the East's emphasis on the corporate, rather than individual, character of the doctrine of redemption. One reference will suffice to summarize:

> Certain fundamental intuitions and convictions divide Orthodox from Western interpretations of Christianity, such as the stress on the corporate and cosmic aspects of redemption, the vivid sense of communion with the departed, the rejection of the legalistic and rational approach to religion.[37]

This communal emphasis establishes different theological criteria for analyzing Bulgakov's novel, especially its two title characters, from those which might come readily to the minds of readers reared in cultures shaped by Western Christianity. It encourages the view of the Master (and of Pilate) as representative of all mankind. Also, it sheds light on how to approach the question of whether the Master (and Margarita, as well) is truly redeemed.

Another important quality of the redemption which results from the Incarnation has to do with the description of the final state of redeemed man. Orthodoxy uses a vocabulary quite foreign to the West on this point. Sergius Bulgakov says that the happy result of the Incarnation "is understood by Orthodoxy as, above all, the deification of man, as the communication of the divine life to him."[38] Elsewhere he says, "The Lord has created man in his image in order to have him for his friend, to let him participate in the divine life, and by dwelling in him to make him a god through his grace."[39] Benz specifies that redemption "is not primarily the restitution of a legal relationship that has been upset by sin. Rather, it is fulfillment, renewal, transfiguration, perfection, deification of man's being."[40] Transfiguration, apotheosis, deification, divinization—these are not terms used in the West with regard to the doctrine of soteriology. In the Western traditions, man in heaven will experience the fullness of humanity, something which in his fallen state he cannot know on earth. But he is never going to become a *god*. Both East and West speak of God-manhood when referring to Christ's Incarnation. The Orthodox Church, however, uses exactly the same language when referring to man in his eternal state—as the West does not.

If the final state of redeemed man is God-manhood, the question then turns to who we are to understand are the redeemed. Here a matter which can be stated with theological precision in the West becomes quite murky in the East —and perhaps suitably so for our novel. Benz remarks, "The doctrine of eternal damnation has always met with intense resistance in the East."[41] Adding that "[f]rom the beginning, the Eastern Church secretly inclined toward the theory of universal salvation," he elaborates:

> The Judgment at the end of our eon will not be the ultimate judgment, will not forever set apart the saved and the damned. It will only assign men their place in a new age of the universe (eon) in which everyone will have a fresh chance to ascend to glory.[42]

Although he acknowledges that the Church officially disavowed this doctrine of universal salvation, "nevertheless a hankering for it persisted within Eastern Orthodox religious thought, and the Eastern theologians have repeatedly revived it."[43] Adrian Fortescue tries to understand this topic from a Western point of view: "Their opinion seems to be that all the dead sleep and wait passively in a middle state till the day of judgement."[44]

Sergius Bulgakov speaks with similar inexactness about the eternal fates of human souls, including those which would likely be considered in the West to be among the lost:

> Upon those who never belonged to the Church or have fallen away from it, the Church passes no judgment, but leaves them to the mercy of God. God has left us ignorant of the destinies of those who have not known Christ and have not entered into the Church. A certain hope is given us by the teaching of the Church on the descent of Christ into Limbo and His preaching on hell.... Nevertheless, the Church has never officially defined the destiny of non-Christians, adult or infant.[45]

Even assuming that the unregenerate are punished, he notes that two (ultimately incompatible) tendencies have existed from antiquity: eternal punishment for the lost and universal salvation. "From most ancient times doubts have existed as to the eternal duration of these torments; they are sometimes viewed as a provisional pedagogic method of influencing the soul, and a final restoration...is hoped for."[46]

Zernov's understanding is compatible with the above:

Eastern Christians have never been attracted to these clear-cut answers [of the Christian West] to the mystery of death. Their underlying conviction is that the end of physical existence closes only one stage in human ascent towards God, and that the seeds of good and evil sown on earth continue to bring forth fruit long after the death of the individual. The final reckoning can be made only after death and those who failed to learn how to love in freedom are not deprived of the possibility of improvement in their position through the compassion of their friends.[47]

It might seem that the attitudes expressed here would lead logically to a belief in Purgatory. But the Orthodox do not have such a doctrine. They do, however, believe in prayers for the dead, which can "even snatch from hell and lead to paradise those whose condition does not present unsurmountable obstacles."[48] The same theologian, while denying that there is a special *place* of Purgatory, allows that "the possibility of a *state* of purification is undeniable..." and also offers "the possibility of liberation from the pains of hell and of passing from an estate of reprobation to that of justification."[49]

The murkiness of the Orthodox view of the afterlife seems particularly congruent with what we find in the closing chapters of *The Master and Margarita*, especially as we think of the two title characters and of Pilate. Their final fates seem to pose one of the thorniest issues for theologically attuned interpreters of the novel. But perhaps, given the above, they need not do so. One should not look for a Western-style precision on a topic about which the Eastern Church offers only imprecision. Eastern Orthodoxy provides ready accommodation for the notion that the Master, Margarita, and Pilate may enter the eternal company of the redeemed.

Doctrinally and historically, what begins with the Incarnation concludes with the Resurrection. Easter and Christmas are of roughly equal importance on the Western Church calendar, but Easter reigns supreme in the East. R. M. French writes of "the central position which Easter occupies in the spiritual life of Orthodoxy."[50] Sergius Bulgakov speaks similarly:

> The feast of Easter is the heart of Orthodoxy, and at the same time a living testimony to its plenitude and truth. It is at once the palpable action of the Holy Spirit, the manifestation of Pentecost, and a manifestation of Christ risen on earth, an invisible manifestation, because it happens after the Ascension.[51]

The Easter service is a celebration of great joy. It centers on the midnight hour of Easter Eve. Again Sergius Bulgakov elaborates:

> If we wish confirmation of the idea that the church services are not only commemorations but that the event commemorated really happens in the heart of the Orthodox service, we will find it the night before Easter, a service which is as vitally connected with the Passion as shadows with light, sadness with joy, suffering with happiness. But in the light of

eternity, in the light of the Resurrection of Christ, that sadness is extinguished and disappears; it becomes simply a remembrance of something past. A Paschal hymn expresses this sentiment: "Yesterday I was buried with Thee, O Christ; with Thee today I rise from the dead."[52]

It is no accident, or secret, that, out of 365 days in the year, Bulgakov chose for his novel the time frame of the second half of Holy Week, culminating on Easter Sunday. Once again, *prima facie* evidence encourages us to think that there is religious significance for this choice. In addition, as will be explored later, the mood of the two main characters in the closing pages of the novel coincides perfectly with the mood attributed to the Orthodox observance of Easter in the preceding quotation.

While all branches of Christendom have traditionally adhered to a belief in the activity of angels, including fallen angels, in human affairs, once more we move into an area of doctrine which has received special attention from the Eastern Orthodox. The modern imagination, to the extent that it is secular, does not take angels seriously as literal entities. Orthodoxy always has done so and still does. Sergius Bulgakov explains:

> ...side by side with the angels of light there are fallen angels or demons, evil spirits, who strive to influence us, acting upon our sinful inclinations. Evil spirits become visible to those who have attained a certain degree of spiritual experience. The Gospels and the whole of the New Testament give us unshakable testimony in a manner wholly realistic; it does not accept an allegorical exegesis and even less refuses to explain these texts by the simple influence of religious syncretism. the spiritual world and the existence of good and evil spirits are evident to all those who live the spiritual life.[53]

Implied here, of course—as will be elaborated upon in the next chapter—is that Mikhail Bulgakov's focusing on Satan and his followers is, consistently on his part, a rendering of aspects of the angelology which is so prominent in Orthodoxy. It is also to be noted that Margarita and eventually the Master are among those to whom evil spirits become first visible and then recognized for what (who) they are. Perhaps these two have attained a "certain degree of spiritual experience."

The final area of Orthodox teaching which needs discussion because of its direct relevance to *The Master and Margarita* is the apocalyptic vision of the impending end of time. Yet again, we have a theological concern which is common to both West and East but which has greater status in and greater importance for the East. Calian speaks of "a maximizing of the eschatological and pneumatic in the East to a height not known in the West."[54] Sergius Bulgakov concurs: "...the soul of Russian Orthodoxy is, in its depths, always open to the emotion and the presentiment of apocalyptic thought."[55] Indeed, he goes to far as to say, "A non-apocalyptic, non-eschatological Christianity is a dangerous counterfeit to the real thing and a secularization of it."[56]

Apocalypticism is of the greatest importance to our understanding of Bulgakov's novel, because the author devotes the entire last portion of his work to a fictional development of the concept. Further, it is only in those final few chapters that he reveals the keys which unlock the meanings inherent in the work as a whole and allow us to see the coherence of plot elements which, by themselves, seem disconnected. Without a clear understanding of this final section, we might well think that the novel is as incoherent as some of its critics, with a sense of regret, have concluded that it is.

In both Bulgakov's novel and Orthodox theology as a whole, the apocalyptic vision is more than a final doctrine chronologically. It is the consummation, the capstone which validates all of the doctrines which precede it and which confirms their truth, just as the fulfillment of a prophecy proves the accuracy of the prophetic envisioning of the truth and evokes full, unhindered sight. No longer do we see through a glass, darkly.

> The advent of the "Lord's Day" signifies therefore neither the ending, nor the rendering absurd, nor the emptying of time. Indeed, the whole meaning, the whole point and uniqueness of early Christian eschatology is just this, that in the light of the coming of the Messiah and the "drawing near" of the messianic Kingdom, in the light of its manifestation in the world, time becomes truly real, acquires a new and special intensity. It becomes the time of the Church: the time in which the salvation given by the Messiah is now accomplished.[57]

Both the canonical and the apocryphal sacred writings of Christian antiquity include works devoted primarily to the apocalyptic vision. By far the most important of these is the last book of the New Testament, the Revelation of St. John the Divine, alternately known as the Apocalypse. (St. John himself, in his opening words, calls it "the Revelation of Jesus Christ.") All apocalyptic visions grow out of a curious combination of faith and despair.

> Apocalypses were usually written at a time of crisis and danger. One of their purposes was to strengthen the believer at a time of persecution and to encourage him to stand firm.... Although apocalypses spring from profound faith and burning conviction, the writers generally despair of the present and pin all their hopes on the future. They look for some great divine intervention in the near future, often on a world-wide scale, to put an end to an intolerable situation.[58]

St. John's Revelation was written against such an historical background of persecution—by an omnipotent state, Rome. Moscow, called sometimes the Third Rome, provided the Russian Orthodox with a parallel setting in modern times. Since the Revelation was often interpreted futuristically, that is, as referring to the end of the Christian dispensation, when persecution would again be prevalent, as it was at beginning of the Christian age, such a conjunction of ideas was natural. Various Russian Orthodox writers in the twentieth century made the same connection. For instance, Sergius Bulgakov, after giving a typical description of apocalyptic writing, asserts:

> At this very hour, the Russian Church, the greatest among Orthodox Churches, lies beneath the yoke of the most terrible persecution history has ever seen. In the eyes of the unbelieving, its very existence is menaced. But to the eyes of those who believe, the Russian Church appears as chosen among all Christianity, that it may, after having passed through a trial by fire, testify in spirit, in truth, and in liberty.[59]

It should come as no surprise that Sergius Bulgakov's favorite book of the Bible was the Revelation; the last theological treatise which he wrote was about it. His "favorite, constant prayer," according to James Pain, was, "Even so, come, Lord Jesus."[60] These are the last words of the last book of the Bible. Sergius Bulgakov links succinctly the subjects of apocalypse and history: "In the light of the apocalypse I comprehend the historical tragedy which is being unfolded before us...."[61] There is a consanguinity between the imaginations of Sergius and Mikhail Bulgakov on these points. An interest in the Book of the Revelation comes to the fore at the end of *The Master and Margarita*. Viewing history in the light of apocalypse seems to fit the novel perfectly. It gives to the novel's social satire a cosmic setting. Equally applicable, when we think first of the Master's portrayal of Yeshua and then of the appearance of the risen Lord at the end of the novel, is Sergius Bulgakov's statement, "The Revelation shows the figure of Christ, whom we know from the gospel, in a light which shines nowhere else...."[62]

There is substantial evidence in Mikhail Bulgakov's writing excluding *The Master and Margarita* that he made the same connection between the desperate straits of life in Stalin's Soviet Union and the Apocalypse that Sergius Bulgakov (and others) made. The most important instance is in his early novel about the Bolshevik Revolution, *The White Guard*. One of the two quotations comprising the epigraph to this novel comes from Revelation 20:12: "...and the dead were judged out of those things which were written in the books according to their works...." In the first chapter a priest, discussing the Revolution, turns to the Book of the Revelation for a parallel and quotes: "And the third angel poured out his vial upon the rivers and fountains of waters; and they became blood."[63]

At the end of *The White Guard*, a syphilitic comes to Alexei Turbin (like Bulgakov himself a professionally trained venereologist) for treatment. He is obsessed with the Book of the Revelation and sees parallels between its apocalyptic message and his times. He calls Moscow "the city of the devil" and "the kingdom of the Antichrist."[64] Alexei Turbin agrees,[65] though he fears that the patient's obsession with religion threatens his sanity. (Perhaps we should think here of the Master, and even Bezdomny.) Yet in his own subsequent dream the same parallel haunts Alexei.[66] The syphilitic, Rusakov, says, "...it is only *above* that we can obtain complete relief."[67] This is strikingly similar to the Master's rhetorical question, "Where else can such wrecks as you and I find help except from the supernatural?"[68] The syphilitic also quotes the same passage from the Revelation, about the third angel pouring his vial, that the priest had cited much earlier.[69] In the case of both quotations, there is a direct linkage with the contemporary setting: "Great and terrible was the year of Our Lord 1918."[70] Thus, the references to the Revelation serve as an envelope device, providing the cosmic setting within which the historical events of *The White Guard* occur and are to be understood.

Rusakov appears for a second and final time within the scope of just a few pages, on pages 295-96 (297 being the final page of the novel). Again, he refers to the Book of the Revelation. This time he reads from chapter 20 about the Final Judgment. His concluding reference is from Revelation 21:4: "And God shall wipe away all tears from their eyes: and there shall be no more death, neither sorrow, nor crying, neither shall there be any more pain: for the former things are passed away." The last paragraph of the novel shows Bulgakov following up on this passage and interpreting the events of 1918-19 according to the same apocalyptic vision:

> Everything passes away—suffering, pain, blood, hunger and pestilence. The sword will pass away too, but the stars will remain when the shadows of our presence and our deeds have vanished from the earth. There is no man who does not know that. Why, then, will we not turn our eyes toward the stars? Why?[71]

Any reader of *The Master and Margarita* can discern that there are several foreshadowings in this paragraph of the ending of that novel. The first thing which is mentioned as passing away is suffering. At their transfiguration the Master cries, "Burn away, past!" And Margarita echoes, "Burn, suffering."[72] Those things which pass away parallel closely the judgments represented by the Four Horsemen of the Apocalypse: war, famine, pestilence, death.[73] Shadows— which, as has been noted, constitute a recurring image in *The Master and Margarita*—have been left behind. Our vision passes beyond the sphere of the earth (the sublunary sphere) up to the stars, representing the world beyond change and also beyond distorted perception.

The point, then, is that in both novels, *The White Guard* and *The Master and Margarita*, Bulgakov establishes a framework of cosmic, eternal values within which he sets the action belonging to the twentieth-century Soviet Union. Both novels conclude on an apocalyptic note which is established through reference to the Revelation of St. John. Both appeal to the supra-earthly state. In both cases the device of the dream is employed to accomplish the mingling of the natural and the supernatural realms. Of course, the supernatural element is much more pronounced in *The Master and Margarita*, but even *The White Guard*, for all of its surface realism, is sufficient to justify Bulgakov's general view of himself as a mystical writer and an analysis of him as an apocalyptic writer.

There are yet other pieces of evidence from Bulgakov's writings that the Apocalypse appealed to his creative imagination. For example, in *A Cabal of Hypocrites* there is a reference to the Antichrist. In this instance, Bulgakov, ever the master ironist, twists the idea so that the term applies to his hero,

Moliere. Then, Moliere is called Satan—and by a priest, at that.[74] In *Black Snow: A Theatrical Novel* an editor, Rudolfi, tells Maxudov, the hero and another of Bulgakov's harried artists, that he must delete three words before his novel can be published: *apocalypse, archangels,* and *devil.*[75] Not only are all three of these terms religious ones, but they are of the same order as those which figure prominently in *The Master and Margarita.*

After these evidences, external to the novel, that the Revelation has had a long-standing appeal to Bulgakov's imagination, it is observable that some main themes of the Revelation coincide with some main themes of Bulgakov's work. Internal evidence will be presented in the chapter on "The Apocalypse." But just a brief listing of some of those themes will initially make the point.

> John has used symbols to describe the end of the world [in order to express] the following truths: (1) that God is in control of history and has the initiative; (2) that there is a real struggle in history between good and evil; (3) that the supreme clue to the understanding of God's character, actions, and purpose is to be found in the life, death, and resurrection of Jesus of Nazareth, and that these events have a direct bearing on everything that happens in history; (4) that the struggle will go on to the end of time and that no power in history itself can cure the evil: "both grow together until the harvest"; (5) therefore God himself must in the end cope with evil, and history be "swallowed up in eternity"; (6) heaven is the most real place and state of all.[76]

Although Bulgakov omits none of the above points in his novel, he gives especially detailed treatment to the conflict between good and evil; and, in good Orthodox fashion, he embodies these concepts. He even goes so far as to give extensive consideration to the fallen angels. References to Satan and the lesser devils are commonplace in Jewish apocalyptic literature, not excluding the Book of the Revelation. D. S. Russell includes these beings in his summary of the apocalyptic vision:

> The age-long story from the beginning to the end, has a single theme— the dramatic conflict between the kingdom of God and the kingdom of Satan; thus there emerged in apocalyptic an "antagonistic" conception of history and the world in which demonology was incorporated into the monotheistic faith of Judaism.[77]

Not only is the Revelation a substantive influence on the content of *The Master and Margarita,* but the technique of the novel seems also to be indebted to a significant degree to the same source. There is, for one thing, the time structure. All recognize that the novel takes place in the second half of Holy Week. What may not be equally well known is that the Book of the Revelation speaks of two half-weeks, with the second half bringing terrible judgment upon sinful man. So the structural device borrowed mainly from the Gospels is reinforced by the Revelation.

But more important is the method of discourse. Both the Revelation and *The Master and Margarita* employ a kaleidoscopic shifting of images and symbols, moving quickly from plane to plane of meaning and even mixing planes in the same passage. Commentators on the Revelation typically express frustration in imposing a single-line chronology or other neat schematization upon St. John's material. Surely, the Revelation is the most difficult of all biblical books to interpret. Russell provides a relevant statement about the technique of apocalyptic literature which could as easily apply to *The Master and Margarita* as to its actual subject, Jewish apocalyptic literature: "The apocalypticists give full rein to their imaginations in extravagant and exotic language and in imagery of a fantastic and bizarre kind. To such an extent is this true that symbolism may be said to be the language of apocalyptic."[78]

After this summary of doctrines pertinent for a reading of *The Master and Margarita*, there is one ancillary matter: the Apocrypha. It is clear, as later chapters will demonstrate and as certain earlier critics have done, that Bulgakov draws on material from the apocryphal books, especially those attaching to the New Testament, rather than the Old Testament. The Orthodox Church is vague on the authority of the Apocrypha—again, suitably so for purposes of interpreting *The Master and Margarita*. Sergius Bulgakov is representative. In a long section on the subject, he says, "Protestantism has arbitrarily impoverished its Bible by excluding the deutero-canonical books; this is beginning to be understood now and there is a tendency to give them again their value."[79] He does not, however, offer much clarity about how the apocryphal books are to be regarded: "...the non-canonical books have a certain authority as the Word of God, but less authority than that of the canonical books."[80] That Mikhail Bulgakov used the Apocrypha is beyond question. Just what he understood about its status is as unclear as Sergius Bulgakov's statement.

It could be said that Mikhail Bulgakov's use of the Apocrypha suggests that he is Gnostic, since Gnosticism influences some of the apocryphal works. The counter suggestion is that Bulgakov's borrowing reinforces the quality of Satanic parody, since somewhat tainted sources are drawn upon. If the Apocrypha is untrustworthy, what better ancient source would there be for a diabolical version of (and diversion from) the biblical Passion story? However, probably the more fruitful approach is to agree that Bulgakov sees a certain authority in the Apocrypha and uses the evidence in tandem with, rather than in contradiction to, his canonical sources. The Apocrypha comments on certain matters which are of interest to Bulgakov but which do not appear in the scriptural canon.

The goal of this chapter, along with the preceding one, has been to make convincing the contention that a theological approach to *The Master and Margarita* is appropriate—and, indeed, is enlightening as no other approach can be. The following chapters are devoted to a detailed reading of many elements of the novel, the purpose of which is to support the general points made in Chapters Two and Three. In the process many of the puzzles which reside in the separate plots and passages should be illuminated. The approach will be to examine the three plot strands separately—first Satan's visit to Moscow, then the Pilate-Yeshua novel-within-the-novel, and then the title plot about the

Master and Margarita. The last full chapter will offer a detailed reading of the final chapters of the book, which comprise the heart of Bulgakov's apocalyptic vision.

Chapter Four

Satan and the
Fallen Angels

❖ ❖

The first plot to appear in *The Master and Margarita* is the one about Satan's visit to Moscow. Of the eighteen chapters in Book One, all but two are devoted exclusively to this plot. In Book Two the center of attention shifts to the title characters, the Master and Margarita. Of the fourteen chapters in this second half of the novel, only four omit the title characters: Chapter 25-28. The first two of these, like the two chapters in Book One not devoted to Satan and company, are about Pilate and Yeshua. Chapters 27 and 28, "The Last of Apartment No. 50" and "The Final Adventures of Koroviev and Behemoth," return attention to Satan and his crew and wrap up their affairs in Moscow. Satan figures significantly throughout Book Two but always as an agent affecting the lives of the hero and heroine. However, in Book One he generally occupies center stage. Those events which belong to the Satanic incarnation but which occur in Book Two (excepting Chapters 27 and 28) will be discussed in later chapters, in relation to the Master-and-Margarita plot line.

The opening chapter, which is one of the best in the novel, sets the stage exquisitely for all of what follows. Satan appears in Moscow and speaks to two atheists, Berlioz and Bezdomny. The main subject of the conversation is Jesus Christ. Whereas the atheists deny the historical reality of Jesus, Satan affirms it emphatically. The ostensible purpose of his coming to Moscow, he being the only specialist in the world on black magic, is to decipher manuscripts of the ancient necromancer Herbert Aurilachs which had been unearthed by the National Library. His real purpose, as we learn early, is to search the hearts of modern Muscovites. So, from the very beginning, the basic concerns of the novel are set forth. Satan comes in his own right but also as a parody of the incarnate Christ. He immediately brings to the fore that question from the Gospels, "What think ye of the Christ?" In short, he forces upon the attention of his two auditors (and us readers as well) the issue of the intermingling of the natural and the supernatural. The first chapter, therefore, opens up the central theme of the novel.

It is especially in the plot about Woland that one has the greatest difficulty in knowing when a little detail has symbolic significance and when Bulgakov is merely having fun, giving free rein to his imagination.

Without question, Bulgakov's original intention was to write a novel about the Devil. Chudakova tells us, "In the first two versions there is as yet neither Master nor Margarita."[1] Proffer declares that "the key idea for the novel was the gospel according to the devil" (and she adds that this subject "required that Bulgakov immerse himself in scholarly research on religious and historical subjects, just as his father, the professor of theology, had").[2] She notes further that "Woland is the one character who is actually present in all of the different strands of the novel, which is, in part, a reflection of the fact that Bulgakov's original plan was to have him be the main character."[3]

Further evidence that the Devil was central in Bulgakov's thinking about the novel is provided by the early titles, all of them focusing on the Devil, that Bulgakov considered. One which goes back to 1928-29 was *The Consultant with a Hoof.*[4] Others mentioned by Chudakova are *A Black Magician, The Road Tour [of Woland?], Son of W[...?],* and *The Hoof of the Engineer.*[5] The second chapter, about Pilate and Yeshua, was first entitled "The Gospel According to Woland" and later "The Gospel According to the D[evil]."[6]

Thus, although one should take literally Bulgakov's imputation of the role of hero of his novel to the Master (note the chapter title "Enter the Hero" for the Master's debut),[7] there could be no novel without the presence in it of Satan. At one time, obviously, Bulgakov could conceive of it without the Master and Margarita. A natural guess would be that Bulgakov came to want human characters with whom readers could identify; also, their presence would give focus to the thematic concern of mixing the natural and the supernatural realms. But what he could not do without was the presence of the supernatural character, Satan.

As God came into the world in the form of a man, according to the Gospels, so here Satan comes in a human disguise, that of Professor Woland. This is hardly a Russian name. Lakshin explains that the name *Faland,* which means "deceiver," or "cunning," was used by medieval German writers to denote the Devil. A quite similar-sounding Woland, or "Herr Woland," appears in *Faust* as one of the allegorical names for the Devil.[8] Stenbock-Fermor corroborates these points, elaborating, "*Junker Voland* is the name by which Goethe's Mephistopheles introduces himself at the beginning of the Walpurgis Night."[9] Proffer agrees, then goes on to insist that Bulgakov intended that the name of the visiting professor begin with a *W* instead of with Goethe's *V,* possibly because "an upside down W looks like the Russian (and English) M—which, in turn, can be interpreted as a link to the Master, or, more likely, to Mikhail Bulgakov himself."[10] (It is at just such a point that one cannot be sure if

Bulgakov was setting out a clue for us or if we are falling into the error of over-interpreting.)

Throughout Christian tradition many characteristics have accrued to the Devil. He deceives; he tempts; he punishes; he plays tricks upon the innocent; he plays the buffoon; he engages in riotous living; he suffers because of his sin. It is interesting and important to note which of these characteristics Bulgakov includes and which he does not. First, there is nothing of the comic buffoon in Woland. Second, he does not go around playing tricks on people. These two roles he leaves for two of his underlings, Koroviev and Behemoth. More important than these points, he does not tempt people.

Rather, the most significant role of Woland in this novel is that of meting out punishment. This punishment is always just, never arbitrary or capricious. Only those human beings who deserve evil treatment receive it from Woland. Indeed, he finds himself in the unenviable position of dispensing good to those who have found favor in the eyes of the Lord: he is minister of justice. Certainly, he also deceives, but again his victims are only those who have already turned their eyes away from the truth, the light. He does, in addition, suffer because of his own evil. Although he does not express the towering rage or the excruciating anguish of the Satan of Milton's *Paradise Lost*, he does "bitterly" say, "I am always alone" (p. 42). Loneliness, separation from God—this is, according to traditional Christian teaching, the ultimate suffering for those who go to hell.

Critics of the novel have commented frequently and at length about the character of Woland, with varying degrees of accuracy. Deck notes that Woland leaves it to his subordinates to play pranks, tricks, jokes. "Woland remains above these antics and performs a more philosophical function."[11] Proffer concurs: "It is noteworthy that Bulgakov is careful to credit all of the mischievous tricks to Koroviev, Begemot [Behemoth], et al., often emphasizing that Woland knew nothing of these things. Woland presides over the Variety performance only briefly, for example, and disappears before the truly scandalous events take place."[12] Lakshin, describing the traditional Devil's role as twofold, to tempt and to punish, states, "Woland seems intentionally to narrow his functions. He is not as inclined to tempt as to punish."[13] Proffer gives an illustration: "Woland has seen Berlioz's fate—*not* caused it."[14]

But some good critics have then overreacted. Lakshin asserts that Woland "offers an example much more in the way of goodwill and nobility and even, I would say, an unexpected morality."[15] He says, also, "How slight is the resemblance between this thoughtful humanist and the merciless demon of the netherworld!"[16] And Proffer, calling Woland "an extremely sympathetic character, all told," thinks that "it is he, and not the Master, who comes closest to embodying Bulgakov's own views and character."[17]

The best antidote to these exaggerations comes from a character who knows the true nature of Woland. Matthew calls him the "spirit of evil and lord of the shadows"(p. 357). It is no wonder that Woland sneeringly expresses implacable hostility toward Matthew, even as he accepts the Lord's instructions sent through this messenger whom he disdains. Satan knows his role, here given in the words of Eastern Orthodox euchology: "Render evil unto them, O Lord, render evil unto them, even unto the proud ones of the earth."[18] In short, although Bulgakov's Satan does not embody every aspect of the traditional conception of the Devil, there is nothing in his character which lies outside of that conception. The subject of Satan's role will be discussed further toward the end of this chapter.

The names of Satan's companions deserve special consideration. Of the four who accompany him, two have names which can be traced to biblical or apocryphal sources, while the other two apparently have names of Bulgakov's devising. The name of Behemoth appears in the Bible (Job 40:15). The name of Azazel appears, as well as Behemoth's, in the Jewish apocalyptic literature of the Pseudepigrapha. Sometimes these names, as well as others, have been used for the Devil himself in one or another of his aspects. Bulgakov uses the names to make them distinct characters, much as did Milton in *Paradise Lost* with such characters as Beelzebub, Belial, and Mammon. Clearly, Bulgakov wants us to see Woland's four traveling companions—Azazello, Behemoth, Koroviev, and Hella—as in league with and in liege to Satan.

Of the four, Azazel is particularly prominent in traditional Christian demonology. (Milton, too, mentions him by name.) There is enough information on Azazel to fill many pages. Indeed, Milne says that the character of Azazello opens up "veritably fathomless pits of exegesis."[19] However, not all of this voluminous material offers help in illuminating the character of Bulgakov's Azazello.

Bulgakov lets us know which particular legend about Azazel he has mainly in mind in portraying Azazello. In the final section, when Satan and the fallen angels appear out of the disguises which they have used during their earthly sojourn, the "real guise" of Azazello is that of "the demon of the waterless desert, the murderer demon" (p. 377). This legend links Azazel with the story of the scapegoat which is treated in the sixteenth chapter of the Book of Leviticus, though Azazel is not mentioned by name in that canonical book. According to this account, on the Day of Atonement the priest was to use two goats, one to be sacrificed to God and the other to be symbolically loaded with the sins of Israel and driven into the desert, the opposite of the sanctuary, the desert being the place to which sin should be consigned. Azazel's role in this story, then, would be as the devil of the desert to whom ransom had to be paid. (We recall here the importance of the concept of ransom in the soteriology of Eastern Orthodoxy.) In addition, the scapegoat sent to Azazel would serve as a reminder to him of his own ultimate fate. Milne notes that the name *Azazel* itself means "scapegoat."[20]

Azazel thus is integrally related to the Old Testament typology which prefigures the sacrifice for man's redemption, both of the goats together forming a type of Christ. It seems likely that Bulgakov's choice of this particular name of a devil, out of all of the devils' names available, is an indication of his abiding concern to focus attention upon the vicarious atonement of Christ. Milne remarks that the typological significance of the two goats as prefiguring the sacrifice of Christ was "clearly and prominently stated in the article on Azazel in Brokhaus-Efron, one of Bulgakov's reference books."[21]

The Book of Enoch is the primary source in antiquity for information about Azazel, though he appears also in the Apocalypse of Abraham and the Testaments of the Twelve Patriarchs. Although most of this information is on matters other than the scapegoat story, this element is not excluded. Charles, citing the Book of Enoch, notes that the scapegoat was to be sent "to die in a hard and rough place in the wilderness of jagged rocks, i.e., Beth Chadure or Beth Chadude," which "was a definite locality near Jerusalem."[22] This was the very location to which Azazel had been consigned. Charles again quotes the Book of Enoch to this effect:

> And again the Lord said to Raphael: "Bind Azazel hand and foot, and cast him into the darkness: and make an opening in the desert, which is Dudael and cast him therein. And place him upon rough and jagged rocks and cover him with darkness, and let him abide there for ever, and cover his face that he may not see light. And on the day of the great judgment he shall be cast into the fire."[23]

There are many other elements to the story of Azazel. Of these we shall look at the following: that Azazel was the first (and the leading) angel to fall from heaven, that Azazel taught first women and then men carnal ways, that Azazel taught men the arts of war, that the wicked dead are sent to Azazel, and that the scapegoat story is not unconnected to these other stories.

It is Lea's view that "the first clear mention of a personal devil (Beliar-Satan, Sammael, Mastema, Azazel) occurs in the *Testaments of the Twelve Patriarchs*," a pseudepigraphal work which he says dates probably from the Maccabean age.[24] Similarly, the Book of Enoch sees Azazel as personal, since he teaches unrighteousness to humans. But the author depicts the fallen angels as stars. And he sees "a single star representing Azazel, falling from heaven, which is followed by many other stars representing all his host."[25] In that Azazel is the leading fallen angel whom others follow in the fall of the angels, he plays the same role elsewhere ascribed to Satan, or Lucifer. Significant for our purposes is the importance of Azazel. Bulgakov is choosing no minor demon when he selects Azazel for embodiment in his Azazello on the visit to Moscow.

Whereas the story of the fall of Satan traditionally associates him with the tempting of Adam and Eve in the Garden of Eden in the third chapter of Genesis, the coming to earth of Azazel is related to the time very shortly before the Flood of Genesis 6 (Noah's Flood, as it is popularly known), an event which occurred many long generations later. The key Bible verse here is Genesis 6:4, a verse which has been much discussed in the commentaries. It says, "There were giants in the earth in those days; and also after that, when the sons of God came in unto the daughters of men, and they bare children to them, the same became mighty men of old, men of renown." The debate has raged: were these partners the sons of Seth and the daughters of Cain, or were they fallen angels and human women? The latter interpretation has been of long standing, and it is within it that Azazel figures. One version, not canonical, is that he and Shemhazai were the first two fallen angels to father sons by human mothers.[26]

One source explains, "Azazel was familiar to the Rabbis as the seducer of men and women."[27]

These same two fallen angels (Shemhazai = Semjaza) "are mentioned in the Book of Enoch, including the earliest chapters, as being responsible for the bloodshed and lawlessness which prevailed on the earth following the descent of the angels."[28] But it is Azazel in particular, the first who fell, who is blamed (in I Enoch 9:6) for having "taught all unrighteousness on earth and revealed the eternal secrets which were preserved in heaven."[29]

One of Azazel's acts was "to devise the finery and the ornaments by means of which women allure men."[30] A number of citations could be given for this point; it is not an obscure one. And it is this point which causes Proffer to say, "Azazello, usually identified as the demon of the waterless desert, has many different roles; and the one which Bulgakov was obviously thinking of is that of the fallen angel who taught men magic and women how to paint their faces."[31] Proffer offers no support for this assertion, and I think that she is mistaken, as the previous discussion has made clear.

What Azazel taught to the men includes the making of armaments out of metals. Citing yet again the Book of Enoch (8:1-2), Charles comments, "And Azazel taught men to make swords, and knives, and shields, and breastplates, and make known to them *the metals* (of the earth) and the art of working them...."[32]

Other charges against Azazel could be added.[33] But these, as well as the ones cited in the immediately preceding paragraphs, seem to have no direct referents in *The Master and Margarita*.

The next point comes closer to possibly having application to Bulgakov's novel, though ultimately it does not. Russell explains that "in the Apocalypse of Abraham it is said that the righteous dead go at once to Paradise (ch. 21) and the wicked dead to Azazel and the Abyss (chs. 12, 14, 21)."[34] Russell comments, also, that the Abyss and its torments "can be identified with Azazel" and that "the wicked or the heathen are Azazel's `portion' who have been assigned to him from the beginning."[35]

The question here is whether the Master and Margarita go with Azazello down into the Abyss, a place of suffering and torment. They do not; this matter will be discussed in Chapter Nine. Rather, they go to a peaceful place. They do not follow the fallen angels "to the abyss of fire and to the torment and the prison in which they shall be confined for ever."[36] So this part of the story of Azazel seems not to be used by Bulgakov—though there is every reason to presume that Bulgakov in his erudition knew all of the stories mentioned about a character whose name he employed.

If we stand back from the ancient sources about Azazel and simply ask what the character of Bulgakov's Azazello is, what is probably most striking is that Azazello is not a party with his fellow demons in their high jinks—the pranks, the tricks, the fun and games. These divertissements are left to Koroviev and Behemoth. Azazello is truly demonic. Of all of the devils in the novel, he is the most physically repugnant in appearance. When he goes on a mission, as when he brings the cream to Margarita (and many other examples from the novel could be given here), he is a deadly serious emissary of Woland and his infernal realm. He is the one—the murderer demon—who brings death to the Master and Margarita with the poisoned wine. Of course, as with Satan himself, his evil deeds result in ultimate good. But that fact relies on God's initiative, not Azazello's. Azazello, despite his "real guise" at the end of the novel, knows his "department." He does what he must do, as we might extrapolate from ancient legends, he might prefer to do. He is as clearly attached to the concept of the Satanic incarnation as Satan himself is.

The name of Behemoth, unlike that of Azazel, appears in the Bible, in Job 40:15. The rest of chapter 40 (verses 15-24) describes him. This passage is part of a long section in which the Lord explains to Job, after Job's series of testings, that he, the Lord, is absolute master of all things, that he created the great land creature Behemoth and (in Job 41:1-34) the sea creature Leviathan. In this account, though Behemoth eats and drinks prodigiously, he is no more than a very large animal, one of the chief of God's creations.

It is in apocryphal books and later legend that Behemoth takes on aspects of a monster and becomes associated with the diabolical. The name itself is a plural noun, the literal meaning of which is "cattle."[37] Later commentators, including Aquinas, understood the name "to signify the demon."[38] Thus, according to Lea, "As with the serpent of Genesis, so also Satan was identified with the Leviathan and Behemoth of the book of Job."[39] The pseudepigrapha develops the legend that Behemoth, the male land monster, and Leviathan, the female sea monster, become consorts.[40] Charles cites the Book of Enoch (60:7-10) as recounting the parting of the two monsters.[41] And Ginzberg explains that God had to keep them from propagating; "else the world could not have continued to exist."[42] Therefore, God deprived Behemoth of "the desire to propagate his kind."[43] The Book of Enoch has Behemoth consigned to "a waste wilderness named Dudain, on the east of the garden where the elect and righteous dwell."[44] Ginzberg asserts that this desert abode is "undoubtedly identical with the desert Dudael," discounting the possible objection that one desert is located near Jerusalem and the other not.[45] It is, then, the same desert to which Azazel is consigned.

Lea remarks that Behemoth is the name for the devil which signifies gluttony.[46] Ginzberg explains this notion: "He is so monstrous that he requires the produce of a thousand mountains for his daily food. All the water that flows through the bed of the Jordan in a year suffices him exactly for one gulp."[47] There is some canonical precedent, albeit lacking pseudepigraphal extravagance, for this matter. Job 40:23 says, "Behold, he drinketh up a river, and hasteth not: he trusteth that he can draw Jordan into his mouth." Lea summarizes the allegorical meaning applied to this feat: "The swallowing of the Jordan by Behemoth means that Satan swallowed the human race, with the exception of a few saints, until the time of Redemption...."[48]

Behemoth, along with Leviathan, also figures into the eschatological scheme of Jewish apocalyptic literature. Citing II Baruch 29:4-5, D. S. Russell notes that at the time of the final judgment, "...the great mythical monsters, Behemoth and Leviathan, will be used as food for the righteous in the great 'messianic banquet.'"[49] Farrer mentions a line of interpretation which links the two monsters with the dragon of the twelfth chapter of the Revelation and the two beasts of the thirteenth chapter. Noting that the Septuagint, the ancient Greek translation of the Hebrew Old Testament, rendered the plural noun *Behemoth* with the plural form of "wild-beast" (one word in Greek), instead of the tame-sounding "cattle," he comments that Leviathan and Behemoth became, respectively, "the dragon and the (wild) beasts."[50] The final chapter of this study will attend to Bulgakov's fascination with and use of the Book of the Revelation.

On the basis of this background, what are we to say of Bulgakov's choice of the name of Behemoth for his big, fat black cat? Obviously, having the devil appear as a black cat is a commonplace in literature on witchcraft, so much so that citations are unnecessary. Bulgakov's Behemoth is huge for a cat, but he does not begin to rival the land monster of the pseudepigrapha or even the mammal of the Book of Job. The cat Behemoth is not the only animal which Bulgakov endowed with human traits; one thinks immediately of the dog Sharikov in *The Heart of a Dog*. But Bulgakov surely knew about the Behemoth of ancient Jewish lore, and he had to have this material in mind when he chose the name.

The general answer is simply that Behemoth was linked with Satan and thus was among the names which could be used for the evil spirits of the novel. If Bulgakov started with the idea of a black cat, the choice of the name of an animal which was sometimes used as a synonym for the Devil would be a reasonable one. Also, of course, the ancient Behemoth is a big animal, and Bulgakov's cat is big as cats go. Bulgakov refers to "the gluttonous Behemoth" (p. 349), which description fits with the ancient legend. And Proffer notes that in Goethe's *Faust* the poodle (Mephistopheles in disguise) turns into a hippopotamus—just at the moment when Faust is translating from the Gospels.[51] It is of more than passing interest that there existed in the 1920s a popular satirical magazine entitled *Begemot (The Hippopotamus)*, which specialized in satirizing bureaucrats, profiteers, thieves, and hooligans.[52] Surely, this association must have delighted Bulgakov. He could gather together more than one association into a single richly symbolic name.

There is yet one more possibility about which one can only speculate, since one often must remain unsure of the connections which flitted through Bulgakov's fertile mind. Perhaps his choice of an animal as one of Woland's crew is related to the fact that in the Book of the Revelation one of Satan's key emissaries on the earth is called the Beast—usually understood as a synonym for the Antichrist. If there is any merit to this speculation, another might follow: that Koroviev, the ex-choirmaster who acts as Woland's interpreter, is an echo of the False Prophet of that same book, the Revelation.

It should be remembered that the black cat is only a disguise for the fallen angel under consideration. And it is not his only disguise. At one point, he takes on the disguise of "a large fat man in a tattered cap" (p. 344). One character who comes to accept the reality of the supernatural, the Master, knows that Behemoth is "not entirely a cat" (p. 288).

To the extent that the old lore about Behemoth helps us understand Bulgakov's cat, it applies only to the disguise. Whereas the real guise in which Azazello is revealed at the end of the novel links him directly with the ancient

Azazel, the real guise of Behemoth bears no resemblance to the ancient Behemoth. He is revealed as "a slim youth, a page demon, the greatest jester that there has ever been" (p. 377). It is not at all clear what Bulgakov has in mind here, nor do other critics help here. Perhaps the author has no ancient figure in mind.

Despite the obviousness of the primary source of the name of Bulgakov's cat, this character has many attributes which bear no relationship to this connection. The outlandish pranks and antics, which the reader of the novel does not need to have rehearsed here, have no necessary connection to the old land monster. In sum, Bulgakov's Behemoth is a much less faithful representation of the ancient source than is Azazello.

The name of Koroviev is of a different order from those of Azazello and Behemoth. This name is a Russian one, not a name of ancient vintage. Nor is his synonym of Faggot, or Fagot. Deck notes, "Koroviev-Faggot is the most gratuitously ludicrous of Satan's retinue, and appears to belong neither to the serious heritage of Abadonna nor to the lore of black magic."[53] His name is clearly an assumed one. When asked who he is, he responds hesitantly, as if inventing an answer on the spot: "My name is...er...let's say...Koroviev" (p. 94). The name itself comes from the Russian word for "cow." There is no apparent significance to this etymological choice, nor is there any evident linkage with the fact that the name of Behemoth means "cattle."

The name of Faggot, as Piper observes, means "bassoon."[54] Stenbock-Fermor notes that his name "designated a small musical instrument."[55] If there is any particular significance to this choice of name, it might simply be that this musical connotation fits loosely with his being an ex-choirmaster, a point which he is at pains to underscore.

On the point of his being an ex-choirmaster, there may be an additional significance. Perhaps Bulgakov is hinting that Koroviev also is to be understood as one of the fallen angels, one who once led an angelic chorus before he fell (hence *ex*). And, since he is an ex-choir*master*, perhaps he was once an *arch*angel, though there is no clue to which one he was. In that case, his leading of the Theatrical Commission workers in their involuntary and continuing singing is to be read as a parody of an angelic chorus. This parody would be of much the same sort as the parodies, depicted elsewhere in the novel, of the Last Supper and the Christian Mass.

One supposition for Koroviev's having a human name rather than a demonic one is that he is Woland's "interpreter" (p. 94), the one who mediates between the Devil and the Russian populace—hence the Russian name. He might be considered, in a way, the Devil's John the Baptist, the one who goes before and prepares the way. He is the first of the hellish retinue to appear in the novel, preceding even Woland.

In one passage Koroviev is described as "magician, choirmaster, wizard, or the devil knows what" (p . 249). It seems that only the Devil does know. We readers are left in the dark.

The part of Koroviev's character which has evoked the greatest amount of critical comment is the real aspect in which Koroviev appears at the end of the novel. He is called a knight who "once made an ill-timed joke," specifically, "a somewhat unfortunate pun" on darkness and light (p. 377). On the basis of this passage, Stenbock-Fermor concludes that Koroviev-Faggot is "a reincarnation of Faust, but of a Faust who instead of being the devil's master is now his servant and is doing penance for the pun which offended the devil...."[56] Faust's pun was, "You call yourself a part, yet stand whole in front of me," which pun, Stenbock-Fermor says, "was a refutation of the words by which the devil had introduced himself and which form the epigraph of the novel."[57] Proffer is among those who accept this interpretation.[58]

On the other hand, Beatie and Powell assert that Stenbock-Fermor's identification of Koroviev and Faust "cannot be taken seriously."[59] Milne, also, rejects that identification, for the compelling reason that "the 'pun' cited by Stenbock-Fermor contains no reference to light and darkness."[60] Then Milne offers two alternatives of her own. Perhaps Koroviev is Mephisto, since Mephisto's reply to Faust does contain a reference to light and darkness.[61] Her second, and preferred, guess is that Koroviev is Goethe himself, since he is the author of Mephisto's words.[62] She then works a slight variation on this second possibility by suggesting that the name *Fagot* refers not just to the author but to the work itself, noting that her capitalized letters in "FAust by GOeThe" might provide a source for the name Fagot.[63] Fortunately, Milne sits lightly on her suggestions, for they seem highly unlikely. Though this reference does seem to cry out for allusion-hunting, so far it is one of the doors in the mansion which is the novel which remains closed to critics.

Hella, the witch, is the fourth and last of Woland's company. She appears only sporadically and is not characterized in depth. Devils, of course, can be either male or female.[64] She often appears naked, as does Margarita when she becomes a witch; and one of Hella's functions in the novel seems to be as a foil to Margarita. Hella has a perfect figure, except for a livid scar on her neck.

The name of Hella has no source in ancient Jewish lore. If there is a literary source for the name, it might come from Norse mythology. Hel is the Norse goddess of the underworld. She is half white and half black and looks like a corpse.[65] Only the second part fits Hella.

Milne's opinion is that "Woland and Bulgakov both forget about her [Hella] on that last transfiguring flight, an omission which indicates that Bulgalkov had not devised for Hella any further level of significance."[66] One need not disagree with the gist of this statement (except for the word *forget*), to suggest that Bulgakov needed only four, including Satan, to serve as a parody of the Four Horse*men* of the Apocalypse and that there was no place for Hella.

The critic who has best illuminated Bulgakov's Hella is Laura Weeks. She locates the antecedent of Hella in ancient Middle Eastern mythology about Lilith. Lilith is probably best known in legend as Adam's first wife; but the story has it that she later became the wife of Sammael, king of the demons, and she was traditionally considered both a vampire and a seductress.[67] Not only is Weeks persuasive in linking Hella with Lilith, but she offers a good explanation for why Hella is absent on the journey of Woland and his henchmen into the abyss:

Her absence from that scene...could be explained by the fact that Lilith, unlike Satan and the fallen angels that serve him, is mortal and will die with the coming to power of the Messiah. Thus, she would have no part in the eternal punishment of Satan and the others.[68]

Thus, Hella is a member of Satan's retinue on his visit to Moscow, but she is different from the others. She plays her part, especially in the hair-raising scene involving punishment for Rimsky, one of the functionaries in that version of hell which is the Variety Theater. Yet it is not appropriate for her to accompany Woland on his final ride from earth to the beyond.

One more infernal character, Abadonna, must be mentioned, though he is not exactly one of Woland's retinue: he does not travel with or otherwise align himself with the Satan's retinue. His major appearance in *The Master and Margarita* is at the conversation between Woland and Margarita just before Satan's Ball commences, that occasion which, as will be seen, is a parody of the Christian Mass and which is set in Apartment 50, one of the locations symbolizing hell. Abadonna says nothing. However, Woland describes him cursorily and explains his function. Abadonna appears in the figure of a man wearing dark glasses, glasses which make a powerful impression on Margarita. He is "utterly impartial," even "equally sympathetic to people on either side" of a fight or war (p. 258). Woland says, "There never has been and never will be a case when Abadonna comes to anyone too soon" (p. 258). When Margarita asks if Abadonna can take off his glasses, Woland replies, "No, that is impossible" (p. 258).

Bulgakov's Abadonna is obviously the same figure of which St. John writes in Revelation 9:11: "And they had a king over them, which is the angel of the bottomless pit, whose name in the Hebrew tongue is Abaddon, but in the Greek tongue hath his name Apollyon." The Hebrew name, or word, appears six times in the Old Testament "as a synonym for Sheol or Hades, the universal graveyard, the land of death, darkness, silence, and oblivion, the destroyer of life and hope."[69] To this Old Testament word both St. John and Bulgakov give human qualities.

Abadonna is the Destroyer, is the one who brings death, is Death itself. He cannot bring death to someone until the appointed time has come; hence, he cannot take off his glasses at Margarita's request. He never comes too soon, because he is not his own master. Like Satan himself, he is under the ultimate control of God. Thus, he, along with Satan, reinforces the overarching theme of the Satanic incarnation: that it is God who really rules over all, both the human world and the netherworld. Indeed, the passage in which he cannot take off his glasses may be a parodic echo of Exodus 33:20, in which God tells Moses, "Thou canst not see my face: for there shall no man see me, and live."

When one of the fallen angels, Koroviev, first appears in the novel, "...the sultry air coagulated and wove itself into the shape of a man—a transparent man of the strangest appearance" (p. 4). According to a popular medieval notion, angels can take on earthly forms, including human form; but the bodies are constituted of air. Their bodies are not those of real men, which are made of the dust of the earth, not of air. It is to this same medieval idea that the learned

John Donne repairs in his famous seventeenth-century English poem "Air and Angels." Angels may take on human appearance, but they are not actually human beings. They can only parody the true Incarnation of Christ, who took on a body of flesh and blood and thus became fully human.

Both good angels and bad angels can take on earthly forms, but there is a difference:

> Angels when they visit men assume human shape, when their bodies are formed of air with other elements.... So it is with demons, except that they take the lower air while angels take the higher. The shapes assumed by demons are usually most foul, and, if God permitted them to appear in deformity like their sin, no man could endure the sight.[70]

So it is altogether appropriate that Bulgakov's devils have uniformly bizarre and unpleasant appearances: Woland's unmatching eyes; the fang, walleye, and nasal accent of Azazello; the marring scar on Hella's neck; the outlandish clothing of Koroviev, as well as his initial shape (seven feet tall and incredibly thin); the very "cat-ness" of Behemoth. Bulgakov does not make infernal evil pleasant; he is too orthodox to do so. In these unpleasant appearances he gives ample warning not to read guileless benevolence into the actions of the devils.

Whenever Satan is about his business, we find the setting to be illumined by moonlight. The novel can be examined episode by episode according to the presence of the moon or the sun; Bulgakov is very careful about this matter. Examples abound; here a few will suffice. Satan arrives at sunset; with his coming the sun disappears and the moon rises. The second chapter of the novel, which is the first installment of the story of Yeshua, is set in blazing sunlight. A common Christian appellation for the day is *Good* Friday. But the searing sunlight is mightily oppressive to that unbelieving man, Pilate, who is the son of an astrologer—that is, a moon- and star-gazer. As soon as this chapter ends and we return to Satan in Moscow, the moon rises. The major events of Book One will occur at night (or indoors), not in sunlight: the scene at Griboyedov House, the first scene at the insane asylum, the show at the Variety Theater, and so forth. When a man escapes from Satan's presence in the Devil's Moscow headquarters, Apartment 50, he emerges into "the sunlit courtyard" (p. 200). Late in the novel we read that fragments of the sun still shine on Moscow (p. 373). This city is not a part of the Kingdom of Light; yet God is still interested in it, has not written it off, has not altogether withdrawn from it the presence of grace. His light is still available, though it is partly concealed by the diabolical influence.

Satan explains that his intention in coming to Moscow—an intention, incidentally, which has nothing to do with the intentions of Mephistopheles in Goethe's *Faust*—is to find out about the state of heart of the Muscovites: "Have the Muscovites changed inwardly?" (p. 121). The answer comes a few pages later: No. External circumstances have changed; there are buses and telephones and other accouterments of modern life. But men's hearts are the same in all ages:

> They're people like any others, but thoughtless...but they do show some
> compassion occasionally. They're overfond of money, but then they
> always were.... Humankind loves money, no matter if it's made of
> leather, paper, bronze or gold. They're thoughtless, of course, but then
> they sometimes feel compassion too.... They're ordinary people—in fact,
> they remind me of their predecessors, except that the housing shortage
> has soured them. (pp. 124-25)

Parenthetically, the last clause is one illustration of Bulgakov's intermittent,
and actually quite frequent, satire of Soviet society. This study may shortchange
this dimension of Bulgakov's contemporary satire, though only because it is
not central to the novel, not because it is absent or insignificant. Many other
commentators have written at length, and usually appropriately, on this
subject. Although such satire is not the major concern of the novel, just as it is
not in the preceding quotation, certainly Bulgakov delights in taking satiric
potshots all along the way. Many examples could be mentioned. One of
Bulgakov's favorite targets, for reasons which grow primarily out of his own
sad personal experience, is the state of letters and arts. For instance:

> ...if you wanted to make sure that Dostoevsky was a writer, would you
> really ask him for his membership card?... A writer isn't a writer because
> he has a membership card but because he writes. How do you know
> what bright ideas may be swarming in his head? (pp. 350-51)

It is the prominent literary figure Berlioz who is the recipient of Woland's
harshest scorn. The driving concern of the members of MASSOLIT for nice
vacations and other perquisites has its obvious referent in real Soviet life.

Bulgakov takes aim at other targets, as well. At one point, Koroviev throws
the Master's case history into the fire and destroys it in order to keep the
keepers of the insane asylum from tracking down the missing Master.
Koroviev says with satisfaction, "Remove the document and you remove the
man" (p. 288). This is certainly an ironic twist on the malevolent use to which a
Soviet citizen's papers are often put. Additional objects of Bulgakov's satire
include the tight housing situation, the drunkenness of the Russians, the robot-
like bureaucrats, the despicable character of many persons in theater life, and a
host of others.

However, these barbs are all tangential to Bulgakov's main concern, which
is spiritual. Or, better, they are to be understood within the context of his
spiritual concern—much as is the case with Solzhenitsyn when he comments
on political matters but wants them to be understood within the context of the
moral vision which governs his writing. It is the human heart, not the theater
or the economy or the government or any other arena of the social surface,
which absorbs Bulgakov's attention. What Woland observes is that the
Muscovites are not a new brand of humanity; there is no New Soviet Man.
Bulgakov has sounded this note before. In his story "The Adventures of
Chichikov," which brings Gogol's famous character of *Dead Souls* to life in

Soviet Russia, we find that rogues still flourish, just as they did in pre-revolutionary Russia. That the Communist Revolution did not change human nature, as it intended and promised to do, is also a major point of Bulgakov's novella *The Heart of a Dog.*

In Bulgakov's view, human nature is fixed and is therefore beyond manipulation by humans. This fixed human nature Bulgakov understands to be dual, mixing good and evil—which conception a theologian draws from the Christian doctrines of Creation and Fall. So Woland observes that the Muscovites have, on the one hand, compassion and, on the other, greed and thoughtlessness. In this regard, the Muscovites are no different from human beings of any time or place. Human nature is not only fixed but also universal. These qualities of the human heart are the definitive issues of Bulgakov in *The Master and Margarita* (and elsewhere, throughout his writings, though that is another subject).

Of the several issues which, by appearing at the opening and the closing of *The Master and Margarita*, provide an envelope effect and thereby demonstrate their significance, we may observe a most important implied question about the spiritual life of the modern Muscovites. The novel opens with a conversation about Jesus Christ, one which focuses on the response of men to Jesus' import. At the end Jesus reappears. Both of these sections on Jesus lie outside the novel-within-the-novel about him and Pilate. The reality of Jesus Christ is accepted by Bulgakov himself and not just by the sometimes deluded Master and Bezdomny. This is a novel about beliefs. The key question is always, "What think ye of the Christ?" Of course, its presentation is usually oblique, via the Satanic incarnation. The responses of the various characters are what determine their fates at Bulgakov's hands.

The Muscovites represent natural man, man in the unredeemed state. Satan *qua* Satan is of course glad to learn that they are atheists and thus under his control. But it is precisely for such sinners that Christ came to earth. And in this novel it is for these that Satan comes. It is of God's doing that Satan comes, for his appearance is presented as proof of the existence of God. In a state which promulgates a doctrinaire disbelief in God's reality, none of the traditional proofs or evangelistic approaches will serve. The only approach left is an indirect one, one which is designed to force men first to recognize the reality of something other than God—something which their party-line outlook also rejects but which, if ever accepted, would lead logically to an acceptance of the reality of God, too. All of those chapters in which Satan and his followers appear are, cumulatively, devoted to explaining this, the seventh proof of God's existence. Most persons in the novel do not believe, however much evidence is forced upon them, and for their rejection they receive their just reward. Two do come to believe, the Master and Margarita; that is, they believe that the Devil really is the Devil. For their belief they, too, receive their appropriate reward. Both deniers and believers must have direct experience of the seventh proof, which is the crucial test in this novel, and both groups get it.

The standard reaction of Muscovites to the presence of Satan in their midst is that "it can't be." This is another one of those matters which appears at both the beginning and the ending of the novel. As Satan remarks to one of them,

"Whatever I ask you about—it doesn't exist" (p. 42). Bulgakov, speaking *in propria persona*, puts these denials in proper perspective when he asserts, "But that, of course, is pure fantasy—the Caribbean doesn't exist, no desperate buccaneers sail it, no corvette ever chases them, no puffs of cannon smoke ever roll across the waves. Pure invention" (p. 59). One who must see to believe has no more seen the far-away Caribbean than he has seen Jesus. The one is no more real to the strict materialist than the other. Such a one has all the sophistication of the cosmonaut who returned to earth to report that he had not found God up there.

It is no wonder that Woland, himself of supernatural reality, after having in the first chapter asserted that Jesus really did exist, quickly goes on to twit the atheists when he says, condescendingly, "But surely...you of all people must realize that absolutely nothing written in the gospels actually happened. If you want to regard the gospels as a proper historical source..." (pp. 40-41). And he breaks off in mid-sentence. What, logically, would be the conclusion to that sentence? Bulgakov seems to be inviting each of his readers to finish it. Woland's question is of the same order as—indeed, essentially appositive to— that question in the Gospels, "What think ye of the Christ?" In terms of the novel, Woland's sardonic assertion that nothing in the Gospels ever happened is an untenable view. Even the distorted picture of Jesus Christ in the novel-within-the-novel does not take such an extreme position. Despite all of the divergences from the canonical account, many of the essential details of the biblical narrative remain.

One of those Muscovites whose heart we see plumbed is Bezdomny, or Homeless. Because he is such an important, albeit puzzling, character, a full chapter, number eight, is devoted to him. Suffice it here to say that it is his contact with Woland which arouses in him some degree of awareness of supernatural reality, and he can no longer go on his old naturalistic way.

Bezdomny is not the only unbelieving Muscovite whose soul is laid bare to the reader. In all of the others, however, there is something definitely evil, something which calls forth just punishment. On the spiritual spectrum of belief and unbelief, they cluster at the end of unbelief.

Among these is George Bengalsky, Moscow's best-known master of ceremonies and the person who presides over the black-magic show at the Variety Theater. Proffer tells us that Bulgakov himself was once a master of ceremonies of a small theater and that this experience provided him "with the material to create the character of Bengalskii."[71] It is this character who, in an effort to pacify a very nervous crowd, insists that there is "nothing supernatural" (p. 123) to the magic tricks of Woland and company, and he offers his own naturalistic explanation, mass hypnosis, for one of them. This explanation is of a piece with those offered in the Epilogue by the "educated and cultured people" for the whole visit of Woland and his gang. For his temerity Bengalsky must experience the seventh proof personally: his head is cut off. Unlike Berlioz, who also lost his head, Bengalsky has his head put back on. His crime is less than Berlioz's, though of a similar nature. Still, his punishment is one of the three most severe ones in the novel, along with that of Berlioz and that of

Baron Maigel, who is stabbed to death; and Bengalsky is never again able to return to his normal occupation.

Head imagery is significant in *The Master and Margarita*. Indeed, Beatie and Powell declare, though extravagantly, that "the 'head' is, in fact, the predominant motif" in the novel.[72] Donald Fiene also comments substantially on this imagery.[73] The many references to "head" are thoroughly catalogued in these two sources. Missing from them is an explanation of the significance, especially theological significance, of this recurring motif. One possibility is that the biblical imagery of Christ as the head of the Church, which is the Body of Christ, is a useful point of reference. The severed head of Berlioz is used, in parodied form, as a communion cup from which to drink to life everlasting (p. 272). In the case of Bengalsky's temporarily severed head, we might draw also a parallel to the severed head of John the Baptist. As John the Baptist was the forerunner of Jesus, so Bengalsky, as the master of ceremonies at the Variety Theater's magic show, serves as the forerunner at that one point in the grand parody of the Incarnation provided by Satan's visit to Moscow.

Another Muscovite who challenges the reality of the Devil and who therefore must experience the seventh proof personally is Arkady Appolonovich Sempleyarov, chairman of the Moscow Theaters' Acoustics Commission and guest of honor for the festivities of that fateful evening at the Variety Theater. This important personage demands an explanation, a naturalistic explanation of course, for the magic tricks of the evening. As a punishment for his rejection of the supernatural, there follows the public revelation of his infidelity: Faggot announces Sempleyarov's four-hour tryst at an actress's flat the night before. Such is the price for denying the reality of the Devil.

Another who tastes the seventh proof is Rimsky, the treasurer of the Variety Theater. (How Bulgakov relished imposing a fictional punishment on those denizens of the theatrical world, whom he so heartily despised—just as Dante damned his enemies in the *Inferno*!) Rimsky cannot figure out the telegram ostensibly (and actually) sent from the far-off city of Yalta by Likhodeyev, the house manager of the Variety Theater, to whom he had talked in Moscow that very morning. He was in "an extremely perplexing situation. He had to find an immediate, on-the-spot *natural* solution for a number of very unusual phenomena" (p. 106, emphasis added). Then he remembers a nearby Turkish restaurant named The Yalta and, adding into his calculations a drunk Likhodeyev, concludes that his problem is resolved. But the simple, though naturalistically impossible, truth is that Likhodeyev is the better part of a thousand miles away. Rimsky's straining after a natural explanation for a supernatural event is akin to those explanations offered, to the point of silliness, by the "educated and cultured people" in the Epilogue. Who can believe that the Devil has come to Moscow? After all, who can believe that God once came in person to Jerusalem?

The first and most important demonstration of the seventh proof involves Berlioz, the atheistic literary editor. In fact, it is the death of Berlioz which is the subject matter of the chapter, number three, entitled "The Seventh Proof." When Berlioz first meets Woland in the opening pages of the novel, he rather "like[s] the look of him" (p. 7). He is one of Satan's own and has an intuitive affinity for him, though on the intellectual level he rejects the concept of the Devil.

Their conversation about Jesus turns Berlioz against Woland, because Woland belittles his reasons for disbelieving in the historicity of Jesus. That Bulgakov places Berlioz in a bad light throughout is one of the many clues that Bulgakov is countering atheism with his novel. That he uses the Devil himself to do so tells us much about how we are to view Woland. On the question of the historicity of Jesus, Berlioz tells Woland that "we take a different attitude on that point" (p. 14). Woland counters sharply: "It's not a question of having an attitude.... He existed, that's all there is to it" (p. 14). Berlioz is capable of "pick[ing] his way around the sort of historical pitfalls that can only be negotiated safely by a highly educated man" (p. 6). But the way of this cultured despiser of Jesus Christ is destruction, not the light of truth.

Berlioz rejects the reality of the Devil as firmly as he rejects the historical existence of Jesus and the reality of God. When Woland queries, "And the devil doesn't exist either, I suppose?" (p. 42), it is Bezdomny who blurts out, "There's no such thing as the devil!" (p. 42). But the context makes clear that Berlioz agrees. He had mouthed to Bezdomny, "Don't contradict him" (p. 42). Berlioz's denial of Jesus is no more vigorous than his denial of Satan—to Satan's face!

When confronted by Woland, Berlioz resolves his befuddlement in the time-honored Soviet way of dealing with belief in supernatural reality: he considers Woland "a lunatic" (p. 41). It is the way of last resort. Earlier, quoting Schiller and Strauss against Kant's proof of God's existence, Berlioz had suggested that Kant belonged in an insane asylum (p. 9). Bezdomny will soon, for his flirtation with the supernatural, be placed in such an institution, as will the Master—and for the same reason. And Berlioz wishes the same fate for Woland himself.

The seventh proof is about to be demonstrated to Berlioz: that the Devil exists and thereby proves that God exists. Berlioz's death, beheading by a street-car, happens just in the manner that Woland had said it would. Denial of the Devil's existence results in physical destruction.

Proffer suggests that "there is a kind of vengeful cruelty in Bulgakov's manner of disposing of him."[74] She is wrong. Bulgakov allows Berlioz to receive clear testimony to the truth which resides outside the ken of his atheism. Indeed, Proffer herself earlier offers a hint in this direction:

> If the erudite Berlioz had been less distracted he would no doubt have begun to suspect the identity of this foreigner, merely by looking at the cigarette case with the triangle of diamonds (the inverted triangle being a sign of the devil, and anti-trinity) or by wondering why his cane has a poodle handle.[75]

Actually, Berlioz would not have had to know Satanic symbolism to have perceived Woland as some sort of supernatural entity. Woland has spent time with Kant and Pontius Pilate. If, when he announces these occasions, he might well be considered merely a lunatic, the ring of authenticity in his detailed account of Pilate in Jerusalem should give Berlioz pause. And he must be elevated to at least the level of magician when he produces the very brand of cigarettes requested. Even the label *magician* is inadequate when Berlioz feels a twinge in his heart and Woland thereafter suggests that Berlioz has had a slight heart attack. Woland coyly speaks hypothetically, but Berlioz should recognize that something is afoot here which transcends his categories of thought. The same is true when Woland announces what is not public knowledge: that Berlioz has an uncle in Kiev.

Berlioz has two major appearances in the novel: one in the opening chapters (Chapters One and Three) and one at Satan's Ball (Chapter Twenty-three, specifically page 272). The former ends with the beheading of Berlioz. In the latter, the bodiless head appears before Woland. Woland talks to it. Then Berlioz's head turns into a goblet. In between these two appearances there occurs a passage in which Berlioz was supposed to appear in person but did not do so: the dinner scene at Griboyedov House. Twelve members of the management committee of the writers' union are awaiting their chief. This scene serves the symbolic role of antitype of the Last Supper of Jesus and his twelve disciples, as we shall see shortly.

On one level the severed head of Berlioz symbolizes the state of the natural man; recalling the Pauline image in I Corinthians of the Body of Christ, we see that a body lacking a head is like man apart from Christ. On another level Berlioz serves as an antitype of Christ. His death (like Christ's, prophesied) is historical (again like Christ's). His funeral is held on Good Friday. His pallbearers are three men and a woman; Satan's retinue is comprised of thee males and a female. Berlioz was the top man of Griboyedov House, which we shall see is a type of hell.

Toward the end of Satan's Ball, Berlioz's head, now fully conscious, reappears. This final scene including Berlioz focuses on Bulgakov's twin concerns about facticity and about the centrality of beliefs. Indeed, the two merge into one, for in the novel the chief issue has to do with believing that facts are facts and not denying factual matters.

Underlying the author's concern for facticity, Woland says to Berlioz, "It all came true, didn't it? Your head was cut off by a woman, the meeting didn't take place and I am living in your apartment. That is a fact. And a fact is the most obdurate thing in the world" (p. 272). Woland's prophecies had not been idle speculations but foretellings of actual events.

Then Woland moves on to the centrality of beliefs. He describes Berlioz's belief that human life stops when one's head is cut off. This *theory* (that is the word which Woland uses) is false, of course, as the very conversation in which it is stated demonstrates. Yet Woland, devilishly, calls the theory "intelligent and sound" (p. 272). Satan is gladdened when men hold such a theory. But then, since "the devils also believe and tremble" (James 2:19), he offers an alternate theory: "that a man will receive his deserts in accordance with his beliefs" (p. 272). Note the word *beliefs*. What a man believes is the all-important issue. And Berlioz's answer to the question "What think ye of the Christ?" had been such that his deserts are now "to depart into the void" (p. 272). Woland then transforms Berlioz's skull into a goblet from which he has "the pleasure of drinking to life eternal" (p. 272). One could hardly ask for a clearer rejection of atheism. Neither in this novel nor in the Bible do the devils ever adhere to the world view of atheism.

Why did Bulgakov choose the name of a non-Russian Romantic composer of music, Berlioz, as an antitype of Christ? Since he also brings into his novel the names of Rimsky, Stravinsky, and Strauss, Bulgakov may be making an indirect statement about his taste in music, perhaps about the philosophical underpinnings of Romantic music. Little help on this subject is to be found from other commentators, but a few speculations on the use of the name of Berlioz are possible.

Hector Berlioz left us two compositions which seem to have a bearing on this novel. His *Symphonie Fantastique* includes a witches' sabbat and demonstrates his taste for the grotesque. His *Damnation of Faust* is based on Goethe's *Faust*, which quite obviously had a place in Bulgakov's mind when he wrote *The Master and Margarita*. The latter is the more important of the two for our purposes. Many critics have observed the link between Bulgakov's novel and Berlioz (and Goethe). Some presuppose that Bulgakov liked and approved of Berlioz and his point of view.[76] That assumption may be incorrect; it may be similar to the notion that Bulgakov sympathizes with the Devil. After all, there is a strong streak of Satanism in the Romantic period, a view which sees the rebel as ineluctably heroic; and this view is at odds with Bulgakov's depiction of Woland.

The Faust legend is the West's primary literary myth about the Devil's entering the sphere of human activity. Goethe's Faust is sentimentally saved. Berlioz reworks Goethe and has his Faust damned. Bulgakov seems to rework the myth in quite another way. His Faust (if the Master is indeed his Faust figure) is saved but not sentimentally. Bulgakov seems to reject the Romantic perspectives of both Goethe and Berlioz. The originally Christian imagery which they accepted only as legend to be appropriated to their own uses, a common practice among the Romantics, he accepts as a depiction of literal truth. That Bulgakov uses the name of a Romantic composer, Berlioz, as his antitype of Christ suggests strongly that he is not merely working a minor revision on the Romantic treatments of the Faust story but is standing the legend on its head. Or, better, he might be saying that the Romantics had turned the true story of man on its head in the first place by their treatments of the Faust legend and that he is righting it.

There is no question that the Faust story was a trigger for Bulgakov's imagination. His novel's epigraph comes from Goethe's *Faust*. He began, as we have noted, by focusing on the Devil's coming to earth. But just what relationship are we to find between that hoary legend and this novel? Most of the commentators on the novel have pointed out a connection between the two, usually emphasizing Goethe's treatment of the story. Elisabeth Stenbock-Fermor has led the way in viewing the Faust legend as the key to a proper reading of *The Master and Margarita*. Certainly, she has demonstrated that Bulgakov's borrowings from this source were extensive. Yet she provides a quite inadequate transition from pointing out the Faustian parallels to showing, as promised, Bulgakov's "real intentions"[77] in terms of the Faust legend. Her article, seminal for many commentators, offers no coherent, overarching interpretation of Bulgakov's novel. Indeed, it concludes with unsatisfying vagueness.

Were one to locate in Goethe's *Faust* a key to the meaning of *The Master and Margarita*, one could expect, at a minimum, that some sort of equation would be limned between Mephistopheles and Woland, between Faust and the Master, and between Gretchen (Margaret) and Margarita. Yet Stenbock-Fermor's emphasis falls on a correspondence between Koroviev-Faggot and Faust and another between Bulgakov's Frieda and Goethe's Gretchen.[78] Also, when she offers, on behalf of Goethe, "the purifying and inspiring power of the moon, dear to Romantic poets,"[79] we think of how different—virtually opposite—is Bulgakov's moon symbolism.

Of course, there is a certain linkage between Mephistopheles and Woland: both are devils come to earth to intervene in human affairs. But Proffer enlightens when she points out dissimilarities. "Like Mephistopheles, Woland is passing as a traveling scholar, but unlike Goethe's character, Woland remains a dignified personage even as he mocks the limited imaginations of his interlocutors."[80] Notice throughout that it is only in minor and superficial ways that Bulgakov's characters imitate Goethe's—though certainly enough to keep calling Goethe to mind. Bulgakov's echoes of Goethe serve to highlight the difference of outlook between the two authors. Demonstrating that "Woland reveals himself to be more than just a literary borrowing from Goethe," Proffer observes,

> ...Bulgakov's Woland is not the witty drinking companion of Faust who tempts "so that men will strive." He is, rather, Lucifer the fallen angel—solemn, majestic, and only occasionally witty. Bulgakov's Devil is close to Marlowe's version of Mephistopheles—a tormented figure who carries his suffering with him.[81]

Even more emphatic is the difference between Goethe's Faust and the Master. Whereas the former embodies the self-sufficient man's thirst for knowledge and for dominance over nature, the latter is clearly in need of aid from outside himself in his effort to cope with life and its realities. (He finds that aid primarily in Margarita, who serves frequently as a type of Mother Mary and of the Church.) The call to Faust is to be strong and self-reliant; the Master is called upon to be neither. What parallels there are between Faust and the Master emerge only in the manner of irony or parody—or ironic parody. So Helen Muchnic is generally on the right track when she calls *The Master and Margarita*

> a humorous, intricate, philosophic work that seems to be a version of Goethe's *Faust*, but is really a parody of it, transforming the Goethian conception of a world in which illimitable striving, whatever crimes it may entail, is the essence of virtue, into a demon-ridden one where helpless men are ruled by incomprehensible fate, where the highest good is an artist's mysterious knowledge of truth and reality, and the finest virtue is self-abnegating devotion.[82]

If there is a character in Bulgakov's novel who is Faustian, it is Margarita. She is the one who makes a pact with the Devil: she agrees to be the queen of his ball. Yet she does so not at all out of a sense of personal striving for captaincy over her own fate, but rather out of a willingness to sell herself for her beloved Master. She, too, is self-abnegating. She is like a mediatrix, if not a redemptrix. This contrast is a vital one between traditional Christianity and Romanticism. The only thing in common between Bulgakov's Margarita and Goethe's Margaret (Gretchen) is the name. Stenbock-Fermor is therefore correct in linking Gretchen with the pitiable Frieda—who also is spared through the mediation of Margarita-the-active-agent, though that linkage weakens the claim that Goethe's *Faust* provides the key to interpreting Bulgakov's novel.

Thus, we may conclude that the Faust legend serves only as an ancillary and tangential element for the interpretation of *The Master and Margarita*. One view of the novel is that the Bible provides matter for literary allusions and that *Faust* gives us the key which unlocks the mystery. The view offered herein is exactly the opposite. It is the Bible's story of redemption, duly expanded and explained by Christian theologians through the centuries, which offers us the key to Bulgakov's vision of the human situation. The Faust story, especially as presented by Goethe, is one which deals with ultimate human realities, and thus it provides Bulgakov with a grand body of allusive material which he can turn to his own Christian purposes.

We return, then, to the role of Satan in this novel, a role which has been touched upon before but one on which we can now focus with adequate background. He is a minister of God to bring justice. He functions only under God's heaven, and he knows as much. When he brings misery to unbelieving human beings, he is not acting arbitrarily. These unbelievers, after all, are in his power already; he gains nothing through their punishment. Rather, he is executing justice on human beings who live in a moral universe governed by immutable laws. As Yeshua is God's minister of love, so Woland is God's minister of justice.

Woland himself explains (to Margarita) that mercy and forgiveness lie outside his "department." Margarita had asked him to exercise compassion toward Frieda, who had stifled her baby with a handkerchief. He demurs. Then he explains why: "Each department must stick to its own business. I admit that our scope is fairly wide, in fact it is much wider than a number of very sharp-eyed people imagine" (pp. 282-83). Satan's realm, as great as it is, has strictly defined boundaries. As an early anonymous reviewer noted, "Although the Devil does some mischievous damage, his function seems in the main to be that of a scourge of God; he is much less a tempter of the pure to sin than a tempter of the sinful to uncover their sins and be punished."[83]

Out of respect for the concept of justice, Woland then informs Margarita that she herself can provide the forgiveness which Frieda craves. As for compassion, which is what Margarita had requested of him, he says, "Sometimes it creeps in through the narrowest cracks. That is why I suggested using rags to block them up" (p. 282). Such are the ways of the universe which God rules and within which Satan has only an assigned department. And so

Margarita, symbol of the mediatrix Mother Mary, does what Satan cannot do: she forgives Frieda.

Satan, we must always remember, is the one who wills forever evil, yet does forever good, as the above-cited passage illustrates and as the epigraph to this novel reminds us. And he does so for a good reason: divine providence rules the world. "All things work together for good to them that love God" (Romans 8:28). But evil-doers receive their just recompense. As an earlier-cited line from Orthodox liturgy says, "Render evil unto them, O Lord, render evil unto them, even unto the proud ones of the earth."[84]

When, in the Old Testament, God allows Satan to test Job, the Devil is forbidden to harm Job personally. This restriction is in accordance with the rules governing the operation of the world. Job does not belong to the Kingdom of Darkness. Neither do the Master and Margarita, and so all of Woland's dealings with them must work to their ultimate benefit—not because of Satan's sentimental softness but because of God's just providence.

Even Azazello's killing of the two title characters is seen, in the light of eternity, as for their own good. Azazello, the murderer demon, kills also Baron Maigel; but that character goes to hell, because that fate is what he deserved. Both executions are in accord with the principle of justice. When the staff members of the Variety Theater are located after Woland had scattered them, all of them—Likhodeyev, Varenukha, and Rimsky—ask to be locked up in a strong room for their own protection. Their incarceration contrasts directly with the freedom which is the reward of the believing Master and Margarita. The contrast between bondage (under Satan) and freedom (under God) is a motif which runs throughout the novel.

An indirect evidence of providence crops up time after time in the common expressions of language which invoke the Devil and hell. Following their encounter with Woland, the Master says to Margarita, "...the devil knows what it was!" (p. 362). She replies, "Just now you unwittingly spoke the truth.... The devil *does* know what it was and the devil, believe me, will arrange everything!" (p. 362). Other characters also speak the truth unwittingly. The man who disappears out of his suit, which remains at his desk and at work, swore once too often. He said, "I'm damned if..." to Behemoth, who replies, "You'll be damned, I think you said? Very well!" (p. 188). A woman on the stairway leading to Apartment 50 says to a man about to re-enter the apartment, "Oh, go to hell" (p. 207). When he goes into the apartment—which, we shall soon see, is a symbol of hell—he is punished: clawed about the head by Behemoth. In an inverted form the same principle operates when Varenukha, at his request, is released from being a vampire and returned to ordinary life. He says to Woland, "Thank Go— I mean your maj-..." (p. 290).

The examples of inadvertent truth-speaking when humans use such words as *Devil, damned,* and *hell* abound. But this last-cited one by Varenukha is particularly serviceable for highlighting the negative correspondence between God (as distinguished from Yeshua) and Satan. The primary parallel comes, of course, in the Satanic incarnation, which has already been discussed. Satan is to God (who never appears directly in the novel) as the moon is to the sun, as the shadow is to the substance. Indeed, this correspondence is the context when

Woland gives Matthew the important "lecture" about the value of shadows. But Satan, even as a minister of justice, is never to be perceived as good, as God is good. His implicit acknowledgment to Matthew of the parallel between himself and shadow is a recognition on his part of his own evil. We have already noted Satan's aloneness when he said, "I am always alone," and he said it "bitterly" (p. 42). Isolation, alienation from God—this is the essence of hell. Even the Master (as representative man), who often feels alone, is not, in the final reality, alone; it is always the Master *and* Margarita.

Still, like God, the Devil is always to be understood as a real being, one who is supernatural. Bulgakov's depiction of Woland squares perfectly with St. Paul's conception: "For we wrestle not against flesh and blood, but against principalities, against powers, against the rulers of the darkness of this world, against spiritual wickedness in high places" (Ephesians 6:12). Thus, when the police come armed to Apartment 50 to arrest Woland and his crew, they score a direct hit on Behemoth; but it is of no effect, inflicting no wounds (p. 351). They are fighting spiritual wickedness, not flesh and blood; but they do not know so.

When Satan, as God's shadow, comes unto his own in Moscow, he appears in several locations, which then serve as symbols of hell. Four buildings are gutted by fire—traditionally hell's element—all of the fires having been set by the diabolical visitors.

One is the haunted apartment, which becomes Satan's dwelling place and which had belonged to Berlioz, the antitype of Christ. Proffer informs us that the apartment was the very one in which Bulgakov himself had lived—and hated: He called it the "damned apartment 50" and the "nightmarish apartment No. 50."[85] (Bulgakov used actual locations so regularly that even today a visitor to Moscow can locate many of the sites which appear in his work.)

Woland's occupancy of the apartment transfigures it; and, appropriately, it takes on religious qualities, albeit inverted ones. The apartment is described as having stained-glass windows through which "poured a strange ecclesiastical light" (p. 202). The table is covered with an altar cloth, on which is a plate of solid gold. Also present are candles and the odor of incense. All of these are elements of that parody of the true Mass, the Black Mass, which is soon to occur during Satan's Ball (and which will be treated later). There is also a fire in the fireplace, though it gives off no heat. At the Ball the habitues of hell will issue forth from the cavernous fireplace.

A full chapter is devoted to the finishing-off of Woland's abode: Chapter Twenty-seven, "The Last of Apartment No. 50." Most of the chapter charts the hapless efforts of the authorities to resolve the mystery of this place. Of course, in real life this apartment building still stands. But in the novel it ends in conflagration—set by the demons from hell. The setting for that scene from hell, Satan's Ball, is destroyed. It is the first of the four buildings to burn, a precursor of things to come.

The second of the four buildings destroyed by fire is Griboyedov House, another symbol of hell. This is the headquarters of MASSOLIT, a typically Soviet acronym for the literary establishment which Bulgakov despised. Proffer sees this site as "the key location for the contemporary satire of the novel."[86] If not necessarily that, it is certainly the locus for Bulgakov's justifiably venomous satire on the literary elite of the Soviet Union. And Bulgakov makes sure that we understand that this presumed elite is populated by second- (and lower-) rate writers and just plain hacks.

This Griboyedov House, which pampers its habitues with the best restaurant in Moscow, is of course Herzen House, which was in Bulgakov's time and still is now the headquarters and watering hole of the Soviet Writers' Union. Why does Bulgakov change the name from Herzen to Griboyedov? In the novel the commonly held story is that the house was once owned by Griboyedov's aunt. Edwards, noting that this story is unconfirmed, suggests that this fact emphasizes "the unreality of the writers' situation"; recalling that Griboyedov's most famous play was entitled *The Folly of Being Wise* (more commonly translated *Woe from Wit*), he adds, "There is a pleasing irony in Bulgakov's implicit application of the title of Griboyedov's play to an organisation of writers who in his view are excessively concerned with the intellect at the expense of the spirit....."[87] Proffer sharpens the point when she writes of "...the distance between the original and the Soviet variation—the difference between...Alexander Griboedov, the first important Russian playwright, and the building which bears his name, inhabited by characters just as negative as his corrupt aristocrats—but infinitely more vulgar and insignificant."[88]

As in the case of the burned-out haunted apartment, here again the element of parody is clearly present. The highlight of Chapter Five, "The Affair at Griboyedov," is a parody of the Last Supper. Twelve of Berlioz's lieutenants wait for him in a room in "the upper story" (p. 57), but the antitype of Christ does not appear. His body has been broken—not to save them but to condemn them. The twelve members of the management committee leave the room at midnight. Later they do eat, after hearing of their leader's broken body. Their conversation is about who will have a place in the summer resort of Perelygino—their version of Paradise. This is a thinly veiled reference to Peredelkino, which still serves as the prime literary colony for Soviet writers. This conversation may well be intended as a parallel to the talk among Christ's disciples about who will have the places of prominence in his coming Kingdom. Bulgakov may also have had in mind John 14:2: "In my Father's house are many mansions..... I go to prepare a place for you."

At midnight the jazz band strikes up, the dancing begins, and shrieks of "Alleluia" are heard (p. 58). These elements correspond to details of Satan's Ball, which of course is itself a parody of the joyous Orthodox service occurring at the midnight hour which introduces Easter every year. Griboyedov and the activities within it are pointedly labeled "in short—hell" (p. 58).

At midnight there appears, as "a vision in this hell," a man who seems like Satan himself and who "surveyed his domain" (p. 58). It is Archibald Archibaldovich, the maître d'hôtel. A story had been circulating that he was once a pirate on the Caribbean. He has a pointed black beard—just like the one, for whatever reason, which adorns the face of the doctor at the insane asylum who admits and initially quizzes Bezdomny.

Just how are we to understand Archibald Archibaldovich? Critics recognize his connection with Satan. Haber calls him "the diabolical director of the restaurant."[89] Ullman calls him "the Devil's Double."[90] Wright says that the restaurant is "presided over by its Satan, the manager Archibald Archibaldovich."[91] Proffer describes him as "a satanic figure," one "who involuntarily calls up associations with pirates and walking the plank."[92] When Bezdomny, after his initial encounter with Satan, rushes into Griboyedov to tell the sad news about Berlioz, it may be the presence of Archibald Archibaldovich which causes Bezdomny to "sense that he's [Woland's] here!" (p. 61).

One supposition is that Satan temporarily takes over the being of Archibald Archibaldovich. A parallel case is that of a female nurse at Dr. Stravinsky's clinic, who appears in the guise of Azazello—or, better, he in hers. One of the doctors looks at her and sees "a wide, crooked man's mouth with a fang sticking out of it. The nurse's eyes seemed completely dead" (p. 212).

If Archibald Archibaldovich provides a human form for Satan to use in Chapter Five, "The Affair at Griboyedov," the case is different in his other major appearance in Chapter Twenty-eight, "The Final Adventure of Koroviev and Behemoth." When the two infernal rascals appear in the scene which culminates in their burning the house down, Archibald Archibaldovich immediately recognizes them and commands that they be admitted. He seems also to guess at the impending disaster. Exercising what Bulgakov calls "his phenomenal sixth sense" (p. 354), he goes to the larder, removes two heavy fillets of smoked sturgeon, grabs his silk-lined overcoat, and departs the premises. This man has gained some understanding that there is a supernatural reality which is beyond his control. He implicitly acknowledges the powers of evil with whom he has been in league and accepts them as real. However, his deficiency is that he has accepted the shadows as if they were the substance. He does not perceive that they point to something outside themselves as the ultimate reality, as do the Master and Margarita. He accepts Satan as Satan but not as a parodic parallel to God. Thus, he is one character in the novel who accepts the reality of the supernatural but remains without the benefit of redemption.

If this explanation of a fascinating minor character remains somewhat frustrating, the problem lies with the difficulty which we have in accepting Bulgakov's skewed and kaleidoscopically changing correspondences. For they violate what we might call our innate desire for symmetry and order. Archibald Archibaldovich is a classic case of Bulgakov's eschewing straight allegory in favor of ever-shifting symbolism. At one time he fuses with Satan; at another time he does not. But he is not at all alone with regard to this kaleidoscopic shifting of symbols by Bulgakov.

And so Griboyedov House burns—"to a cinder" (p. 359). In all, four symbols of hell do so. As Griboyedov burns, Woland, sitting to the east of the fire and also facing east, still has his eyes shining "with the same fire, even though he sat with his back to the sunset" (p. 357). His body is of air, not earth. But he partakes of the same infernal element which consumes one of the earthly images of hell.

The other buildings are about to burn. Although these fires receive scant coverage in the novel, the principle is the same: they are symbols of hell. One of these is the building which contains the Master's basement apartment. Though the Master was once happy in his little flat as he worked on his novel about Pontius Pilate, the hostile reception of it brought him great anguish. It is this unhappy abode which, at the end of the novel, is exchanged for the pleasant cottage which is to be his (and Margarita's) eternal dwelling place. Much earlier, Margarita had dreamed of a hut, a log cabin, by a little bridge. A mournful, desolate hut (p. 217), it represents, in the style of a dream, the miserable apartment of the Master. It is, like Griboyedov House, "in short— hell" (p. 217). It is this cabin which, at the end of the novel, is transfigured into the Master's "home for eternity," his "reward" (p. 381). Fire can be purging and purifying as well as destructive. As Azazello sets the fire in the Master's apartment, the Master says, "Burn away, past!" And Margarita cries, "Burn, suffering" (p. 369).

The fourth building which burns is the Torgsin Store, a state-run store for tourists—only foreign currency accepted. Tourists today will know this kind of store as a *beriozka* in Russia, a *kashtan* in the Ukraine. Once again, Bulgakov vents his ire on a Soviet institution which he finds an abomination, as do many others, by making it a symbol of hell. It provides a classic occasion for Bulgakov's intermittent satire of the oppressive Soviet system.

So Satan and company have come to earth. They have done their jobs. We shall examine their departure in Chapter Nine, "The Apocalypse."

Chapter Five

Pilate and Jesus

❖ ❖

The second of the three plots of *The Master and Margarita* is the novel-within-the-novel about Pontius Pilate and Yeshua Ha-Notsri. It appears in three widely separate places in the novel and is comprised of only four of the thirty-two chapters: Chapter Two ("Pontius Pilate"), Chapter Sixteen ("The Execution"), and Chapters Twenty-five and Twenty-six ("How the Procurator Tried To Save Judas of Karioth" and "The Burial").

Some commentators have found these combined chapters the best part of the whole novel. D. G. B. Piper, for one, calls this plot "the most important and powerful section of the book."[1] Shirley Gutry considers the early scenes of this plot "truly magnificent. There is nothing to compare with them in Bulgakov's prose or in Soviet literature of the thirties. The ripeness is there as well as the mastery of an accomplished artist."[2]

The style of this plot is "majestic"[3] and "consciously elevated,"[4] quite in contrast to the "the comic style found in the Moscow narrative,"[5] with its idiosyncratic style and its sometimes raucous and uproarious elements. And the narrative is strictly objective throughout, again unlike the frequently subjective approach of the parts set in Moscow. Says Gutry, "In the Jerusalem narrative, where the narrator disappears, Bulgakov's prose style is, in contrast, elevated in tone and much more involved, with an intricate syntax."[6]

There are two primary questions about the Jerusalem narrative, and they are integrally related. First, who is telling this story? Second, how are we to interpret the character of Yeshua, or Jesus, since his portrait in this narrative is quite different from that in the Four Gospels of the New Testament? Bulgakov does not allow us to give a simple answer to the first question, though what we can determine is certainly enough to lead to a firm answer for the second question.

However, even answering these two questions does not get us quite to the heart of the issue of this plot. For the main character to whom we must attend is neither the author (or authors) of the account nor Yeshua but Pilate. The Master (let us assume for the moment that the Master is the author of the novel-within-the-novel) is called "the creator of Pontius Pilate,"[7] by no less an authority than Woland, and the Master does not disagree. Whoever created Pilate created Yeshua, but it is Pilate who is specified. It is Pilate who is called the Master's "hero" (p. 381), that is, his central character. So it is not surprising that much more space is devoted to the depiction of Pilate than to that of Yeshua. Further, Pilate is the primary active moral agent in this drama; Yeshua is the essentially passive recipient of the result of Pilate's initiative. Yeshua is present as the moral touchstone by which we are to evaluate Pilate (just as he is the touchstone by which to evaluate all of the Muscovites who appear in Bulgakov's novel). Milne is of like mind: "The centre of identification is Pilate; the wandering philosopher Yeshua is described as he impinges upon Pilate...."[8] Ullman and Johnson concur; Proffer speaks of "the Pilate novel."[9] Since Yeshua is the touchstone, we must understand him before we can understand Pilate.

But, first, who is the author of his narrative? As was observed in the "Overview" chapter, the three segments come ostensibly from three different sources. Woland, or Satan, tells the first part. The second comes from a dream by Bezdomny. The third is from the Master's novel, as being read by Margarita. Yet all critics apparently would agree that "everything intrinsic to the three installments of the Pilate story argues that it be viewed as a single text."[10] Proffer's view, which is closer to the truth than she may know, is that "the devil is the only author of the story of Yeshua...."[11] Milne's coy, but not incorrect, assessment is that the author is "Woland—which is to say the Master, which is to say Bulgakov."[12]

On the subject of the authorship of the Jerusalem account, Johnson's extensive remarks are as helpful as anyone's:

> In fact, from the outset the reader forgets that Woland is talking, that Ivan is dreaming, or that Margarita is reading because the same objective, omniscient third person narration is present in all three segments. It is phraseologically marked by long, complex sentences with numerous participial clauses, inverted word order, and exotic, defamiliarizing names and epithets.... In this manner the three separate installments of the Pilate-Ieshua story are combined into a single, coherent entity which can be seen as the Master's novel. After all, in the case of Woland and Ivan, the narration does not correspond on the phraseological level to what the reader knows of their speech characteristics, but it is identical to that of the text identified as the Master's novel.[13]

Not only is Johnson persuasive here, but she proceeds to harmonize effectively the ostensible three sources into one actual author.

> Woland could have witnessed the events of two thousand years ago, and thus he could be reporting facts to his unbelieving modern-day audience. Yet he could also be recreating what the Master has independently divined. After all, the text which Margarita reads is itself not the original which the Master wrote and later destroyed but the manuscript which Woland "resurrected." The devil, of course, could have easily caused Ivan, his impressionable and ignorant listener, to dream the continuation of the story.... Thus, the supernatural powers of the devil and the creative insight of the artist could both be equally responsible for the narration of the same true events.[14]

Certainly, it is the case that in the opening chapter Woland is able to read the mind of Bezdomny (of Berlioz, also) and even to finish his thoughts. (The case for Bezdomny as author—which, though plausible, I reject—is discussed in Chapter Eight.)

That a manuscript has both a natural source and a supernatural source—this is just what historic Christianity has declared about the Bible. We need not trouble ourselves here with the various theories offered by theologians on the subject of divine inspiration of the various human authors of Holy Writ. The oblique nature of Bulgakov's symbolic correspondences does not allow us to press the point. All that is necessary is to see the parallel between God's inspiration of the biblical writers and the Devil's inspiration of the Master.

To see this parallel allows us to avoid two errors made by some critics, both of which are represented by Proffer. We need not diminish the biblical account, as she does when she says that "Bulgakov wishes the reader to believe that his narrative is more likely, more convincing, and better written than the Gospels."[15] Nor shall we ascribe the authorship of the Jerusalem chapters directly to Bulgakov himself.[16] Rather, we shall know just how to mistrust this diabolically distorted account of historical reality. We shall understand that, when we see Jesus through the diabolical filter of moonlight, we see only the shadow of the real Jesus Christ.

In the final analysis, although it is likely that the human authorship of the Pilate story belongs to the Master, the more important matter is to recognize the sublunary origin of this version. For this understanding is what allows us to explain the distorted, or apocryphal, elements in the plot.

It is easy enough to list details in the novel-within-the-novel which differ from the account in the Gospels. For instance, Yeshua is twenty-seven years old, not thirty-three. He says that he has no relatives. He blames Matthew for writing lies. He enters Jerusalem on foot, not on a donkey. He wears filthy rags, which the Roman guards spurn, rather than a seamless robe which they greedily gamble for. He is poked in the stomach with a lance, not in the side; and this piercing occurs before he is dead, not afterwards.

But the overriding matter is that all of these details, as well as all others which could be listed, have their origins in the canonical record. They are not fabricated out of thin air. They distort the canonical account and set it askew. But it is precisely the canonical account which they distort. It is always to it that they have a necessary relationship; they do not have a life of their own. Indeed, critics of the novel recognize the relationship between the novel-within-the-novel and the Gospels, however they choose to interpret that relationship. Irving Howe is correct when he says that this "version of the Christ story approximates the spirit of primitive Christianity" and that this version's Jesus "is a figure Dostoevsky would have recognized and loved."[17]

What has usually been too little noticed, especially by critics who insist upon using the novel-within-the-novel to support their case that Bulgakov holds an unorthodox view of Christianity, is that very many canonical details are retained intact. Here are some of them, among which are ones which are so obvious that it is easy for critics to neglect to mention them. Judas betrays Jesus, for which the price is thirty pieces of silver. Pilate sentences Jesus. Pilate asks his famous "What is truth?" question. The Jewish religious leaders, Caiaphas in particular, insist that Jesus be put to death, even at the cost of the freeing of Barabbas. Jesus is crucified, and the crucifixion occurs on Mount Golgotha and on Friday. The event is accompanied by a major storm.

Then, there are many details which are neither direct repetitions of the biblical account nor obvious distortions of it; rather, they are imaginative reconstructions of the biblical narrative which generally do not depart from the letter of the account and which at all points retain the spirit of it. For instance, Yeshua does not know exactly who he is by birth; according to the Bible, he was born of a virgin mother and had no human father. Yeshua has no home; in Matthew 8:20 Jesus says, "The foxes have holes, and the birds of the air have nests; but the Son of man hath not where to lay his head." Yeshua asserts that Pilate is mistaken in his statement that he, Pilate, can cut the thread of life of Yeshua. In John 19:11 Jesus replies to Pilate, "Thou couldst have no power at all against me, except it were given thee from above...." This response squares with Jesus' previous declaration to his disciples in John 10:18: "No man taketh it [my life] from me, but I lay it down of myself. I have the power to lay it down, and I have the power to take it again." On the cross Yeshua is offered a soaked sponge from which to drink, as is the case in the Bible; what is supposedly water is vinegar in the Bible but poison in the novel. Yeshua pleads that one of the thieves alongside him be given a drink of water, too. This is a naturalized reworking of his promise of Paradise to that thief; both versions demonstrate mercy. Yeshua "blamed no one" (p. 327) for his death; in Luke 23:34 Jesus exclaims, "Father, forgive them; for they know not what they do." All of this meticulous attention to detail is to be seen as Bulgakov's attempt to be faithful to the realism of the biblical narrative—as faithful as he can possibly be, given the diabolical source of the Master's version.

Yeshua was buried on the Eve of the Passover feast, as the Bible also has the story, and Bulgakov employs the Passover typology in good Eastern Orthodox fashion to emphasize the ransom element of Christ's death. (See the section in Chapter Four, above, on Azazel and the scapegoat.) Above the temple in Jerusalem there are "two gigantic seven-branched candlesticks" (p. 313) which are lit for the Passover. (These are to be contrasted with the parodying two candelabra at Satan's Ball.) "They seemed like fourteen huge lamps that burned over Jerusalem in rivalry with the single lamp climbing high above the city— the moon" (p. 313). We have here a contrast between the Kingdom of Light, represented by the candles, and the Kingdom of Darkness, represented by the moon.

Bulgakov also inserts—or has the Master insert—parallels with the Messianic prophetic passage of Isaiah 53 to underline Christ's salvific role. (Or so most orthodox Christians interpret Isaiah 53.) Isaiah's Suffering Servant receives the traditional thirty-nine stripes, or lashings, as does Christ in the New Testament. Similarly, Yeshua is beaten and whipped. "With his stripes we are healed" (Isaiah 53:5). Yeshua is described as having a bandage on his head, a large bruise under his left eye, and a scab of dried blood in the corner of his mouth. Isaiah 53:5 says, also, "But he was wounded for our transgressions, he was bruised for our iniquities." The first promise in the Old Testament of the coming of the Messiah speaks of the bruising which he will sustain from Satanic force (Genesis 3:15).

Not only does Bulgakov's Master retain a great number of canonical details, but he also allows Yeshua to express views which can be understood only by recourse to the belief that Jesus Christ is divine. Even an account inspired by Satan, who, after all, does believe that Jesus Christ is God but who tries to obscure that view of things from mortal men, cannot totally obliterate the divine presence. For instance, when Pilate asks his "irrelevant" question, "What is truth?", Yeshua is able to tell him the truth about his (Pilate's) internal state, something beyond mere powers of observation: "At this moment the truth is chiefly that your head is aching and aching so hard that you are having cowardly thoughts about death.... It even hurts you to look at me" (pp. 21-22). Yeshua also predicts, "Your suffering will be over soon."[18] And we have already seen that Pilate does not have the power to do away with Jesus. When, in John 10:18, Jesus said that he had the power to lay down his life and to take it up again, he finished by saying, "This commandment have I received of my Father." In Yeshua's rebuke to Pilate in Chapter 2, there is an obvious thematic congruence with Woland's assertion in Chapter 1 that a human being does not have the power to rule himself, that even his death can come unexpectedly and is outside his control. Apparently, then, Bulgakov is giving us hints that we should withhold the easy judgment that Yeshua was a merely mortal, natural man—even though, as we shall see, the Devil seems to want to have the Master depict him so. Despite the diabolical filter, some evidences of Yeshua's divine status seep through. Why the presenting of these evidences is important will become clear when Yeshua appears outside the Master's novel—at the end of Bulgakov's own novel.

But Bulgakov never makes matters easy for his readers. Sometimes, even when he drops hints that Yeshua is to be seen as retaining supernatural powers, he allows those readers who would be akin to the "educated and cultured people" of the Epilogue (p. 383) to find a naturalistic explanation. For instance, when Yeshua says that he knows that Pilate wants to pet his dog, Banga, and Pilate asks him how he knows, Yeshua replies, "You moved your hand through the air...as though to stroke something, and your lips..." (p. 23). So maybe Yeshua is just a close observer of human behavior? But what about such an item as Yeshua's knowing that Pilate was suffering a severe headache? Here no alternative naturalistic explanation is offered.

The apocryphal, or non-canonical, details of the novel-within-the-novel, some of which have already been mentioned, remain. However, in the light of the background presented in the last several pages, they now seem much less confusing that at first glance they might have appeared, and they no longer seem an adequate basis for declaring Bulgakov heretical. In fact, ironically, many of the modifications of the biblical account now serve to reinforce through symbolism that very biblical narrative from which they diverge. And those which do not do so can now be seen as harmonious with the overall interpretation being offered in this chapter. Specifically, they serve to freshen our view of Jesus; they make us try to imagine the story of Christ's passion apart from the accretions of the centuries, which tend to dull our minds and to reduce the drama of the story to formulas encased in creedal and liturgical texts. For example, there is no symbolic value in the fact that Yeshua is twenty-seven or in the fact that he entered Jerusalem on foot or in the fact that he wore filthy rags. Such deviations fit perfectly with that common Russian literary "technique called *ostranenie*, or 'making it strange.'"[19]

Those alterations which carry symbolic weight are of greater interest, since they serve to reinforce the message carried by the biblical narrative as traditionally understood. Thus, for example, the hour of the storm is shifted from early to late afternoon. Why? One guess is that the reason is so that it can merge into the setting of the sun. The storm is a symbol of judgment, and the crucifixion is traditionally understood as God's judgment upon sin and the Devil, to be consummated at the end of time. Darkness is a natural image for evil, and it is so applied in the Bible (*e.g.*, John 3:17-21). Consistently and repeatedly, Bulgakov uses the same imagery. With the death of Christ, the Sun of Righteousness (Malachi 4:2) sets, and men who rejected his light are left to the enveloping darkness of night. Also, Bulgakov associates a storm and earthquake with nightfall when he apocalyptically describes the end of Moscow (p. 327) in terms which correspond closely to the description of Jerusalem as a "smoking caldron of wind, water and fire" (p. 179).

Another revision which carries symbolic weight is that the sponge, ostensibly soaked with thirst-quenching water, contains poison in the Master's novel, not the vinegar of the biblical story. Pilate's several reiterations of the word *poison* demonstrate his sense of guilt toward the killing of Yeshua. But it is important to note that Yeshua does not drink the poison. Rather, he dies of "sunstroke" (p. 303). Once again, Bulgakov invokes the symbolism of sun and moon. It is God, the one who gives life in the first place, who now takes away Christ's life from him—not Pilate, not the Devil. In ultimate theological terms, a good thing is happening on Good Friday, and God is in control. Christ's death is God's provision of a vicarious atonement for the sins of men.

Another cluster of apocryphal elements which symbolically reinforce biblical themes comes from those passages in Matthew's parchment which Pilate reads: "There is no death.... Yesterday we ate sweet cakes.... We shall see the pure river of the water of life.... Mankind will look at the sun through transparent crystal...greatest sin...cowardice" (p. 326). None of these items can be found in the Gospel according to St. Matthew—or any of the other three Gospels, for that matter. But that there is no death is clearly a biblical teaching—

if it is understood to mean that all men possess immortal souls and will never be annihilated. This very point is presented elsewhere in Bulgakov's novel, most notably in Woland's conversation with the skull of Berlioz at Satan's Ball. Seeing the pure river of the water of life is precisely what happens to the Master and Margarita at the end of the novel (p. 381), as the believers' hope is fulfilled. Seeing the sun through transparent crystal is another symbolic expression of that hope. It is based on Bulgakov's sun-moon antinomy, the sun always representing the revelation of truth. During life in this dark, evil world, man's vision is distorted by the diabolical moonlight. Someday all will be changed, and believers will see God, will see Truth in all of its fullness.

The argument of this chapter has been both that Bulgakov's intention is not to rewrite the Gospels according to an unorthodox conception of them and that the account in the novel-within-the-novel is not his own personal version but that of someone under the influence of the Devil. If the distortions do emanate from a diabolical intention, on what general basis are these crafted?

The first thing to say here is that the Devil does not at all accept the standard Soviet interpretation that Jesus Christ never existed historically. The point would be of major import to anyone in the Soviet Union who had an opportunity to read the novel. The second thing to say is that all commentators on the matter acknowledge that Bulgakov's original design was to have the story of Pilate and Jesus told by the Devil, a conception which, as we have seen, was modified to include the human authorship of the Master.

What, then, is the view of the Passion story which Satan wishes to pass along to mankind? It is that Jesus was merely a man, not in any way God, or the God-man. Thus, he prefers to allow into the account which he inspires only those elements which show Jesus as a man. In other words, his choice is to give us a naturalistic account. We begin with the name: not Jesus the Christ, or Jesus the Messiah, but Yeshua Ha-Notsri—that is, Jesus of Nazareth. We are to think merely of a man from a small town, one with delusions of grandeur, even of divinity. The crucifixion is conveyed with grimly naturalistic detail. We read, "...the mosquitoes and horseflies had settled on him so thickly that his face was entirely hidden by a black, heaving mass. All over his groin, his stomach and under his armpits sat bloated horseflies, sucking at the yellowing naked body" (p. 178). Death by crucifixion is grisly, horrible. So nothing saccharine or "sanctified" is to be permitted in this account. Throughout, the diction of the account is stripped of particulars which might remind modern readers of any sacred associations. We read of execution, not crucifixion; of gibbet, not cross; of Golgotha (Bald Mountain in the Ginsburg translation), not Calvary. Christians commonly name churches for Crucifixion, Cross, Calvary—but not for the alternative, yet equivalent, terms used in the Master's novel.

Most important, the conclusion of the story comes with the burial of Yeshua. There is no resurrection. Thus, the very point of the story of the Good News according to historic Christianity is obviated. The resurrection is, by far, the most important part of the story of the Four Gospels which is omitted. According to the teachings of historic Christianity, it is this alleged historical occurrence which gives supreme meaning to those events in ancient Jerusalem. Without it, the whole edifice of the historic Christian faith crumbles. What the Devil wants human beings to think about those events can include almost any other detail, but it cannot include this one.

Bulgakov had, I think, two main reasons to present the account as he did. One was to show how the Devil might interpret the central Christian story. He allowed the Devil to get as close to the truth as he could, as good liars do. Who, after all, could accept the incredible Soviet version which denies the very historicity of Jesus? The Devil is shrewder than the Soviets.

But, second, Bulgakov wished, as a Christian writer, to avoid the error all too easily slipped into by Christian believers that Jesus Christ was to be perceived as God but not really man. No Christian would admit to holding this view—the term for it is Docetism—which has universally been held by the Church to be heretical. But it is an easy error to fall into, especially when Christians live in an environment (such as the Soviet one) which gives approval to any view which denies the deity of Jesus Christ. No, Bulgakov, working behind his author of the novel-within-the-novel, wants us to see just how terrible the events on that hill outside of ancient Jerusalem really were. One might even say that he wants to rub our noses in the dirt. But he does so not out of a sense of rejection of orthodox teachings but precisely to bring those teachings to life for those of his readers who understand his Christian intention. Indeed, his strategy is in perfect keeping with the Eastern Orthodox teaching as articulated by Sergius Bulgakov: "In order to accept death, God had to set aside His Godhood and, as it were, cease to be God."[20] The Devil may want us to see Jesus as man only. Bulgakov wants to make sure that we see that Jesus Christ was not only God but also man, a man who suffered horribly in an effort to fulfill his redemptive mission during his stay on this earth.

This point is reinforced by the appearance, at the end of Bulgakov's novel, of a Yeshua who is now risen and in total command. That appearance is of utmost importance in understanding Bulgakov's own personal view of Jesus Christ. There is no resurrection in the Master's novel, but there is a resurrection in Bulgakov's novel.

We can now understand why the Master's Yeshua would show cowardice. He cringes in a most un-Christlike way and cries, "Don't beat me" (p. 18). His apparent teaching about cowardice is another, and more difficult, matter. Arthanius, Pilate's chief of secret service, reports that, on the occasion of Yeshua's death, his "only words were that he regarded cowardice as one of the worst human sins" (p. 303). However, it is Pilate, not Yeshua, who asserts that cowardice "is the most terrible sin of all!" (p. 317). And Pilate never thinks to lay the charge of cowardice to Yeshua. Appropriately, Pilate, with his guilty conscience, applies the notion to himself. "Had *he* not shown cowardice, the man who was now Procurator of Judea...?" (p. 317).

There is no compelling reason to think, as does Proffer, that Arthanius lies to Pilate when he reports these words of Yeshua. Arthanius and Pilate do speak to each other in a code of language of circumlocutions which both of them readily understand, but the evidence does not support the claim that "Arthanius regularly lies to Pilate."[21] Nevertheless, Proffer shows proper care in ascribing the notion that cowardice is the worst sin to Pilate and not to Yeshua.

Although the historical Jesus never even said that cowardice was *one* of the greatest sins, for Bulgakov to have the Master's Yeshua say so would have special force for religious believers in the Soviet Union. Solzhenitsyn has frequently expressed similar thoughts, especially in *The First Circle*. And Bulgakov himself has expressed the idea before. The priest who appears in the first chapter of *The White Guard* comments, "Faintness of heart is a great sin."[22] "The cowardly" head St. John's list (in Revelation 21:8) of those destined for eternal punishment. Those who are being persecuted cannot endure if they are cowardly. Further, governmental rulers who submit for the sake of their own security to what they recognize as unjust in the apparatus within which they serve are cowards. This is the main context of the treatment of cowardice in the Master's novel, since Pilate is the chief culprit. Cowardice is a great sin because it effects bondage, not freedom; and it is freedom which is Bulgakov's desideratum, as the end of his novel demonstrates. Lakshin is exactly right when he says, "Cowardice is the extreme expression of an internal sense of submission, unfreedom of the soul, and once one has made one's peace with it, it is difficult to free oneself from it."[23] Finally, one wonders if this choice of theme might have had an autobiographical source. It is at least possible that Bulgakov thought of himself as cowardly for keeping his head down and not expressing his full vision throughout his writing career, until he chose to invest his secret writing time in *The Master and Margarita*.

If Yeshua's reported line about cowardice seems to diverge from the teachings of the historical Jesus, the line that "there are no evil people on earth" (p. 24) sounds downright heretical. Margot Frank finds the assertion "incongruous."[24] T. R. N. Edwards calls it "simple-minded" and likens Yeshua to a Holy Fool.[25] Yeshua's "faith in human beings" (p. 22) is especially jarring for Western Christians, Calvinists most of all, who emphasize that all men are evil. And Bulgakov himself seems not to espouse universal salvation, since his unbelieving characters are condemned. This statement by Yeshua is part of the skewed picture of Jesus which is offered by the novel-within-the-novel.

Nevertheless, this concept of Yeshua's might not seem so antithetical to Christian doctrine for one nurtured by Eastern Orthodoxy. For the Eastern Church teaches the deification of man, and sometimes this doctrine verges on universal salvation. Nicolas Zernov, a major Orthodox theologian, has written, "All mankind is involved in the process of deification and the saints are those who, having advanced nearer the ultimate goal, can uplift the rest."[26] This statement is suitably vague, befitting Orthodoxy's mystical theology, but it does seem to allow sufficient latitude to remove the onus of heterodoxy from Yeshua's creed. No men are evil in the sense that the fallen angels are evil. All men are redeemable and may even, for all that we can know, finally be redeemed. Ernst Benz, again with fitting imprecision, describes the Eastern Orthodox "conception that all men are created after the image of God, that Christ died for all, and that all are called to the resurrection in the new life."[27] Perhaps it is needless to say that this idea of human goodness remains at a far remove from the sentimental notion of innate human goodness spawned by Rousseau and the Enlightenment, which sought to eliminate God altogether from the picture of the human drama.

The apocryphal portrait of Yeshua Ha-Notsri affects, of necessity, the depiction of Matthew the Levite. Matthew is the only faithful disciple of Jesus who enters into this fictional account. But this lone follower is all that the Master needs, for he allows Matthew to play the roles of various other disciples of Jesus as he chooses to bring those stories into his narrative. After all, the version is a distorted one, and he need not be beholden to his sources for accuracy of detail. Thus, at one point, Matthew briefly denies God; here he represents Peter, who denied Christ. Matthew is the one who takes the corpse of Yeshua for burial; in the New Testament this role was performed by Joseph of Arimathea. At another point, Matthew sits under a sickly fig tree; Nathaniel was sitting under a fig tree when Jesus called him to be a disciple (John 1:48-50). Matthew 28:18-22 records the story of Jesus cursing the fig tree. He tells his disciples that, if they have faith, they can do the same and can even move mountains: "And all things whatever ye shall ask in prayer, believing, ye shall receive." At the end of Bulgakov's novel, the mountains do move—there is an earthquake. It destroys the Moscow which has persecuted some modern disciples (p. 375).

Matthew's parchment is particularly important. Its correspondence to the Master's manuscript is obvious; both tell the story of Yeshua. However, the correspondence is, once again, askew. It is Yeshua, the disciple's "Master," who asks Matthew, "Please burn this manuscript of yours" (p. 20). It is the Master himself, the author, who burns his manuscript. In both cases, thanks to Bulgakov's writing of *The Master and Margarita*, "Manuscripts don't burn," as Woland explains to the Master (p. 286). At least, these manuscripts cannot be destroyed, for they bear witness to the ultimate reality of human history, the story of God's incarnation. The manuscripts abide, just as facts remain facts. Historical reality is what it is, and nothing can alter facts.

Why did Bulgakov choose Matthew to be the one disciple who would represent all of the others? Michael Glenny says that he did so to demonstrate that the Master's account was based on the Gospel according to St. Matthew (plus, of course, the Master's own variations from the text).[28] But Donald Pruitt finds John's Gospel to be the most important canonical source, and he lists "several significant parallels between the novel and certain facets of the trial reported only in St. John."[29] It is the case that some aspects of the Pilate story are found only in John's Gospel. At the same time, the Master's version of the story of the conversation between Yeshua and Dismas has its source only in St. Luke. The only reasonable conclusion is that Matthew's parchment represents all four of the Gospels. And it does so in just the same way that Matthew represents all of Christ's followers except Judas.

Still, why Matthew? If only one follower could represent both the Twelve Apostles (minus Judas) and the four Gospel authors, the choice would have to be limited to either Matthew or John, for Mark and Luke were not among the Twelve. Matthew wrote the first book of the New Testament. His Gospel was written earlier than John's. It also sticks closer to straight graphic narrative, with fewer theological comments. And Priscilla Deck adds this interesting, albeit inconclusive, speculation:

According to Irenaeus, in Christian iconography the four Gospel writers are represented pictorially as follows: John is represented by a lion, indicating power; Luke is depicted as a calf, signifying the priesthood; Mark is portrayed as an eagle, symbolizing the spirit; and Matthew is portrayed as a man. Bulgakov's version of the story of Yeshua's death stresses that this was a human event and that Yeshua was a man. Thus the choice of Matthew, as the disciple who represents man, is a logical one.[30]

This is an intriguing possibility. And Milne's comments dovetail neatly as she observes that Matthew is a tax collector, that is, one who is occupied with material stuff.[31] She describes the Matthew of the novel as "the memoirist who gets everything wrong, and yet not so terribly wrong after all...."[32] In any case, the important thing to see is that, through the process of truncation, the Master focuses in Matthew all of the Gospel writers, as well as all of the faithful disciples.

Discipleship is a major theme in *The Master and Margarita*, and it provides one of many links between this plot and the title plot. We shall see later the parallels between Margarita and Matthew, plus other parallels of discipleship. Matthew is the compassionate believer who wants to spare Yeshua his execution. While he understands the divine plan inadequately, his faithfulness is exemplary in a disciple. His doubts and temporary denial humanize him; the disciples were in no way superhuman, in a realm beyond our own. They belong to history, not myth.

There are interesting and important correspondences between Matthew and Pilate. They are the two characters called upon most directly to respond to the question, "What think ye of Jesus Christ [Yeshua]?" On the surface, the contrast is stark: Matthew tries to spare Yeshua the execution ordered by Pontius Pilate. However, in Bulgakov's hands, the similarities outweigh the dissimilarities. About himself Matthew says, "I'm a coward!" (p. 173). Pilate reached the same conclusion about himself. By the end of Bulgakov's novel, we see that Matthew is redeemed. As we shall see, so is Pilate. Both Matthew and Pilate reappear toward the end of Bulgakov's novel, outside the novel-within-the-novel, along with Yeshua Ha-Notsri. In his reappearance Matthew shares in the glorification of his Lord. Now he is the confident messenger of his Lord to Woland. No longer is he afflicted with cowardice and doubt. This reappearance assigns Matthew to the sphere of transcendent reality, not merely that of apocryphal myth, as surely as Yeshua becomes the risen Lord and Master.

Judas, because of his unfaithfulness, is the one of the twelve disciples who cannot be represented by Matthew and must appear in his own right. Judas of Karioth (Judas Iscariot) is the antithesis of Matthew. It is Judas who gives Yeshua supper, in a parodied version of the Last Supper as recorded in the New Testament. Besides being the archetypal false disciple, Judas serves as a parody of Yeshua himself, particularly in their respective deaths. As Judas betrays, so he is betrayed—by Niza, whom he desires to have as a mistress. The contrast here is to Margarita's fidelity to the Master. Niza sends Judas to the Garden of Gethsemane, which location serves to establish the death of Judas as a parody of the death of Jesus. When Judas dies, "the lifeless body lay with arms outstretched" (p. 315)—a parody of the crucifixion. As Pilate ordered the death of Yeshua, so he was the instigator of the death of Judas—through the sly indirection of his conversations with his right-hand man, Arthanius. However, Pilate's effort to exonerate himself from the guilt of consigning Yeshua to death by having Judas killed must be seen as pitifully inadequate. At the same time, Judas's spiritual significance is underlined when Pilate and Arthanius talk near the end of the novel-within-the-novel. Pilate, seeking reassurance that the hated Judas is indeed dead, asks, "So he will not rise again?" (p. 323). Arthanius, not at all believing in the resurrection, replies, "He will rise again...when the trumpet call of their messiah sounds for him. But not before" (p. 323).

As we have noted, Pilate is actually the central character of the Master's novel. And he appears, along with Yeshua and Matthew, in Bulgakov's own novel. But the novel-within-the-novel is essentially the story of man, not God; and so the main character is Pilate, as representative man, not Yeshua. It is Woland, of all personages, who specifies that Pilate is the "hero" (p. 380) of the Master's novel. Pilate belongs to historical reality (the Master's novel) and also to transcendent reality (the closing chapters of Bulgakov's novel). He belongs to both time and eternity.

An early reviewer, Raymond Rosenthal, said, "Pontius Pilate is the most moving and fully realized character in the novel, indeed the only real character."[33] This comment is an overstatement. But Rosenthal has sensed, as have many later critics, that one cannot fully understand *The Master and Margarita* without coming to terms with the significant role of Pontius Pilate.

Pilate is repeatedly referred to as the son of an astrologer; his lineage is of one who studies the moon and believes in its power. Bulgakov's use of sun-and-moon imagery is worked out with special care in regard to Pilate. "The sun, which had lately seemed to scorch Jerusalem with such particular vehemence" (p. 30), is unbearable to the astrologer's son, and he seeks "to find some shade from the pitiless heat" (p. 31), though he finds no peace by moonlight either, because of his sense of guilt for his treatment of Yeshua. The events of the crucial day in the life of Pilate, Good Friday, are traced according to the symbolism of light and darkness. Although he finds the sun oppressive, it is during daylight hours that he unwittingly fulfills God's design to provide redemption for human beings through the death of Christ. At twilight he eats bread and drinks wine by the "half-darkness of the storm" (p. 298). He is in the presence of partial light; but he does not perceive its symbolic import, and so the elements for the Eucharistic celebration are not transfigured into their sacred value. After Pilate finishes giving Arthanius the order to have Judas killed, the Procurator notices that the "sun had set and twilight had come" (p. 307). The twilight causes a sharp change in Pilate's appearance. He seems "to have aged visibly" and looks "hunched and worried" (p. 308). As the evening shadows play their tricks on his eyes, he has a moment of superstitious fear and thinks that he might have seen someone sitting in his chair.

Pilate is so plagued by his sense of wrongdoing in assenting to Yeshua's death that he tries to assuage his guilt by taking a compensatory action. In the

New Testament Judas commits suicide by hanging himself. In the novel-within-the-novel, Pilate orders Judas to be murdered. The considerable space devoted to this apocryphal story of Judas is additional evidence that Pilate, not Yeshua, is the main character of the Master's novel, for Pilate is the initiator of the plot to kill Judas.

In passages of most wonderfully subtle indirection, he instructs Arthanius to eliminate Judas and then hears Arthanius report back on the completion of the task. Pilate says to Arthanius, "The fact is—I have received information that he is to be murdered tonight" (p. 305). Of course, Pilate has received no such information. He is telling his agent what he wants to have happen. Pilate's actual words to Arthanius are that the agent "take all possible steps to protect Judas of Karioth" (p. 306). But Arthanius understands and participates in Pilate's charade. Double-checking, he asks Pilate, "You say he will be murdered, hegemon?" (p. 306). The very next line is a giveaway to the reader about Pilate's real intention: "'Yes,' answered Pilate, 'and our only hope is your extreme efficiency'" (p. 306).

Arthanius pays two men to kill Judas, and he personally inspects the corpse before returning to Pilate to report his "failure" to protect Judas. With the same superb circumlocution by which Pilate and Arthanius arranged to get rid of Judas, they now establish their story about his murder. Although Arthanius has ostensibly failed, Pilate calls him "a man who never makes a mistake" (p. 324). Shortly thereafter, Pilate has Matthew brought before him. When Matthew says that he wants to kill Judas, Pilate tells him that the deed has already been done. When Matthew asks who did it, Pilate answers, "I did it" (p. 328). Seeking Matthew's approval, he adds, "It is not much, but I did it" (p. 328).

Pilate shows inordinate interest in Judas. Why? Clearly, Pilate is trying to exculpate himself for his role in the execution of Yeshua Ha-Notsri. Similarly, he is not displeased that Matthew has played his role in the burial of Yeshua. And he wants to talk with Matthew to learn more about Yeshua.

However, Pilate's do-it-yourself atonement is of no avail. Even as he "trie[s] to deceive himself," he realizes that his having Judas killed is "a trivial substitute" by which he was "striving to compensate" for something which "he had irretrievably lost" (p. 308) that morning, when he sentenced Yeshua. "His self-deception consisted in trying to persuade himself that his actions that evening were no less significant than the sentence which he had passed earlier in the day. But in this attempt the Procurator had little success" (p. 308). He has had his chance to come to terms with the truth of Yeshua, but he has missed it and now cannot compensate for his error, try as he might. Deck correctly observes, "Despite his efforts, Pilate is aware that the displacement of his own guilt onto Judas does not really free him, and that a human life is not like a monetary commodity which can be repaid in such a fashion."[34]

While Arthanius is out taking care of Judas, Pilate falls asleep and has a dream, in which he sets off along a "path of light, straight up toward the moon" (p. 317). Yeshua is alongside. In the dream Pilate wishfully imagines that there was no execution of Yeshua. However, "the blue pathway" is "slippery as butter" (p. 318), in contrast to the obdurateness of facts, and collapses. Pilate admits that he has acted in a cowardly manner and that cowardice is the greatest sin, but he pleads for pity from Yeshua—a great turnabout from Pilate's perception that morning of the relationship between them but one which holds true to the end of Bulgakov's novel. It is Yeshua who says to Pilate, "You and I will always be together..... Where one of us goes, the other shall go too. Whenever people think of me, they will think of you..." (p. 317). Pilate replies, "Remember to pray for me" (p. 317), and he weeps with joy when Yeshua nods in agreement. Yet, as soon as he awakes from this pleasant dream, Pilate realistically remarks, "Even by moonlight there's no peace for me at night.... Oh, ye gods!" (p. 318). When Pilate is awakened from his dream for his nocturnal interview with Matthew, three candles are brought in, "and instantly the moonlit night retreated to the garden as though Arthanius had taken it with him" (p. 325). Pilate is now in the presence of Yeshua's disciple, and only a dim analogue of the sun's light shines, since only the disciple and not his Lord is present.

This linkage between Pontius Pilate and Yeshua Ha-Notsri is true in historical retrospect, but it is even more importantly true in regard to eschatological considerations. The novel's ending confirms this linkage, as Pilate escapes his suffering through Yeshua's intervention. Their fates are linked. It was precisely the function of the Incarnation to connect God and man in an eternal, indissoluble entity; Christ came to redeem and (in Eastern Orthodox terms) to deify man, that is, to join man to himself.

We see in this sequence of events a foreshadowing of Pilate's ultimate salvation. He is a sinful man, one who represents abhorrent political power, at that. He never devotes his life to faithful discipleship. Yet he is not in the same category as those atheistic Muscovites like Berlioz who glibly deny supernatural reality. He knows that he has been thrust into contact with something which is greater than he can fathom. As the son of an astrologer, he remains open to supernatural truth, albeit in such a limited manner that he cannot recognize the Sun of Righteousness when he appears right before him. Since he represents not disbelievers but all of mankind, those for whom Christ died, in some ways he parallels both the Master and Bezdomny. Both of these characters stand on the broad middle ground between wholehearted disciple and doctrinaire denier, though one (the Master) ends up saved and the other (Bezdomny) apparently not (at least, within the novel). Together, in the Moscow story, they combine to explicate the fate of Pilate (man).

Confirmation of Pilate's middle status between confirmed believer and confirmed disbeliever comes from elements in his first appearance in the opening installment of the Master's novel (Bulgakov's second chapter). While Pilate is irked by Yeshua's lack of common sense, his stance toward his captive is always sympathetic, never hostile. For instance, when he asks Yeshua whether he has spoken against Caesar, Pilate phrases the question so as to offer Yeshua the escape route of a safe, acceptable answer. From the beginning, he obscurely realizes that he has more to learn from Yeshua than he has gleaned so far. When he thinks of Yeshua, thoughts of immortality teem in his brain. He perceives that apart from Yeshua there is no cure for his savage headaches except death.

Despite these "intimations of immortality," Pilate cannot arrive at intellectual assent to what Yeshua stands for. He suffers from hemicrania; half of his head aches. His hemicrania is, symbolically, the reverse side of the coin of schizophrenia, from which the Master and Bezdomny are said to suffer in the Moscow chapters. The latter is the naturalist's perception of a believer in the supernatural. The former is a judgment from a supernaturalistic vantage-point on the naturalist. Half of his mind is in a diseased state; he can perceive healthily only that truth which resides in the realm of nature. The Master's ache in the left temple is a parallel symbol.

The motif of poison figures in here. Pilate recurrently says that he needs poison, as does the Master. Yeshua does not need mercy-killing, since he can endure the justice dispensed in a divinely ordered cosmos. Pilate, on the other hand, observes only chaos and not cosmos. The poison which Pilate wants, and which would put him out of his misery, the Master and Margarita get. And it is in Falernian wine, Pilate's favorite, that the poison is slipped to them by Azazello.

Also, Pilate hates the smell of rose oil, a smell which pleases Margarita. Although roses and their odor remain somewhat elusive symbols, several critics have commented on them. Perhaps, the rose is to be understood here as a symbol of the Holy Spirit, and we are to think of the sweet-smelling savor of sanctification. Perhaps, it simply represents love, of which the rose is a traditional symbol. Perhaps, it represents both of the above. In any case, Pilate's reaction diverges from that of the loyal and true Margarita. And not only Margarita but also the Master loves roses. Gutry says, "For him, the roses that blossom in the spring are a symbol of love and beauty, the forces of life."[35] But, as for Pilate, "The flower is to him a strange and painful touch of beauty in a world consumed by evil."[36] Deck observes that "roses symbolize love and Pilate is both unloved and unloving."[37] Milne links roses, "the Master's favourite flower," with both "the symbol of earthly love in medieval literature and of divine love in Dante's *Paradiso*."[38]

These motifs have the force of conjoining Pilate, in his plot, and the Master and Margarita, in theirs. In both cases, they represent mankind in contact with God; God intervenes in the affairs of mortal human beings. In both cases, the key issue is how one is to respond to the evidences of a visitation from the supernatural realm.

One other Pilate-related motif—Pilate's robe of white with "blood-red" lining—presents some difficulties and remains elusive. Elena Mahlow relates it to Revelation 19:11-13, in which a white horse is ridden by one called "Faithful and True," also "The Word of God," who is "clothed with a vestment dipped in blood."[39] Despite the appeal of the concreteness of her supposed allusion, especially since it refers to the Book of the Revelation, it is difficult to see how this reference fits Pontius Pilate. Better is Shirley Gutry's less precise joining of the white cloak with power and the red lining with cruelty.[40] A possible gloss on Gutry is that Pilate's white robe stands for authority but that the red lining symbolizes his shedding of innocent blood (Yeshua's), which is a stain on his function of a temporal ruler who is to be a minister of God for good (Romans 13). Also, it could be that the white robe of Pilate is intended to bring up an association with the white robes of glorified saints in the Book of the Revelation, in which case the blood-red lining could represent Christ's blood shed for him and even now exerting a partial hold on him.

The fact that Pilate falls into the habit of talking to himself also links him symbolically with the Master. This practice is a sign of deficiency, of unwholesomeness. All is not well with the men who do so. One aspect of that deficiency, which applies to both Pilate and the Master, is isolation. These men are in need of aid from an outside agent, as is the universal case of fallen man, according to Christian theology. Pilate expresses his isolating lack of faith when he asks Yeshua, "Or do you think I'm prepared to take your place?" (p. 29). This question implies an ironic reversal of the vicarious atonement which, in orthodox Christian terms, Christ provides through his death and resurrection for all sinful persons, including Pilate. The Master comes to believe that help for him and Margarita can come only from the supernatural. But Pilate announces to Yeshua, "I don't believe in your ideas!" (p. 29). Throughout Bulgakov's novel the key issue is what one believes about Jesus Christ. In the Master's novel Pilate's answer is negative, though the intimations of truth mentioned previously are qualifiers of his rejection.

However, like Yeshua himself, Pilate appears outside the novel-within-the-novel toward the end of Bulgakov's novel. Here the story takes quite a different turn from anything for which the Gospels of the New Testament prepare us. The Gospels drop the story of Pilate with the death of Jesus Christ. What happened to him afterwards? Bulgakov gives us his version. He does not invent it whole cloth; rather, he draws on apocryphal tales pursuant to the New Testament, since canonical accounts are of no avail.

Bulgakov's concluding chapters make good on Yeshua's promise to Pilate that the fates of the two of them will always be linked. In this final appearance Pilate has his suffering brought to an end by the longsuffering love of Yeshua, now the risen Lord. Pilate, who had found no peace by moonlight, now traverses up the moonbeam and beyond the moon itself, which is the source of distortion. The twenty-four thousand moons of penance which Bulgakov (not the Master) tells us Pilate endured are now ended. Margarita, her face "veiled with compassion" (p. 379), seeks to exert her supernatural powers once again and cries, "Let him go" (p. 379). But her intercession is not needed in this case, because the resurrected Yeshua has already pleaded Pilate's cause, as Woland notes.

Woland then tells the Master that he can now finish his novel about Pilate. The Master, who shares with Margarita in the process of transfiguration, or divinization, then shouts, "You are free! Free! He is waiting for you!" (p. 379). As a mere mortal, in the composition of the novel-within-the-novel, the Master was powerless to free his hero; but here he acts as a surrogate of God. In the novel-within-the-novel, Pilate appeared only on Good Friday, the day of death. In Bulgakov's whole novel, Pilate belongs to the world of Sunday, the day of resurrection, as the author carefully specifies: "...on the night of Sunday, the day of the Resurrection, pardon had been granted to the astrologer's son, fifth Procurator of Judea, the cruel Pontius Pilate" (p. 381). Pilate's salvation comes in the chapter entitled "Absolution and Eternal Refuge," the same chapter in which the Master and Margarita are redeemed. That is, it comes at the culmination of what Chapter Nine will show to be Bulgakov's parodied version of the Apocalypse, or the Book of the Revelation.

Pardon had been granted: the passive voice is used. Why? Apparently, because God never appears directly in the novel. There is no person in the novel who has the power to free the sinful Pilate; so the active voice cannot be employed. Certainly, Woland is not the source of the pardon—no more for Pilate than for the Master and Margarita. Only God himself, and not a parodied version of him, can pardon sin. Parallel uses of the passive voice come in the titles of Chapter 24 ("The Master Is Released") and Chapter 29 ("The Fate of the Master and Margarita Is Decided").

There is one more subtle but very important point about Bulgakov's treatment of Pilate. In the Master's first appearance in the novel, he had told Bezdomny that his novel would end with the words, "the knight Pontius Pilate" (p. 137). *The Master and Margarita* has thirty-two chapters plus an Epilogue. Chapter Thirty-two ends with "the cruel Pontius Pilate" (p. 381). It is only with the Epilogue that we conclude with the words "the knight Pontius Pilate" (p. 394). This little clue is indicative of a big point. At the end of Chapter Thirty-two, the Master is completing his novel-within-the-novel. At the end of the Epilogue, Bulgakov himself is completing his full novel, *The Master and Margarita*. Thus, we see that the two novels, the Master's and Bulgakov's, are ultimately one, even though the Master restricts his narrative to the Pilate-Yeshua plot and Bulgakov encompasses both the Jerusalem and the Moscow stories. In the final analysis, both the Master and Bulgakov are telling the story of the relationship between God and man. Pilate, as representative man, does not have his story completed until all persons' stories are completed.

This merging of the two novels demonstrates both the slipperiness which confronts the interpreter of *The Master and Margarita* and the legitimacy of discerning symbolic correspondences between characters who appear in the separate novels—for instance, those between Pilate, the main character of the Master's novel, and the Master, the main character in Bulgakov's novel; also, those between the Master and Bulgakov. Indeed, this reading confirms those many other parallels, often skewed and inexact, which a patient reading of *The Master and Margarita* uncovers time after time.

The important theme of discipleship is reinforced in a surprising way through Banga, Pilate's pet dog. If a cat, Behemoth, can play a role in this novel, so can Banga the dog, especially in a symbolic work. Banga is anthropomorphized when "he wanted to comfort his master and was prepared to face misfortune with him" (p. 309). The word *master* suggests Banga's relationship to the theme of discipleship. Banga, who does not share Pilate's cowardice and is afraid only of thunderstorms and growls at the moon, loves his master. And so he waits with Pilate for Pilate's absolution: "...one who loves must share the fate of his loved one" (p. 378). Banga is to share Pilate's eternal fate with his master. What counts is to belong to the right master. The dog may have no control over this matter of loyalty, but human disciples do.

Upon what basis did Bulgakov assign Pontius Pilate to heaven? How can it be that in this novel Pilate ends up among the redeemed? The dominant inherited view of Pilate is that he erred grievously in consigning Jesus to death, and the New Testament gives no indication that he is a believer. However, Bulgakov does not invent a happy ending for Pilate out of his own imaginings alone. He does have precedent for his version of Pilate's ultimate fate. Learned man that he is, he draws on a persistent strain of thought promulgated by apocryphal texts which followed up on the New Testament and also by medieval legends. The ambiguous character of Pilate fascinated many long before it did Bulgakov.

Actually, although the Gospel accounts give no information about Pilate after the scene in which he announces Jesus Christ's death sentence, all four of them depict Pilate with enough sympathy so as to allow for the later legends which emerged and which enunciated leniency for Pilate. St. John's is the most detailed account. Only here does Pilate ask his famous "What is truth?" question (John 18:38). Only here does Pilate place over Jesus' cross the ascription "Jesus of Nazareth [Yeshua Ha-Notsri] the King of the Jews" (John 19:19), and he refuses to modify the ascription to please the Jewish priests. Consistently, the Gospel writers show Pilate as fearing that he is betraying an innocent man who has done no evil, in whom he can find no fault. He tries to have Jesus released, though he succumbs to pressure from the Jewish leaders not to do so. Matthew's account tells us that Pilate's wife warns her husband against complicity in the crucifixion of Jesus, calling him a "just man" (Matthew 27:19).

Since the Gospels do not carry the story of Pilate beyond the events of Christ's Passion, even though he obviously went on living, it was left to the apocryphal writers of the early Christian centuries to use their imaginations in filling out his account. Their narratives really do not do any violence to the canonical record, though they clearly go far beyond anything which the New Testament authorizes.

The apocryphal books following the New Testament, which are generally little known, contain a number of short pieces which carry forward the story of Pilate. One of them is "The Epistle of Pontius Pilate, Which He Wrote to the Roman Emperor Concerning Our Lord Jesus Christ." In it Pilate writes to Tiberius Caesar:

> Upon Jesus Christ...a bitter punishment hath at length been inflicted by the will of the people, although I was unwilling and apprehensive. In good truth, no age ever had or will have a man so good and strict. But the people made a wonderful effort, and all their scribes, chiefs and elders agreed to crucify this ambassador of truth.... And when he was hanged supernatural signs appeared.... Had I not feared a sedition might arise among the people, who were almost furious, perhaps this man would have yet been living with us. Although being rather compelled by fidelity to thy dignity than led by my own inclination, I did not strive with all my might to prevent the sale and suffering of righteous blood, guiltless of every accusation, unjustly, indeed, through the maliciousness of men, and yet, as the Scriptures interpret, to their own destruction.[41]

We see in this passage both Pilate's cowardice and his unwillingness to put to death a man in whose innocence he believes. Still, he is not depicted as a believer in Jesus the Savior, though his respect for the Scriptures is a hint in that direction.

However, in another apocryphal epistle, this one the "Letter of Pilate to Herod," Pilate is a confessing believer. His wife, Procla, reports to him that she has seen the risen Lord, and he accompanies her, along with fifty Romans, to Galilee, where he sees "our Lord":

> But I prayed in my heart, for I knew that it was he whom ye delivered unto me, that he was Lord of created things and Creator of all. But we, when we saw him, all of us fell upon our faces before his feet. And I said with a loud voice, I have sinned, O Lord, in that I sat and judged thee, who avengest all in truth. And lo, I know that thou are God, the Son of God, and I beheld thy humanity and not thy divinity. But Herod, with the children of Israel, constrained me to do evil unto thee. Have pity, therefore, upon me, O God of Israel![42]

In other words, it was only after the resurrection of Christ that Pilate became a Christian believer. Before the crucifixion he sensed that there was something special about this prisoner, but he was not a secret believer.

Donehoo, an important source on the subject at hand, offers additional information. In his volume we find "Pilate's Letter to Herod," which is compiled from "Epistles of Herod and Pilate" (both the Syriac form and the Greek form, according to Donehoo). In this letter Pilate confirms that Jesus Christ appears in the flesh after the resurrection; and he adds, "And, behold, for his holy doctrines, the heavens and earth seem to leap for joy."[43] Donehoo also cites Pilate to the effect that he believes in the virgin birth of Christ, that he accepts Jesus' miracles as real, and that he "perceived that the wonderful works done by him are greater than can be done by the gods whom we worship."[44] In a passage which has particular relevance to the conclusion of *The Master and Margarita*, Pilate is cited as saying that, on the original Easter, angels were heard from heaven: "And at their voice, all the mountains and hills were shaken, and the rocks were burst asunder, and the chasm of the earth was as if it had no bottom, so that what was in the abyss appeared...."[45]

After his resurrection Christ has kind, mollifying, even forgiving words to say about Pilate. In one text he says to Procla, Pilate's wife, and Longinus, the faithful centurion: "And as each one possesseth in my future presence, being raised up in body and mind, he will thank my Father for my being crucified by Pontius Pilate."[46] In response to Pilate's confession of sin and acknowledgment of Christ's deity, Christ says to him, "All generations and tribes will bless thee."[47] They will do so because Pilate was a necessary agent in the drama which effected the redemption of mankind. Christ adds that he is the one who will judge the living and the dead, obviously including Pilate, in the last day.[48] This passage, too, has a direct bearing on the conclusion of *The Master and Margarita*.

Of the various medieval legends about the final resting place of Pontius Pilate, the most widespread one is that he was buried on a mountain in Switzerland, near Lucerne. It is named after him: Mount Pilatus, now a scenic tourist stop. One version says that Pilate cast himself down from the mountain into the lake. A further embellishment has the Devil taking Pilate's body from the water every Good Friday and setting it on a throne, where it goes through the ritualistic gesture of washing its hands.[49] The details here are so much the same as those which Bulgakov employs that there can be no question about his knowing this story.

Another variant which Bulgakov surely knew was that the storms at Mount Pilatus are to be explained by "the presence of the body and spirit of Pilate, earthbound for all eternity, seeking vain expiation for his crimes."[50] Frank Morison's book gives two other details which are pertinent to Bulgakov's rendition. In one, "Pilate becomes a water-demon, sitting on a stool in the lake, with grey hair and beard, attired in magisterial robes, washing his hands."[51] In the other, wherever, according to various legends, Pilate dwells, there appear scenes of "devilry and incantation," as well as storms and earthquakes.[52] Again, all of these details show up in Bulgakov's concluding depiction of Pilate. The connection between purgatory-like torments of Pilate and the doings of the Devil are particularly instructive.

One could cite many more apocryphal sources about Pilate than have been mentioned here, and not all of the accounts cohere with one another. But these are enough to make the point that Bulgakov's treatment of Pilate was based on his knowledge of some, probably many, of these legends. It seems appropriate to conclude that Bulgakov went to these sources so that he could say certain things about theological issues—most significantly, God's merciful redemption of sinful, undeserving mankind.

Other critics of *The Master and Margarita* also have discovered Bulgakov's indebtedness to these apocryphal and legendary narratives about Pilate—Beatie and Powell, Deck, and Pruitt, to name just a few.[53] Pruitt, for example, notes that "the historical Pilate achieved redemption (and, indeed, sainthood, in the Ethiopian Christian church) because he recognized the Messiahship of Christ and was merely the instrument of God; as such, he therefore could not be held responsible for the crucifixion."[54]

What we can with confidence conclude is that Bulgakov drew from the Four Gospels for his depiction of Pilate before the death of Jesus Christ, and he drew on various apocryphal accounts for his depiction of Pilate after the events of Passion Week. In both cases, he handled the materials in the same way. He used enough details to make the point of his story clear, and his historical sources are discoverable. But there is always an obliqueness, never a slavish indebtedness, about his handling of his raw materials. The true artist makes all things new and fresh. We see his rendering of the story of redemption as if for the first time.

Chapter Six

The Master

❖ ❖

The third plot of the novel—and the most important one thematically—is the title plot about the Master and Margarita. One plot, that of Satan and the fallen angels, is essentially about the presence of the Kingdom of Darkness. Another plot, that of Pilate and Jesus, is essentially about the coming of the Kingdom of Light. These forces of hell and heaven meet on the earth in this third plot; all three realms overlap here in the middle place. Although Bulgakov may originally have intended to tell the Devil's version of the Gospel, in the finished novel Woland and Yeshua are important especially as they affect the fate of the Master and Margarita. It is interesting to know how the Devil might want human beings to respond to the question, "What think ye of the Christ?" It is much more interesting to know how human beings actually respond to that question. Whereas Woland dominates Book One, the two human characters of the title dominate Book Two, the climactic section of the novel.

The Master and Margarita is a book about human beings, as novels generally are. But it shows that Bulgakov believes that the story of mankind cannot be told without reference to the transcendent spiritual dimension. Human beings are not merely social creatures limited to horizontal relationships. For an accurate understanding of human nature and the human condition, one must include the vertical relationships, the links between the natural and the supernatural. Because of the importance of these two human characters, the Master and Margarita, this chapter and the next are devoted to them, though the two chapters essentially comprise one unit and the placement of certain materials within one or the other of them is occasionally arbitrary. More often than not, items applicable to both characters appear in the following chapter, after both of them have been discussed in general.

The character of the Master is one of the most difficult elements within *The Master and Margarita*. Since Bulgakov calls the Master his "hero,"[1] this critical fact is surprising. Nevertheless, the commentators on the novel have much more precise things to say about Woland, Pilate, Yeshua, Margarita, and Bezdomny than they do about the Master. For example, Margot Frank says, "The Master's role and purpose within the general scheme of *The Master and Margarita* is still an unresolved question...."[2] Priscilla Deck says, "The master is a shadowy creation at best," adding that "the master is extremely difficult to visualize."[3]

Indeed, some critics refuse to accept Bulgakov's explicit ascription of the status of hero to the Master and insist on looking to someone else as the main character. For instance, Ellendea Proffer asserts that the novel's main characters are Pilate and Woland, adding, "Certainly, considering the small amount of space given to them, their late entry into the work, and the sketchiness of their characterizations, one would not at first glance think that the Master and Margarita deserve to give their names to the novel as a whole."[4] Her opinion is that the critics' identification of the Master with Bulgakov, "an identification which is dubious," causes them to overlook his relative unimportance, when in fact he is a character about whom we know "virtually nothing."[5] (Surely, however, more pages are devoted to the Master than to Pilate.) And Deck sees Margarita as "really the only character who challenges Woland for centrality in the novel."[6]

Shirley Gutry expresses similar reservations:

> ...the weakness at the center of the book seems to me to lie in Bulgakov's portrayal of his two leading characters. The Master and Margarita are symbols before they are fully realized individuals. Defeated in this world, they go on to enjoy the fruits of victory in their eternal life. The ideas for which they stand thus rule triumphant in the end. The impact of this ending is considerably weakened, however, because little effort is made to portray the Master and Margarita in any convincing psychological depth.[7]

As the next chapter will show, Margarita is a quite well realized character. The question of fictive persuasiveness has to do only with the Master. It is fair to say that he is more important in symbolic terms than in realistic terms. Perhaps, though, the issue is merely one of degree, for all of the novel's characters have their ultimate significance in terms of symbolism.

Frank suggests that the incompleteness of the novel might explain the problems which many have sensed in regard to the character of the Master— and also, to a lesser extent, to that of Margarita.[8] We observed earlier that the novel should be considered as essentially complete. However, there is every reason to think that Bulgakov would have continued to revise it had he lived longer. And it is the case that he inserted the Master and Margarita into a work which was originally designed without them in mind. So there is probably some validity to Frank's suggestion. One might well wish for more informa-tion about this pair than is available.

Nevertheless, what we do know about the Master, in strictly realistic terms, is not inconsiderable. He is "about thirty-eight, clean-shaven and dark, with a sharp nose, restless eyes and a lock of hair that tumbled over his forehead" (p. 131). He has been married, and he has worked as an historian at a museum and also has done translating. Two years prior to the events of the novel, he had won a hundred thousand rubles in a lottery; thus, he was financially able to quit his job and to move into a small apartment, where he could work quietly and uninterruptedly on his novel about Pontius Pilate. The hostile reception of his novel had a crushing effect on him and landed him in an insane asylum. In addition to such facts as these, we know much about his affair with Margarita; from his novel we know much about his view of things; finally, we know the story of his ultimate fate.

Still, there is much that we do not know. We do not even know his name. It is rare in a full-length novel for the reader not to know the main character's name. In this case, the fact of namelessness is fraught with significance, especially when his title is what it is: the Master. This namelessness is certainly a major clue that this novel is a symbolic one in which the usual critical canons brought to bear on realistic novels will not uniformly apply. Bulgakov locates the Master as someone in a particular time and place with his own personal history. But he also imbues him with meaning which transcends the concreteness of historicity. He functions most fully on the level of symbolism; in fact, his symbolic value extends to a variety of levels of meaning.

The title *Master* was chosen with great care to suggest a certain range and direction of those meanings. Lakshin, an early and often astute Soviet commentator on the novel, glimpses a few of the intended associations:

> To Bulgakov, a master is more than a writer. The word is broad: it resonantly responds to various shades of meaning. In it one hears respect for exemplary skill, for perfect mastery of a craft. But not only that. It carries a nuance of dedication, of service to some lofty spiritual task, utterly hostile to that empty life *around* art that is led by the men of letters of the little tables in the Griboyedov Cafe or in the corridors of Massolit. In a certain sense Yeshua too could have been called a master.[9]

Lakshin's associations for the word *master* are limited to the hero's role as an artist, as is true for most critics on this point, though his final sentence quoted above hints at a parallel which, we shall see, is more important than Lakshin realizes. The Master does carefully distinguish himself from the official writing fraternity. When he is asked, "Are you a writer?", he answers, "I am a master" (p. 136). For him, to say so is a matter of pride. One recalls Bulgakov's intense hatred of the literary establishment of his day, and the parallels between Bulgakov and the Master will be developed later in this chapter.

Nevertheless, going by a title instead of a name signifies a rejection of life, as the Master acknowledges explicitly: "I no longer have a name.... I have renounced it, as I have renounced life itself" (p. 136). When Woland asks him who he is, he replies, "I am no one" (p. 285). Of a piece with this withdrawal from life is the fact that he no longer remembers the name of his wife. In the same vein, the Master renounces his novel, which Margarita had called "her life" (p. 141). By voluntarily entering Dr. Stravinsky's asylum, the Master may be said to have abandoned and renounced even Margarita. Loss of personal identity entails loss of a sense of community, of human solidarity. Thus it is that one of the Devil's main goals, as Bulgakov has it in his early story "Diaboliad," is the obliteration of human identity.[10] Therefore, the Master's renunciation of his name is an abandonment of his human dignity and a capitulation to the power of Satan, who, we have seen, inspires the Master's account of Pilate and Yeshua.

As it is at many points in this study, Eastern Orthodox theology is illuminating here. The Orthodox understanding of the Original Sin of Adam is that it placed fallen mankind in bondage to Satan. And this is perhaps the main symbolic function of the Master: he represents all of Adam's race; he is Everyman. In this role the Master corresponds to Pilate, who, as we saw in the preceding chapter, also represents mankind. The Master has created Pilate in his own image. Still, the connotations of the title *Master* are favorable. Orthodox theology helps explain why. Even fallen man retains the image of God within him and thus has great worth. "Sin manifests itself as a distortion, a damaging infecting and tainting of the image of God; but it cannot rob man of his original nobility."[11] Orthodoxy places great emphasis on man as the master of the world, appointed to that role by the Creator. As Adam was a master created by God, so is the character created by Bulgakov.

Orthodoxy also illuminates an additional association of the Master's anonymity.

> The Eastern Church takes quite another view of the role of the individual artist. Most of the Orthodox ecclesiastical painters have remained anonymous. Moreover, an icon painting is not the work of an "artist," as we understand the word. Rather the making of icons is a sacred craft.[12]

This conception opens up a new and valuable way of reading the Master's novel. Now it can be seen as the novelistic equivalent of the making of an icon. It is a portrayal of Christ and his Passion drawn from a human perspective but with the authorial intention of accurately presenting the spiritual truth.

Further, since we have seen that the Master's novel is ultimately identical to Bulgakov's novel, Bulgakov may be viewed as an icon-maker, as well. He, too, is trying to present universal spiritual truth—not just a story containing universal implications, as all good fiction does, but a story delineating the outlines of *the* truth about man and God. Icons remain art objects and can be judged according to aesthetic criteria, and the same is true of Bulgakov's novel. But the usual aesthetic analysis devoted to novels will fall short of baring the soul of *The Master and Margarita*, just as it will in regard to icons. To give an example which is particularly apropos here, the Master is to be perceived as the creation of a novelistic icon-maker, and his character need have no greater relationship to realistic art than does a figure in a painted icon.

In the effort to understand why Bulgakov gave the title of the Master to his hero, most critics simply appeal to high-quality artistry, which is above the reach of most who aspire to be artists. Wright, perhaps sensing that some source for the term is needed to give it a desired specificity, suggests that the hero is a "master perhaps in the sense of a master in a masonic order, as Lakshin has suggested."[13] Edwards points us in a better direction; even though he is probably not exactly on target, he demonstrates the need not to avoid religious categories when interpreting *The Master and Margarita:*

> The Master in many ways suggests a monk, with his conscious withdrawal from society, his lack of concern for material things, his introspection and the singleness of his purpose. In an Orthodox context he is especially close to the *hesychast,* one who in silence gives himself over to thought and prayer with the aim of achieving union with God, opening out his consciousness to perceive the truth.... Hesychasm also implies the rejection of an intermediary priesthood, another important theme in the novel.[14]

In the rest of this chapter we shall view the Master first on the realistic level, though the bare facts of his history have already been listed. Then, and at greater length, we shall examine his various symbolic correspondences to Bulgakov, Pilate, and Yeshua. Finally, we shall study what is quite possibly the most prickly of all issues which the novel raises in regard to the Master: his final state. Why does he receive merely peace and not light?

Our first encounter with the Master comes in Chapter Thirteen, "Enter the Hero." As the preceding discussion has indicated, we should take Bulgakov at his word when he says that the Master is the hero of the novel. The Master, it is true, is weak and ineffectual and usually is passive. In his first appearance he is already in the insane asylum, and he describes himself as "a burnt-out man" (p. 135). But this characterization should not surprise readers of modern novels, which are full of anti-heroic figures. Bulgakov himself offers many anti-heroes in his other works, as Proffer details.[15]

Literary usage awards the term *hero* to the protagonist, the one whose fate is central to the story. Thus, Woland cannot be the hero, for his is not the central drama of the novel. And Pilate is the hero only of the novel-within-the-novel. It is the fate of the Master and Margarita which is the central drama of the outer novel. Thus, Chapter Twenty-nine is entitled "The Fate of the Master and Margarita Is Decided."

Given the novel's title, we could say that there are two main characters, not just one. Margarita shares top billing with the Master, and she receives even more space in the novel than he does. However, she is also depicted as his disciple. Thus, although she is a much more active agent than he is, her status is to some extent a reflection of his own. For instance, he is the creator of the Pilate novel; she merely tries to preserve it. So there is reason for Bulgakov's naming only the Master as his main character, or hero.

In addition, it is not improper to think of the popular connotations of the term *hero* as, in some degree, applicable to the Master. His title is a dignified one. Who is more properly to be considered heroic than one who is a master? Christian theology readily enough explains, through the doctrines of Creation and Fall, how one can be both grand and miserable at the same time. Man may be anti-heroic in his actions; nevertheless, he has nobility and dignity because he is created in God's own image. On the stage which is this world, man is the hero of the cosmic drama, and he cannot be reduced to a lesser status, even by his own sin and weakness. In the Christian story, man is of so much worth that God chose to die, in the person of Christ, in order to redeem him.

The Master has written a novel about Pontius Pilate which treats Jesus Christ as real historical personage. When he submits it for consideration for publication, members of the literary establishment view this work as "an apologia for Jesus Christ" (p. 142) and call the Master the worst of names in their lexicon: "A Militant Old Believer" (p. 143). While the latter is an exaggeration and typifies a smear tactic, the former allegation is actually correct. It is revealing that these Soviet reviewers recognize the novel for what it is; they do not dismiss it as heretical or apocryphal. If Christ really lived, the simpleminded atheism of official Soviet dogma is fallacious. If even they see Christianity in the Master's novel, so should we. In fact, including their allegation is one of Bulgakov's ways of trying to head off the non-religious reading of his own novel, which he was doubtless sure would ensue upon its publication.

It is very important to observe that, from his first appearance in the novel, the Master affirms his faith in the reality of the supernatural order. When Bezdomny tells him about his meeting with Woland, the Master, "slowly and gravely," asserts, "At Patriarch's Ponds yesterday you met Satan" (p. 134). Explaining that we "must look facts in the face," he declares, "The man you were talking to *was* with Pontius Pilate, he did have breakfast with Kant and now he has paid a call on Moscow" (p. 135). He wishes that it had been he, and not Bezdomny, who had had the opportunity to meet the Devil in person.

Also, the Master gives clear indication that he knows that the Devil is the one who has inspired his novel about Pilate. When Bezdomny asks him to say what eventually happened to Yeshua and Pilate, the Master shrinks back from thinking further about the subject, and then he adds, "Your friend from Patriarch's Ponds could have done it better than I can" (p. 148).

In short, the Master believes in the reality of the Devil before he ever meets him. Unlike doubting Thomas, he does not need physical evidence before he is ready to believe. His faith grows as the novel develops, and late in the work he expresses his solidified affirmation. But he is never an unbeliever, not even when we first encounter him. Given the novel's premise that one who believes in the existence of the Devil can believe in the existence of God, we readers are prepared, from the very first appearance of the Master, for his eventual salvation.

Nevertheless, in a fit of depression brought on by his rejection at the hands of the literary authorities, the Master burns his novel. Also, he is placed in an insane asylum, since he does not accede to the secular view of his society. On the realistic level he dies there. However, Bulgakov so enmeshes realism and fantasy that the supernatural perpetually invades the natural. We learn from Woland that "[m]anuscripts don't burn" (p. 286), though we know that within the natural order pieces of papers do burn. Since both the Master and Margarita liken their lives to the novel about Pilate (who is representative man), this indestructibility of manuscripts may be read as an indirect espousal of personal immortality. After all, the manuscript's survival is explained only by reference to the supernatural realm. Eventually, we learn that both Woland and Yeshua have read the novel; it lives on the same level where they do. Hell itself burns with a fire which does not consume. And the first chapter about life in the insane asylum, Chapter Eight, "A Duel between Professor and Poet," is bracketed by an opening and closing which describe the beautiful nature setting of the hospital, nature bearing its own witness to the reality of the Creator.

Before we proceed to the important parallels to the Master, let us consider one which has been widely discussed but which is of very little value in illuminating the character of the Master: the professed parallel between the Master and Faust. Since the epigraph for *The Master and Margarita* is drawn from Goethe's *Faust*, it is appropriate to hunt for additional borrowings from this source. However, the search bears little fruit, despite the attention of many critics. In the various versions of his story, Faust raises the Devil, makes a pact with him, sells his soul to him, elevates perpetual human striving to the *summum bonum*, and so on. Although the Master knows about the operatic version of the Faust story, Bulgakov's passive hero is unlike Faust at every significant point. Even Elisabeth Stenbock-Fermor, whose early essay on the subject seems to have encouraged other critics to examine this possible linkage, acknowledges that "we have no indication that there ever was in him [the Master] much of the restless, striving, daring Faust, even though we are told that earlier he was fearless and wanted to travel around the world."[16] Edythe Haber is on target when she says that the Master's personality "is hardly a Faustian personality" and that, in comparison with Faust, the Master "cuts a rather pathetic figure."[17] Joan Delaney says correctly that the Master "is not, after all, the scholar-adventurer Faust."[18] At most, as Delaney remarks, "The Faust theme is used intermittently and with extreme freedom, even whimsy, in *The Master and Margarita*."[19] It is most likely that the Faust legend played a role in Bulgakov's early thinking about the novel. But the character of the Master, as it developed, reflects almost nothing of this original line of thought. Proffer comments that the Master, "who probably began as a modern-day Faust, soon turned into a suffering writer of real ability."[20] Some hints of the Faust legend abide in such matters as the names of Margarita and Frieda and probably in Margarita's "pact" with the Devil and her general activism. But the stories about Faust cast no light on the character of the Master, which one would think would be the locus of any serious borrowing from the Faust legend.

Of the many parallels involving the Master, the one which has been most readily recognized by critics is that which links him with Bulgakov himself. Both are novelists, both write apologies for Jesus Christ, and both make their heroes stand for mankind at large. Both of their novels end the same way, and we have already seen that ultimately both novels are the same. So it should come as no surprise to learn that both novelists are, on one level, the same.

The parallelism between the two novelists extends to the reception which their works received. After elaborating the parallels involving harassment by the literary establishment, Lakshin asserts,

> Here Bulgakov hardly had to invent anything. He had at hand enough material of this sort of criticism by RAPP [Russian Association of Proletarian Writers]. The author of *The Days of the Turbins* had collected in a scrapbook 298 abusively hostile comments on his work as a writer![21]

Lesley Milne observes, "The critical reception of the Master's novel is an almost word-for-word reproduction of the reviews that Bulgakov received between 1926 and 1929 for his plays *Dni Turbinykh* (*The Days of the Turbins*) and *Beg* (*Flight*)."[22] Further, she sees "the pejorative neologism 'Pilatism'" as a "'figure' for the pejorative 'Bulgakovism'...with which Soviet reviewers of the late 1920s made great play."[23] In both cases, the authors were ridiculed for their ostensible adherence to a discredited idea, Bulgakov to the "White" side of the Civil War and the Master to orthodox Christianity. And Gutry cites a letter to Stalin, dated May 30, 1931, in which Bulgakov writes, "I was the lone literary wolf in the wide field of Russian literature in the USSR."[24]

It is no wonder, then, that a critic might find it "eminently reasonable to explain the Master as autobiographical at base."[25] Yet, given the always shifting correspondences that Bulgakov employs in this novel, most critics are appropriately cautious in pressing the autobiographical parallel. Gutry, for example, declares, "To make an absolute identification of the Master as the author's self-portrait is...a mistake. The Master is rather a projection of a discarded part of Bulgakov himself, that is to say, of his noble intentions and his failure in life."[26] Proffer acknowledges that the shift from Woland to the Master in the successive versions of the novel indicates that Bulgakov was coming "closer and closer to his own life" as he worked on *The Master and Margarita*; but she emphasizes that "the Master was far from a self-portrait" (adding, rather obscurely, that "he is what Bulgakov might have become").[27]

Of course, the parallel between the Master and Bulgakov is not exact; correspondences never are in this novel. However, Lakshin's emphasis on similitude rings true—and is nicely put:

> In the description of this character's appearance there is suddenly a hint of something remotely familiar: "He was a man of about thirty-eight, shaven, dark-haired, with a sharp nose, fearful eyes, and a lock of hair hanging down over his forehead." This looks like an attempt at a concealed self-portrait—a face that is very different and yet very familiar. It is as though an artist had painted over a canvas of his: remove the top layer of paint, wash the canvas, and you will see the profile of the author of *The Days of the Turbins* (*Dni Turbinykh*). The same thing may be said of the entire life story of the master, and of the vicissitudes of his destiny. Behind these things one senses much that is personal, endured,

and biographical, but transformed by art and elevated, as was said in the past, into "a pearl of creation."[28]

Bulgakov was about thirty-eight when he began to write *The Master and Margarita*, and the physical description of the Master bears a resemblance to the photographs of Bulgakov.

The psychological description of the Master also seems to have a relationship to what we know of the state of Bulgakov's mind during the period when he was composing *The Master and Margarita*. The Master evidences a dispiritedness throughout most of the novel; he sees himself as a beaten man. He makes cowardice a theme in his novel about Pilate. Similarly, in his 1931 letter to Stalin, Bulgakov describes himself as one who is "very tired," who has "collapsed" and "is renouncing his profession," and who suffers from "faintness of heart."[29] Marietta Chudakova contends, "Guilt...is a motif which is reflected in almost every one of Bulgakov's works."[30] Wright quotes from Bulgakov and comments appropriately: "'A profound depression came over me, and strange premonitions. I began to be afraid of the dark. In short, I was slipping into psychic illness': Bulgakov's description in *The Master and Margarita* would seem to refer, with only slight exaggeration, to his own nervous state at this time."[31]

Readers of the novel know that the Master burned his manuscript; this act is an important event in the book. External evidence tells us that this item was drawn directly from Bulgakov's own life. He, too, burned a manuscript of his, and it was the first draft of *The Master and Margarita*.[32] He did so in 1930 during the fit of despondency described in the preceding paragraph.

Shortly after this time, feeling beaten himself, he wrote a letter, dated February 8, 1932, to his friend P. S. Popov, in which he said, "I want neither tributes, nor curtain calls, generally I want nothing except for the love of Christ to be left in peace...."[33] We know that in the novel the Master's final reward is peace, not light. What this particular fate signifies theologically will be discussed later in this chapter. For now, suffice it to say that Bulgakov accorded the Master exactly the fate which he wished for himself.

Perhaps the most beautifully written paragraph in *The Master and Margarita* is the one which opens the final chapter, Chapter Thirty-two ("Absolution and Eternal Refuge"):

> How sad, O gods, how sad is the world at evening, how mysterious the mists over the swamps. You will know it when you have wandered astray in those mists, when you have suffered greatly before dying, when you have walked through the world carrying an unbearable burden. You know it, too, when you are weary and ready to leave this earth without regret—its mists, its swamps and its rivers—ready to give yourself into the arms of death with a light heart, knowing that death alone can comfort you. (p. 376)

The passage describes directly the mental state of the Master and Margarita, but especially the Master. (Proffer informs us that the phrase "O gods, gods," which

Pilate also uses, comes from *Aida*.)[34] Yet we know that this lyrical passage was written in 1940, as Bulgakov was dying.[35] The paragraph applies to himself as well as to the Master. As he was dying, he prayed. And his last words, which are at one with the theme of Chapter Thirty-two, were, "Forgive me, receive me."[36]

Despite the depiction by Bulgakov of weakness as a leading trait of both himself and his main character, it should be noted, for the sake of balance, that both Bulgakov and the Master achieved a considerable accomplishment: the writing of a lasting piece of art which expressed their deepest spiritual impulses. In other words, they persevered despite their anguish, driven by their commitment to deeply held beliefs. At this point, a comment by Bulgakov's one-time friend Valentin Kataev, apparently intended to be derogatory, may be apropos:

> He liked to lecture—he had something of the mentor in him. The impression was created that the higher verities were vouchsafed only to him, verities not only of art, but of human life in general. He belonged to that fairly widespread type of person who is never in doubt, who lives by unshakable rules, decided once and for all. His moral code contained all the preachings of both the Old and New Testaments, as if they were unconditional.[37]

Wright, in assessing the effect of Bulgakov's personal crisis of 1930, suggests, "It may well be that his basic world view has not really changed: That the old values...still seemed to him to provide man with what he really needs."[38]

Since there is no clear evidence that Bulgakov ever renounced the religious beliefs on which he had been reared, the burden of proof is on those who consider him unorthodox. At a minimum, he allows the Master to share his fascination—perhaps preoccupation is not too strong a word—with the story of the Incarnation. Neither can write his definitive novel without recourse to that story. Neither is so weak as to abandon his effort to do so.

In his kaleidoscopic shifting of symbolic correspondences between characters in *The Master and Margarita*, Bulgakov allows the Master to have some similarities to both Pilate and Yeshua. The parallel to Pilate has already been discussed to some extent in the preceding chapter; so there is no need to add much detail here. Each is called "the hero" of his respective novel. The main connection is that both serve as representatives of mankind. Both are obviously flawed, fallen men, though their different careers cause them to manifest their sinfulness in dissimilar ways, Pilate being a persecutor and the Master being one of the persecuted. Both are guilty of the sin of cowardice. Both are made miserable by the moon; they wring their hands when they gaze at it. Bad things, such as the burning of the manuscript, happen inevitably by moonlight. Sometimes the Master and Pilate even say the same lines—for instance: "Even by the moonlight there's no peace for me at night.... Why do they torment me? Oh, ye gods" (p. 286). Finally, and most importantly, both of these characters are, at the end of the novel, redeemed through the divine intervention of the risen Yeshua.

Proffer sees this Master-Pilate parallel clearly. She says that, if we think of the Master as the author of the Pilate chapters,

> ...the character most like the Master is Pilate himself, a man who lives with fear, though he is not yet destroyed by it, a man who has lost whatever faith he had in people. The Master, for all his surface connections which appear to link him to Yeshua, is as unlike that naive believer in the goodness of man as Pilate is. Like Pilate, the Master has virtually no friends, and has cut himself off from the society he lives in as much as possible, going nowhere, seeing no one.[39]

Milne makes much the same point.[40] Although one might prefer to state the details differently, the main thing here is that it is just to observe this parallel.

Nevertheless, while both the Master and Pilate are representatives of mankind, we should not minimize the differences between them. The primary one is that the Master is a genuine believer in the supernatural, whereas Pilate merely is aware that Yeshua has the key to some important insights which Pilate wishes that he could share. If he were to be transplanted to the cast of characters in modern Moscow, Pilate would stand somewhere between the believers, the Master and Margarita, and the disbelievers, such as Berlioz. In terms of belief and disbelief, which are the central ones of the novel, he would stand somewhere near where Bezdomny stands, just as in the Jerusalem chapters he stands somewhere between Matthew and Judas. The differences between the Master and Pilate are illustrated by their reaction to roses (whatever the roses might mean symbolically); the Master likes them, whereas Pilate hates the smell of the attar of roses.

Right to the end of the novel, though both are redeemed, the Master and Pilate remain different. On the same page both heroes stare at the moon; but Pilate stares "with unseeing eyes," not comprehending its spiritual import, whereas the Master is "smiling at it" (p. 378). The Master believes—and there is no indication that Pilate does—in the seventh proof, that the existence of Satan posits the existence of God, as the moon depends on the sun for its light. Thus, while the heroes of their respective novels are linked by their being representative of mankind, they are not identical, any more than are Bulgakov and the Master. The novel's symbolic correspondences never are exact, as they would be in allegory. And the differences between the Master and Pilate demonstrate two of the responses which have been given to the cardinal question, "What think ye of the Christ?" Neither answer is perfect. Yet in this novel both answers are such that the answerers fall within the purview of God's grace rather than strict justice and are ultimately redeemed.

To liken the Master to Jesus Christ might at first seem far-fetched to the uninitiated and bordering on blasphemy to Christian believers, were it not for three matters already discussed: Orthodox Christology, Orthodox anthropology, and the slanted portrait of Christ embodied in the novel's portrait of Yeshua Ha-Notsri. Sergius Bulgakov liked to use the word *prototype* in discussing Christ, as in the following instance: "We can say of the Logos that he is the everlasting man, the human Prototype, as well as the Lamb slain 'before the foundation of the world'—in other words, predestined to become representative man on earth."[41] So we have solid Orthodox precedent for looking for a parallel between a mortal, who is representative of mankind, and Christ, who also is representative man.

Indeed, the very concept of the Incarnation of Christ gives legitimacy to a novelistic correspondence between Christ and an individual man. It is for this reason that Christ figures appear in so many works of fiction, never more often than in the twentieth century. Bulgakov's Christ figure is uniquely emphatic and detailed; to locate it takes no hard hunting. But the source of the parallel is the doctrine of the Incarnation, as it is for most of the Christ figures in literature. Eastern Orthodox formulations about the Person of Christ are perfectly tailored for the kind of detailed correspondence which Bulgakov presents. Orthodox liturgy places great emphasis on Christ's humanity and the suffering entailed therein.

Perhaps even more important for the parallelism between the Master and Christ is Orthodoxy's view of man, its anthropology. Rather than emphasizing total depravity, as some branches of Western Christianity do, Orthodoxy emphasizes that, despite his sin, man remains a dignified being who is still to be the master over the rest of creation. His redemption not only unites him with Christ and makes him a member of the mystical Body of Christ, the Church, but it also results in his deification. This term, which is unique to the Eastern Church, is the strongest possible identification of man with Christ. Thus, the determinedly realistic depiction of Yeshua makes a parallel with the Master more credible than it would have been had it rested solely on the foundation of the abstract doctrine of Incarnation. Not only does God become man, as all traditional Christians hold; in the Orthodox scheme of things, man becomes God.

Although Orthodox theology is necessary if we are to see the richness and precision of the correspondence between the Master and Christ, the presence of the parallel is apparent even to those who do not turn to this source of illumination. Two early Soviet critics noted the parallel and catalogued some of the relevant details. L. Skorino writes:

> In *The Master and Margarita* there is a character who emphatically duplicates and coincides with the figure of Yeshua Ha-Notsri. This is the Master—just such a good, strange, almost mad philosopher, who it is true, lives in our times, is immersed in deep thoughts, is a pauper, and is a man "not of this world." ...The Master, like Yeshua, is a prophet and herald of the Word and not the Deed. He is satisfied with little, lives in penury, and all his interests are purely in the sphere of the spirit.[42]

Lakshin comments in the same vein:

> As we examine the master more closely, we find in him features similar to Yeshua's—loyalty to his convictions, an inability to conceal the truth despite a secret timidity and fear, an internal independence that does so

much harm to his personal well-being. Like the wanderer from Galilee, the master responds with sensitivity to human suffering and pain.[43]

The parallels go far beyond the ones mentioned by Skorino and Lakshin. Both the Master and Yeshua have moments of fear and cowardice; yet both remain sturdily loyal to their unpopular and dangerous convictions. Both are presented as pathetic figures struggling in a losing battle against the institutionalized authority of their times (both of them thus being like Bulgakov himself on this matter); yet both are transfigured into ultimately triumphant personages. Both suffer greatly. Woland says of the Master, "They have almost broken him" (p. 284). Margarita observes the Master's whitened hair, empty eyes, and "shoulders, bent with the weight they've borne," and sobs compassionately, "They've crippled you" (p. 364). The Master has a bruised forehead; Yeshua has the same wound.

These descriptions of the Master bring to mind the picture of the Suffering Servant of Isaiah 53, a passage which is widely interpreted to be a Messianic prophecy of Jesus Christ. As Yeshua came unto his own, the Jews, and was rejected by them, so the Master is denounced by his own, the literary men of Moscow. After his rejection the Master bleakly cries, "I'm finished" (p. 291). The line sounds suspiciously close to Christ's words on the cross, "It is finished." Margarita says to the Master, "...my poor suffering head" (p. 364); Christ is the Head of the mystical Body of Christ, the Church. (Beatie and Powell see head imagery as the most important in the whole novel,[44] though they overstate.) Yeshua and the Master are both homeless in this world—and here Bezdomny ("Homeless") provides an additional parallel. Yeshua says, "I've nowhere to go" (p. 132); the Master says, "I had nowhere to go...(p. 147). Later, he says, "So let's see what we can find in the other world" (p. 364). Both Yeshua and the Master have disciples, Matthew and Judas in one case and Margarita and Bezdomny in the other. Both have a specific mission to accomplish before their time on earth is over; Yeshua is to meet his fate on Golgotha, and the Master is to finish his novel. The Master desired to travel all over the world; like Yeshua, he was destined to see only one little corner of it. Yet both, as representative men, have global significance.

Both Yeshua and the Master are considered insane—as are Margarita and Bezdomny, indeed all of those who have any perception of supernatural reality. The Master is committed to the mental hospital, an apt image of the Satan-controlled realm and, as we have seen, a symbol of hell. Christ was assigned to come to earth, over which the Prince of the Power of the Air holds sway. He also, according to Christian tradition, descended into hell during the three days between his death and his resurrection. The Master entered the insane asylum in autumn and emerged from it in the spring—the seasons here, with their traditional imagistic functions of death and rebirth, serving the same symbolic purpose as the cardinal days of Holy Week, Good Friday and Easter. The Master entered the asylum voluntarily. "No man taketh my life from me, but I lay it down of myself," says Christ. The Master takes this action for Margarita's sake, not wanting her to suffer, just as Christ died for the Church. (The next chapter will contain an account of the correspondence between Margarita and the

Church.) Just prior to entering the asylum, the Master contemplated suicide: "...the simplest thing would have been to throw myself under a trolley..." (p. 147). Decapitation by trolley was the means of the death of Berlioz, the antitype of Christ. The Master does not follow the course of Berlioz and, especially by naming this unusual means of death, stands in direct contrast to him. The basement room of the Master seems to serve a double purpose. On one level it may be parallel to Christ's descent to earth. In his basement room he never sees the sky, and in this fact there is a suggestion of the distortion which enters into his account of Yeshua. However, the basement room is also the Master's refuge from the world, and he leaves it to enter the world with novel in hand. This moment, he says, is when his life ended. Perhaps there is a parallel here to Christ's leaving his heavenly abode upon the occasion of his Nativity in this world. At the end of the novel, the Master is restored to his room, now trans-figured as he himself is; and Christ returns to his heavenly home following his resurrection.

The parallels cited above pertain to the Master's similitude to Christ incarnate on earth. There are also parallels between the Master and the divine side of Christ's person. The Master's white hair, which on one level represents his suffering, has an additional significance. He enters his eternal state with it. The Revelation of St. John ascribes to the resurrected Lord a head of hair white like wool (Rev. 1:14), "which is the characterizing mark of the Ancient of Days in Daniel vii.9."[45] The apocryphal Book of Enoch (46:1) employs the same description, and with the same association. In his transfigured state the Master remembers his whole novel by heart, as does Yeshua, who has read it. Both have supernatural powers, for both are deified.

The most obvious and important correspondence between the Master and the resurrected Lord is to be found in the Master's final relationship to Pontius Pilate. Like God the Creator (and the second person of the Trinity is frequently considered by tradition and biblical exegesis to be the divine agent of creation), the Master has created a man, Pontius Pilate—and, since Pilate is a repre-sentative man, all of mankind. As God created the world, so the Master, who is the image of God, creates the world of his novel (as Bulgakov created the world of *The Master and Margarita*). Therefore, it is the Master who can and does decide the ultimate fate of Pilate: "...he had set free the character he had created" (p. 381). Thus, Pilate enters his eternal state. The Lord does the same for the Master and Margarita, persons whom he has created. In fact, the freeings of the Master and Pilate are simultaneous. And, significantly, it is the glorified Yeshua who, in the final analysis, frees both of them. Here Pilate and the Master merge into one. Paradoxically, at that very same time Yeshua and the Master are one, since Pilate's freeing is attributed to both. In succeeding paragraphs we have Woland's remark about Pilate's fate: "...his cause has already been pleaded by the man he longs to join," and the Master's sentence: "You are free! Free! He is waiting for you!" (p. 379). This conjunction of roles of the Master will remain puzzling only so long as the Orthodox mystery of the deification of man is ignored; apart from the illumination which comes from Orthodoxy, it may be permanently baffling.

The Master's own redemption deserves further comment. He seems so passive, especially in comparison to Margarita, and in many ways such an unlikely candidate for deification, that it may seem puzzling that Bulgakov chose him, rather than a more forceful or even a more saint-like character, for his hero. Yet perhaps his weakness is exactly right for making the theological point. Once again, Orthodoxy clarifies: "A vivid sense of man's need of the divine compassion of forgiveness is woven into the very fabric of Orthodox religion. The words 'Lord have mercy' are constantly on the lips of the Orthodox and they are repeated, over and over again in the course of worship."[46] The passage from R. M. French goes on to speak of

> ...something very deeply implanted in the religious consciousness of the Orthodox, the feeling of human unworthiness and its need of the divine compassion, the sense of being imprisoned in the dark and crude elements of this world and the appeal for light and liberation.
> Closely allied to it is the awareness of the positive value in suffering and humility, even of humiliation.... The vivid awareness of the other world does much to soften the asperities of this, and that unseen world is peopled by those who have suffered; it is ruled by the Christ Who humbled Himself.[47]

Orthodox liturgy, as G. V. Shann presents it, conveys the same note:

> O Lord, when thou wast crucified, thou, by the nails, our condemnation didst annul; and, when thy side was pierced with the lance, thou didst tear up the handwriting against Adam, and set the world at liberty.
> Adam was smitten in the heel and borne down to hades' depths; but the merciful God went down to deliver him, and to carry him on his shoulder, and to raise him with himself.[48]

This passage could not refer more accurately to the Master if French had had him in mind when writing his commentary, and here we have the explanation for the particular traits which Bulgakov assigns to his hero. Christ died for persons of all types and temperaments (Pilate, Matthew, Margarita); but the Master's disposition underlines the unworthiness and helplessness of mankind to solve his problem of sin. At the very time when God's providence is being worked out for the Master and Margarita in the meeting between Woland and Matthew, the Master ("Oh ye of little faith") is worrying about their future: "But what, in the name of all that's holy, are we supposed to live on? Tell me that, will you? You seem to care so little about the problem that it really worries me" (p. 363).

Nevertheless, the Master is a genuine believer. We have seen that, from the first news of the event, he believed that it was indeed Satan who had come to Moscow. And when, on the very next page after he expresses his worry about how he and his beloved are to get along, Margarita assures him that all will be well, he responds, "All right, I'll believe you.... Where else can such wrecks as you and I find help except from the supernatural?" (p. 364). Thus, when

Azazello comes to kill them, the Master is confident that Azazello has come "for a purpose" (p. 365).

The Master's experience of death is expressed in profoundly Christian terms: "For a few moments a tremor of sadness crept over his heart, but it soon changed to a delicious excitement, the gypsy's thrill of the open road" (p. 373). Death, according to the Christian understanding, is the last great enemy, never to be welcomed eagerly, since the life given by God is good and is not to be dismissed casually. Yet it is not the end of all being but the door to eternal life. So we read of the Master, "He began to listen to what was happening in his heart. His excitement, it seemed to him, had given way to a profound and grievous sense of hurt. But it was only momentary and gave place to one of indifference and finally to a presentiment of eternal peace" (p. 374). The Master's experience corroborates St. Paul's exultant words, "O death, where is thy sting? O grave, where is thy victory?" (I Corinthians 15:55).

Margarita offers essentially the same analysis of her experience of death. She says, "I feel sad at the thought of the journey. It's quite a natural feeling, even when you know it will end in happiness" (p. 374). And we are again reminded of the moving words of Bulgakov, offered *in propria persona* to open the final chapter of the novel, in which "death alone can comfort" the one who, as the world darkens, is "weary and ready to leave this earth without regret" (p. 376).

So the Master is redeemed. But to what state in particular? This is a major and quite vexing question about the novel—but one for which there are some helpful answers. Many critics have dealt with this question, recognizing that it cannot be ignored. Wright accurately observes, "The key passage is the one which has given commentators more problems than any other: that where Matthu Levi requests Woland in the name of Ha-Nozri to reward the master and Margarita not with light but with peace."[49] Here is that passage:

> "He [Yeshua] has read the master's writings," said Matthew the Levite, "and asks you to take the master with you and reward him by granting him peace. Would that be hard for you to do, spirit of evil?"
>
> "Nothing is hard for me to do," replied Woland, "as you well know." He paused for a while and then added, "Why don't you take him yourself to the light?"
>
> "He has not earned light, he has earned rest," said the Levite sadly.
>
> "Tell him it shall be done," said Woland, adding with a flash in his eye, "And leave me this instant." (p. 358)

Most of the commentators see peace, or rest, as a lower reward than light, and thus they see the Master's gaining of peace as a sign of a degree of failure on his part. Proffer, for instance, says, "The Master wants only peace because he is too weak to fight for light."[50] Deck says, "Because he had struggled long and hard, the master is rewarded with peace. Because he gave up the search for truth, he does not receive light."[51] Edwards says that the Master receives rest and not light because of a certain degree of cowardice which he demonstrates.[52]

Some commentators have wrestled at length with the question of the Master's final state. Milne, for one, concludes, "The Master is rewarded 'according to his faith'—or according to his imagination, which in this case is the same thing; and the fact that he is not granted 'light' is an admission of the failure of this imagination."[53] She catalogues three kinds of justice in the novel: retributive, redemptive ("represented by Yeshua, and by Margarita in her compassion for Frieda"), and poetic ("the ideal distribution of reward for good and punishment for evil").[54] The Master receives only poetic justice, not redemptive justice, because of the limitedness of his imagination:

> ...he can imagine for Pilate a dream of ascending a road of moonlight to join the waiting Yeshua. The best that the Master can imagine for himself is "peace" and freedom to work, with Margarita by his side. Poetic justice grants to the Master his dream, as the Master grants Pilate's dream to him, on this "night when all accounts are settled."[55]

Margot Frank has devoted a whole article to "The Mystery of the Master's Final Destination." She asserts that the Master is "denied entrance to heaven.... He is deprived of a basic Christian reward that is vouchsafed even to the wretched Pilate at the end of the book. Instead the Master is relegated to limbo in Woland's territory."[56] This limbo, she says, is "characterized by peace and comfort in the outer layers of Woland's netherworld."[57] She observes, "Only in the outer novel, where the Master is no longer the author, does Bulgakov show Ieshua as the biblical *Khristos*," and she concludes, "This omission appears to be the Master's primary transgression and results in denial of heaven."[58]

Not all critics see the Master's receiving of peace instead of light as a sign of a failure on his part. Wright thinks that this sentence should "be understood not in a negative but in a positive sense, peace being the highest state that can be achieved," and he thinks that "the Master is offered not second best, but the best, and peace is a higher state than light."[59] However, his conclusion is grounded in the faulty premise that Bulgakov is a Gnostic.

Beatie and Powell, who describe the fate of the Master as "one of the most puzzling enigmas of *The Master and Margarita*,"[60] think that the title characters do reach heaven. Noting that "critics have been generally dissatisfied with this reward for all of the Master's sufferings," they remark, "What does not seem to have disturbed them is that Pilate seems to suffer an equally unsatisfactory fate: he does not even seem to achieve peace." They add, "One might well decide that Pilate's 'freedom' is worth less than the Master's 'peace.'"[61] The crux of their argument is that the ending assigned to the Master and Margarita at the conclusion of the novel's final chapter, Chapter Thirty-two, is not their final state. That state is to be discerned only in the Epilogue, through the dream of Bezdomny, who is now Professor Ivan Nikolayich Poniryov. In that dream "...the destination towards which both Pilate and Ieshua, and the Master and Margarita, direct their final journey is not the same as that of Chapter 32, but rather the same as that which Pilate himself had dreamed in Chapter 26."[62] Using Dante as their model, Beatie and Powell assign the Master and Margarita to a certain level of Paradise—not the Garden of Eden, which they say was the character's intermediate dwelling place at the end of Chapter Thirty-two, and not the empyrean—but the moon. They conclude, "All of Bulgakov's heroes find their way to Paradise, though the novelist obscured the path with such skill that, even had the novel been published during his or his wife's lifetime, the references to a religious epiphany would have remained hidden from the average reader."[63]

Marietta Chudakova contributes to the discussion of the Master's final destination by tracing relevant passages through the various stages of the composition of the novel. She tells us that on July 6, 1936, Bulgakov was revising the conclusion of his novel, and to the Master's story he brought "a solution which was perhaps already clear to the author in 1931, but until 1936 had been indicated in the manuscripts only in a sketchy and confused fashion."[64] According to that version, Woland says to the Master, "You are rewarded. Thank that wanderer along the sand Yeshua, whom you created, but do not think about him again. They have noticed you, and you will receive what you have deserved."[65] Most noteworthy here is the fact that the Master is receiving a reward—in other words, something good. Also, he is receiving it from Yeshua, not from Woland. It is very curious that Bulgakov uses the plural pronoun *they*. Yeshua is not a loner here; he belongs to his own company of personal beings, as does Woland to his. It might even be that we have here a hint at the concept of the Trinity.

But later in this same draft Bulgakov places limits on the reward which the Master is to receive. "You will never rise higher; you will not see Yeshua; you will not leave your refuge."[66] Chudakova finds these words "puzzling," as she does the words from a 1933 notebook: "You will not rise to the heights. You will not hear mass."[67] Beatie and Powell think that Bulgakov simply changed his mind on this subject. They maintain that this "unfinished remark...is wrong. The Master does rise to the heights, and he does hear mass—the divine mass sung by the assembled redeemed in Paradise."[68]

What are we to make of all of these conflicting comments? Those critics who see peace as a lesser reward than light are correct: the Master's receiving of only peace is a sign of some sort of failure on his part. But to suggest, as do Proffer and Deck, that the Master is a failed Faust figure who does not strive enough is to lead us in the wrong direction, because it omits the intervention of the supernatural. Milne gets closer when she allows the degree of faith to determine the degree of reward. She is wrong, however, when she denies redemptive justice to the Master. Although Frank correctly emphasizes the difference between the Yeshua of the Master's novel and the risen Christ of Bulgakov's outer novel, she is incorrect when she denies the Master access to heaven and assigns him to some part of Woland's territory. Orthodox Christian teaching never allows that Satan rules independently even over hell, to say nothing of limbo. And in the novel Woland points the Master and Margarita in a different direction from that which he and his demons take. Wright's reading has definite appeal, for the Master's fate should not be viewed as negative. But there is not justification in the text for Wright's assertion that peace is a higher state than light, and his reading is fatally weakened by his seeing Bulgakov as a Gnostic.

The most interesting speculation is that by Beatie and Powell. They correctly recognize that the Master's fate is to be understood as a satisfactory one. He is not shut out of heaven; he does enter the company of the redeemed. And they usefully introduce into the discussion the concept of degrees of heavenly bliss. However, they are too trusting of the accuracy of Bezdomny's dream in the Epilogue. When Bezdomny's dream has Yeshua telling Pilate that the execution at Golgotha never took place, we have a case of dreamy wish-fulfillment on the part of the dreamer, who has taken his place in the atheistic world of Soviet society and has every reason to put a happier face on earlier events than is warranted.

How, then, are we to understand this most difficult matter of the Master's final state? If there is one aspect of the novel for which one could have wished for further revision and clarification by Bulgakov, this is it. However, the text as it stands allows a coherent interpretation which fits with the rest of the reading of the novel offered in this study.

First, to the extent that the Master's fate is less than the best possible, maybe even less than Pilate's, the cause probably lies in Bulgakov's own self-deprecation. Bulgakov surely would have known that readers would see some identification of himself with the Master. He seems to have felt considerable unworthiness about his own life. His multiple marriages and divorces and his compromises with the Soviet literary establishment, along with other things, would not have pleased his theologian-father. It would have violated the author's sense of decorum and honesty to give any hint of making himself seem deserving of a great heavenly reward. If he were to get to heaven at all, it would have to be to a lower stratum of it. Admittedly, these are extra-textual speculations.

Nevertheless, when we look at just the text of the novel, we must conclude that the Master's fate is a good one. Whatever the reasons may be why the Master gets peace instead of light, what is emphatically clear is that peace is a happy state, not a sad one. It partakes of heaven, not of hell. And it is a fitting reward, since peace is exactly what the Master did not have on earth once he went public with his novel. When Azazello greets the Master and Margarita, as he is about to poison them and to send them on their way into eternity, his greeting, "Peace be with you" (p. 365), is to be understood as congenial and kindly, not at all hostile or ironic. In fact, it echoes the refrain of "Peace" which is common as a greeting during the Communion service of a wide range of Christian churches. So the emphasis must be on the goodness of the Master's final state, which emphasis leaves the question about the degrees of reward (peace instead of light) as an interesting but relatively minor question (one to which we shall return).

A number of details from the novel reinforce this insistence on the goodness of the reward. First, the order from the Lord to Woland through Matthew is that Margarita is to accompany the Master into eternity—a happy prospect indeed. She is well aware of the blissfulness of his new situation when she says, upon their arrival in the hereafter, "Listen to the silence and enjoy it. Here is the peace that you never knew in your lifetime. Look, there is your home for eternity which is your reward" (p. 381). She proceeds to describe a happy scene of domestic and social tranquility, in which the Master will always "go to sleep with a smile on [his] lips" (p. 381). This bliss is better than what Margarita had tried to imagine was possible for him, for she had thought only of an earthly peacefulness. Woland tells her so, and in the process he explains that, though he is the one administering the reward, he is acting as the risen Yeshua's agent for justice in doing so. "Margarita Nikolayevna! I am convinced that you have done your utmost to devise the best possible future for the master, but believe me, what I am offering you and what Yeshua has begged to be given to you is even better!" (p. 380).

Not only Margarita and Woland but also the Master himself realizes that his future is going to be a blissful one. Just after he dies, as we have already noted, he experiences "a presentiment of eternal peace" (p. 374). As he takes his ride into eternity, the Master stares at the moon and is "smiling at it as though it were a dear, familiar friend" (p. 378). He knows its symbolic import, and he has a sense of the joy of victory through—and over—death. He heads into "the promised dawn"; he has been "freed" (p. 381). Woland points the Master and Margarita along a path other than the route which he is taking, and they leave his presence forever. The Master receives "Absolution and Eternal Refuge" (the title of the final chapter). Woland takes the Master and Margarita out of this world and into the next, but he does not take them down to his own abode in hell, where there is neither peace nor light.

The question remains: Why did not Bulgakov allow the Master to gain light, as in fact Pilate was allowed to receive? For one thing, the Master had wanted peace, just as Pilate had wanted to be in the presence of Yeshua so that they could talk further. Both receive what they had desired; justice is served. Pilate "vanished irretrievably into the abyss," just as Woland "dived into the abyss" (p. 381). The abyss, therefore, seems to be equated with eternity, or the entryway into eternity, but certainly not with hell itself, as the word *abyss* might at first suggest. There is no particular significance in the fact that the Master leaves Woland before the latter takes his dive into the abyss, except that the Master does not go to hell; all parties—Woland and company, Pilate, and the Master and Margarita—are leaving this world for the next.

Further, Orthodox thought might offer some insight into the Master's destiny, though here we must be quite tentative. A Western Christian's first guess might be that the Master is headed for purgatory, since he apparently does not enter into the direct presence of God, who is Light; and entering into God's presence is the standard definition of heaven. However, there are two problems with this guess. Purgatory entails suffering, which is not any part of the promise for the Master. And the Orthodox Church does not believe in purgatory. Nevertheless, Orthodoxy is suitably vague on the subject of the afterlife—suitably, since it coincides with Bulgakov's vagueness.

> The Orthodox Church recognizes two states in the world beyond the tomb: on the one hand, the beatitude of Paradise; on the other, a state of suffering. The Orthodox Church does not know purgatory as a special *place* or state. There are not sufficient biblical or dogmatic foundations for asserting the existence of a third place of this nature. Nevertheless, the possibility of a *state* of purification is undeniable.... This offers,

consequently, the possibility of liberation from the pains of hell and of passing from an estate of reprobation to that of justification.[69]

If there is no purgatory but only two states, heaven and hell, then the Master must be in heaven, since he certainly is not in hell. The above quotation may be helpful in explaining the Master's fate, because it allows for degrees, or gradations, of destinies. It does not seem, though, that the Master's abode is to be a temporary one, from which he will eventually ascend to a higher location. But that quotation might be quite helpful in explaining the fate of Pilate, who has spent centuries in a state which might be understood as one of purification and is definitely one from which he rises. As for Pilate, another reference from Sergius Bulgakov, again with appropriate vagueness, might be fitting: "God has left us ignorant of the destinies of those who have not known Christ and have not entered into the Church. A certain hope is given us by the teaching of the Church on the descent of Christ into Limbo and His preaching on hell, addressed to all pre-Christian humanity."[70]

As a sort of side note, one more place where Orthodoxy might illuminate the Master's leaving of time for eternity is his final visit to Bezdomny. Immediately after he dies, the Master visits his disciple, bringing Margarita with him. French says, "...according to popular belief the soul does not bid a final farewell to this world until forty days after death, the interval having been spent in visiting the scenes of its earthly life."[71] The period of forty days does not fit; the Master's post-death return to the asylum does. But things are usually askew—and often truncated—in this novel.

In conclusion, it is safe to conclude that the Master enters heaven. His eternal state is one of bliss. At a minimum, he ends up in the new earth. The Book of the Revelation speaks of a new heaven and a new earth, both of which are places of eternal happiness ruled over directly by God and sharply distinguished from hell, that place of everlasting torment. Here Pruitt's suggestion that the "eventual blissful resolution" at the end of the novel may "be viewed as a parody of the expulsion from Paradise suffered by Adam and Eve"[72] is worth considering. For it is true that the cozy cottage which the Master and Margarita are to inhabit for all of eternity in their transfigured state seems much like a transfigured version of the Master's dwelling place on earth.

New heaven or new earth? One or the other is the final abode for the Master and Margarita. Not purgatory, not hell. And it does not much matter which one it is. Bulgakov has not let us know which one it is. If he is intentionally vague on this subject, his approach fits with Orthodoxy's imprecision about eschatological matters. What he makes unmistakably clear is that his hero's final state is one of bliss and happiness, one of a reward which suits his belief in the reality of the supernatural. However we are to sort out the details, the Master is redeemed.

Chapter Seven

Margarita

❖ ❖

Although Bulgakov specifies that the Master is the hero of his novel, in many ways Margarita is his equal in importance. It is difficult to mention the one without mentioning the other, as the title itself suggests. In some ways Margarita actually looms larger than the Master. More chapters in the crucial second half of the novel focus on her activities than do on his. Whereas he represents primarily a state of being, she represents in large measure a course of activity. Indeed, the case could be made that in many ways the character of Margarita is the central unifying device in the novel. She is one of the two main characters in the title plot. It is she who inspires the Master in his writing of the novel, which she in turn calls her life, thus linking the Pilate-Yeshua story directly with the one in contemporary Moscow. Also, it is she, not the Master, who maintains contact with Woland and the plot which revolves about him. And she is the central human character at Satan's Ball, an event which is placed strategically just before the Master is released and he and Margarita embark upon their eternal destiny—and also an event which is laden with symbolic significance.

Given the importance attaching to her character, one might well be surprised at the relative paucity of commentary devoted to her. *The Master and Margarita* contains so many puzzles to be solved that, it seems, this one of the two title characters has been generally overlooked. Bruce Beatie and Phyllis Powell seem to sense the same thing when they say, in passing in a footnote, "The role of Margarita...deserves much more attention than it has received heretofore."[1] The longest chapter in this study is devoted to Margarita.

The general neglect of Margarita by the critics is the more surprising because of the moral questions raised by her actions. Lesley Milne is one who recognizes the problem: "Margarita herself is an ambiguous character—perhaps even more ambiguous than Woland in terms of 'good' and 'evil.'"[2] Although compassion might be said to be her leading trait, she does some things which, on the surface at least, seem morally reprehensible. She vengefully wreaks havoc on the apartment of the critic Latunsky. In more than one scene she is naked in the presence of males. She is said to be unfaithful to her husband when she abandons him for the Master. She gleefully describes herself as a witch. In sum, she is not a simple character who can be passed by lightly.

Book Two of the novel opens with a chapter entitled "Margarita," and for the next several chapters she is the central human figure. In the opening lines of that chapter, she is declared to represent "real, true, eternal love,"[3] an active principle. This characterization gives us a clue to the multiple levels of symbolism involved in the person of Margarita. Her relationship to the Master affords additional insights. Priscilla Deck, one critic who has devoted considerable attention to the character and role of Margarita, says, "Margarita is certainly the most 'real' character in the novel, yet it is she who experiences most fully the supernatural world of fantasy in which Woland too can move."[4] And it is on the fantastic plane that her many symbolic functions emerge. Thus, in this chapter we shall see Margarita as, variously, a symbol of love, of the feminine principle, of Bulgakov's wife Elena Sergeyevna, of the Virgin Mary, of the Church, and of the faithful disciple.

It is only in the second half of the novel that we encounter many episodes which bring together the different spheres of existence: heaven, earth, and hell; and it is in these episodes that Margarita plays a leading role. Thus, it is reserved for this chapter to explicate those scenes. The most important of these is Satan's Ball, or Rout, including the preparations for and aftereffects of it.

We have observed the great significance of the title of the Master. The significance of the name of Margarita is more difficult to assess. However, it is easy enough to identify the source of her name. As many critics have asserted, it comes from the Faust legend, particularly as presented by Goethe, which Bulgakov obviously knew well and drew from. This borrowing brings with it associations of intercession and of purity of love. It is through Margaret—the nickname is Gretchen—that Goethe's Faust is redeemed. Thus, Michael Glenny says, though too simply, "Margarita (as her name suggests) is a Russian Gretchen in modern dress."[5] Deck notes that Gounod's opera *Faust* is generally known in Germany as *Margarita*.[6]

Yet it is apparent that Bulgakov's Margarita is very different from Goethe's Gretchen. Whereas Gretchen is essentially passive, Margarita is essentially active. It is Margarita who speaks first to the Master, not the other way around. She comes to his place, not *vice versa*. It is she, not the Master, who deals with the Devil. Deck properly distinguishes between Margarita and her alleged prototype:

> While Goethe's Gretchen was intended as a pawn to lure Faust into self-satisfaction, Margarita is an active and willing agent of Woland's because she desires something of him. She accepts Azazello's offer on behalf of Woland not to gain some new power in the future, but rather to regain something she has lost. She accepts not out of greed but out of despair....[7]

Further, Gretchen's infanticide is shifted from Margarita onto Frieda.[8]

Margarita's penchant for action makes her more like Faust himself than like Gretchen; certainly, she seems more like Faust than does the Master. So, say Beatie and Powell, "Margarita is Gretchen, but also Faust."[9] Yet, when she makes her pact with the Devil, it is he who approaches her, whereas Goethe's Faust sought out the Devil. Also, we have seen that her motivation is quite in contrast to Faust's. Pacts with the Devil are generally for selfish purposes; not so with Margarita. Thus, elsewhere, Beatie and Powell, recognizing that the symbolic correspondences in this novel are never exact, assert, "Margarita is not a female Faust, though she sometimes functions as one...."[10]

In short, there are echoes of names and activities between the leading male and female characters in *The Master and Margarita* and those in Goethe's *Faust*, and one may assume that Bulgakov had that earlier work in mind as he was in various stages of composition of his novel. But there is no steady, solid paralleling of characters and actions. In regard to Margarita, the borrowing is limited to the name.

Bulgakov does specify one other connection for the name of his heroine. During the preparations for Satan's Rout, at which Margarita is to serve as the queen, Koroviev tells her that she is "of royal blood" (p. 251), and he notes that "the question of blood is the most complicated problem in the world" (p. 251). This seemingly innocuous statement has much meaning for Christians, who believe that remission of sins comes through the shedding of the blood of Christ, the Prince of Peace and son of the King of Heaven. Koroviev continues, "I rather think that a certain king of France of the sixteenth century would be most astonished if somebody told him that after all these years I would have the pleasure of walking arm in arm round a ballroom in Moscow with his great-great-great-great-great-granddaughter" (p. 251). Earlier in the same conversation, Koroviev had explained that "it has become a tradition...that the hostess of the ball must be called Margarita and, second, she must be a native of the place where the ball is held" (p. 250).

All of the critics who comment on this matter identify Queen Marguerite de Valois, wife of King Henry of Navarre, as the source of this reference.[11] Milne notes that this French queen served as the heroine of Dumas's *La reine Margot*, who, during the St. Bartholomew's Massacre, saved her husband's life through her display of courage and compassion.[12] Her exploits "gave birth to the legend of Queen Margot."[13] The connection seems solid. The main point of it, though, seems to be the matter of royal blood. This matter is to be kept in mind for the later discussion of Margarita's correspondence to the Virgin Mary, who was also of royal lineage, a not unimportant matter in the biblical story of Jesus Christ.

The word *margarite* (or *marguerite*) offers other possible connotations. One is that it is a word coming from the Greek language into the French meaning "pearl." Although the word brings to mind the pearl of great price of the New Testament, there is no apparent connection between this association and anything specified in the novel. The word also is the name of a daisy-like flower. Margarita is carrying flowers when she and the Master first meet in early spring. Later, the Master says, "She was carrying some of those repulsive yellow flowers. God knows what they're called, but they are somehow always the first to come out in spring" (p. 137). Bulgakov specifies that the flowers are mimosa (the word is the same in Russian and English). Deck finds significance here: "Margarita's appearance already suggests her affinities with witchcraft, for she is dressed in black and apparently carries mimosa, which is allegedly traditionally carried by witches."[14] Deck may be correct; for, though the Master thinks that yellow is an ugly color, Margarita later says that she had been carrying those flowers so that he could "find her at last" (p. 139). The problem is that mimosa has very tiny flowers, is not the first out in the spring, and is unlikely to grow as far north as Moscow. Other yellow, early-spring flowers— buttercup, forsythia, cowslip, dandelion, even daisy—are unrelated to the legume family of which mimosa is a part. So it is unclear what flower Bulgakov had in mind when he wrote *mimosa* (names of flowers vary from country to country), and thus we cannot discern what, if any, symbolic value these flowers have. But, certainly, early flowers suit Margarita as a symbol of new hope and life, which come to the Master in the spring which follows his autumn-time internment for insanity.

On the realistic level Margarita is a most engaging woman, a model of appealing femininity. When distinguishing her from Dante's Beatrice, Milne calls Margarita "a creature of the Earthly, not the Heavenly, Paradise."[15] Lakshin notes that it is given to Margarita's feminine heart to express the notion that mercy is necessary to make life bearable.[16] As God made man "in the image and likeness of God in a twofold embodiment, the masculine and feminine principle,"[17] so does Bulgakov create the Master and Margarita as representative man and representative woman. Sergius Bulgakov elaborates:

> The duality of the masculine and the feminine principles in man, which corresponds to the primacy of reason or thought in masculine, and of heart and feeling in feminine nature, does not divide human nature, though it inwardly diversifies it and thus goes to make up its fullness. The masculine and feminine principles in man subsist unconfusedly, while admitting of identification in some form of spiritual union. Yet they are at the same time inseparable not only in this sense, that either apart from the other does not possess human nature completed, but also in that the spirit of every human being combines elements of this dual principle, though of course in different ways and in different proportions.[18]

This citation provides insight into the characters of the hero and the heroine in general, and the latter part of it even aids in our accepting Margarita's activity and the Master's passivity.

The Master and Margarita meet in the life-engendering month of May. Her daily visits to him occur at noon, the best of times in terms of the novel's sun- moon symbolism. Both know, upon their initial meeting, that they are the fulfillment of each other's lifelong love needs. According to the Master, Margarita had told him that "we had of course been in love for years without knowing each other and never meeting" (p. 139). Together, they "decided that fate had brought them together...and that they were made for each other to eternity" (p. 140).

But the love affair belongs wholly to the level of fantasy. For in mundane reality Margarita never left her husband, whom she did not love. In fact, at the time of their simultaneous deaths, on the realistic level the Master and Margarita had never met, the Master dying in the mental hospital and Margarita dying in the flat where she and her husband lived. This fact must be an irritant which creates a sense of dissonance for the reader who approaches the novel with expectations of realism. The title characters are soul mates, and it is only on the level of fantasy (which represents the truer reality in this symbolic novel) that Margarita becomes the Master's lover. In her miserable, dull life Margarita represents, along with the Master, Pilate, Matthew, and others, that fallen humanity for which Christ died and which, apart from that vicarious atonement, is deprived of fullness of being. Representative man and representative woman are incomplete and unfulfilled in the natural sphere.

Nevertheless, on the fantastic level Margarita is the lover of the Master, and this fact seems to present a problem to our viewing her as a symbol of the Virgin Mary and of the Church, the Bride of Christ. She seems not unblemished. Why did not Bulgakov just make them man and wife if he wished to employ marriage symbolism? The problem is mitigated considerably by the fact that on the literal level she remains a faithful wife. The Virgin Mary is the "unwedded Bride,"[19] and this, in cold prose, is Margarita's status in relation to the Master. Further mitigation comes from the relatively lenient Orthodox view of divorce and remarriage.

> Western Christians find it strange that the Eastern Church nevertheless allows divorce, and even re-marriage. This practice, however, does not seem to the Orthodox incompatible with their high esteem for marriage. They believe that in marriage two human beings enter into such close organic relations, comparable to those of parents and child-ren, that they are never dissolved even after death. It follows from this that, in its ideal, marriage can never be repeated, but this high standard cannot be imposed upon every Christian, for there are numerous causes which make it very difficult for many members of the Church to experience the love and unity of the true Christian marriage.... In all these cases the Church, as a loving mother, condescends to the weakness of her children, and gives her blessing to a second marriage.[20]

The net effect, for our purposes, of this latitudinarianism is to make Margarita more acceptable for her symbolic roles in Eastern eyes than she might be to Western, especially Roman Catholic, readers. The emphasis on the weakness of those involved agrees with the character of human beings who are needy and not self-sufficient, especially as embodied by the Master. This line of thought serves to underline how thoroughly symbolic the novel is. It is to be expected that a typical novel reader, on his first encountering Margarita, would think of her as a realistic character, since her initial description is in realistic terms. But the fact is that at virtually every point she belongs to the level of fantasy. All of her contacts with Woland and company and even with the Master pertain to the fantastic level. Except for the fleeting scenes when she is seen as a dispirited wife in her own apartment, what else is there to her story?

On the all-important level of symbolism, Margarita is clearly a believer in supernatural reality. When we first meet her, we learn that material well-being does not make her happy. She hankers after spiritual meaning: "...her eyes always glow with a strange fire," and she is already called "that witch with a very slight squint in one eye" (p. 216). In no sense does the real-life wife of the brilliant scientist participate in witchcraft. Her being called a witch is another example of Bulgakov's use of parody and is congruent with a spiritual faith based on the seventh proof, which is, through the Satanic incarnation, what the belief or disbelief of the contemporary Muscovites is judged by. Much of her time is spent in the company of Satan—and is therefore at night and under the influence of the moon. Her openness to spiritual truth is evidenced by the fact that, on the Friday of Satan's visit to Moscow, she awakens "with a presentiment that today, at last, something was going to happen" and a confidence that her previous night's "dream was prophetic" (p. 217). Her dream was about the Master in a cabin by a little bridge, in a setting which looked "lifeless and miserable": "In short—hell" (p. 217). The Master's being in hell on Good Friday parallels Christ's descent into hell. Just as she starts running toward him, she awakes from her dream. The cabin and bridge reappear at the novel's end in a transfigured form as the Master's eternal home, and now Margarita dwells with him.

When Azazello, Woland's messenger, invites Margarita to the Ball that night, she agrees to go as soon as he shows familiarity with the Master's novel (her life) and her beloved's present condition, about which she is promised news at the Ball. Her initial guess had been that her host would want her to go to bed with him, but Azazello assures her that "[h]e does not want you for that" (p. 225). In the overall scheme of the novel, this snippet of conversation is related to the standard practice at witches' balls that the hostess engage in sexual intercourse with the Devil, though at the moment Margarita has apparently not intuited who her host is. This early, Bulgakov calls attention to his varying from the usual "protocols" of witchcraft. For her part, Margarita has faith that her attendance at the Ball is to be "the fulfillment of her presentiment of that morning" (p. 230). Although before her arrival "she had already guessed who her host was to be...she felt quite unafraid" (p. 247), for her serene faith in providence has led her to the conclusion that "he can never harm me!" (p. 231).

When she enters Woland's apartment, she is amazed to find a vast hall which is a kind of microcosm. She reflects, "The oddest thing of all is the size of this place—how on earth can it fit into a Moscow apartment? It's simply impossible!" (p. 249). Of course, it is impossible—"on earth." This is precisely the kind of phenomenon which causes most of the Muscovites to deny the reality of the spiritual when they are tested by a manifestation of its truth. Margarita's response is diametrically opposed to theirs. Although this pheno-menon is impossible according to her natural understanding, she believes anyway. Koroviev explains that the physical impossibility is "easy...for anyone who knows how to handle the fifth dimension" (p. 249), and Margarita is not about to contradict him. When she meets "the man whom the wretched Bezdomny had recently assured at Patriarch's Ponds that he did not exist" (p. 252), her reaction is the opposite of that of Bezdomny and Berlioz. After Satan's Rout she remains "completely unmoved by the fact that she had spent a night in the world of the supernatural," because of her faith in the providential order: "Everything was as it should be" (p. 329). She knows intuitively that crucial truth which Woland later enunciates and which Bulgakov gave primacy by placing it in the novel's epigraph.

If there is any error on Margarita's part in relating to the supernatural, it is the altogether pardonable one of giving Satan too much credit. She tells the Master, "...the devil, believe me, will arrange everything.... Hurrah for the devil!" (p. 362). Whereas the naturalists imagine Satan's range to be narrower than it is—nonexistent, in fact—Margarita seems to imagine it to be wider than it is. For the Devil arranges everything only in the sense that he is God's instrument for doing justice in Moscow. When Margarita says to Woland, "You are all-powerful!", she seems to be engaging in hyperbole, though the occasion, the restoration of the Master's manuscript, is warrant for her ecstasy. And Bulgakov himself confirms her estimate: "...the all-powerful Woland really was all-powerful..." (p. 296). Then again, perhaps Margarita is not mistaken at all, since in the parody Satan represents God as the shadow represents the substance, and to say that Satan arranges everything is to pledge allegiance to supernatural reality and indirectly to imply that God arranges everything. Acceptance of the existence of the Devil is precisely what is called for by the seventh proof for the existence of God.

Although Margarita's main symbolic parallels are, as we shall see, with the Church and especially the Virgin Mary, there is some evidence that she is modeled in part on a real person and that that person was Bulgakov's third wife, Elena Sergeyevna Shilovskaya (last name by a previous marriage; nee Niurenberg[21]). The historical specificity is fitting; Bulgakov tells us exactly where Margarita lived and adds, "Just ask me and I'll tell you the address and how to get there; the house is standing to this day" (p. 215). This is the same kind of geographical detail with which he located the house of the Turbin family in *The White Guard*; the Turbins were based on the Bulgakovs, and the house was their residence in Kiev. Clearly identifiable locations in Moscow appear regularly in *The Master and Margarita*.

Although the novel was, in its initial draft, to focus on Satan, we have noted that, in many ways, Margarita became the central unifying factor in it. She was added only after Bulgakov's marriage to Elena Sergeyevna. According to Piper, Bulgakov met her in May of 1929; she was already married at the time, but she became his lover.[22] Discussing this period of "emotional stress" in Bulgakov's life, Piper says also, "In March 1930, now destitute, he burned the three chapters of his novel."[23] The two were married in 1932. Although the character of Margarita appeared in a notebook of the author in 1931,[24] it was only in 1934, by which time he had returned in earnest to his novel, that she became a major figure in the work.[25] A small detail testifies to the legitimacy of seeing Elena Sergeyevna as a source for Margarita. As Margarita made the

Master a black cap with a yellow "M" on it, so did Elena for Mikhail; the parallel is exact.[26]

The fact that, as we have seen, the Master parallels Bulgakov in important ways makes all the more likely a parallel between Margarita and Elena. It also suggests the tantalizing possibility that Elena's role in the author's life was similar to Margarita's role in the Master's life as the one who gave new heart to a discouraged man and encouraged completion of the novel. To the extent that this parallel holds, Margarita is Bulgakov's loving tribute to his wife. Vida Johnson elaborates:

> The highly lyrical additions to the description of Margarita, the increased emphasis on her "true, eternal" love have strong autobio-graphical motivation. They further support the generally held view that Margarita is modeled after Bulgakov's wife, Elena Sergeevna. Both women nurtured and saved the work of the men they loved. Without Elena Sergeevna's devoted help, *The Master and Margarita* would not have been finished, just as without Margarita's aid the Master's novel about Pilate and Ieshua would have been lost forever.[27]

In the preceding chapter it was suggested that the Master's gaining of only peace and not light may have been a reflection of a sense of guilt on the part of Bulgakov himself. Now we may focus on the possibility that Bulgakov may have felt a sense of unworthiness in his relationships with women, especially since he twice married women who were already married at the time he met and fell in love with them. As A. Colin Wright observes, "...his personal life hardly reflects the Christian ideal of marriage."[28] But more important than this speculation is the fact that the Master falls in love with a married woman, one who is unhappy in her present marriage. It is highly likely that this situation reflects the real-life situation of Mikhail and Elena.

Margarita's correspondence to the Church (and the Orthodox normally would not distinguish between the Orthodox Church and the universal Church) is congruent with the Master's correspondence to Christ: Christ and the Church, the Master and Margarita. The parallels between these pairs proliferate through the novel. Margarita's insistence that the Master's novel is her life is one of these. The novel about Pilate is really one about man in the world, that is, the Church. The subject matter of the Master's novel, Christ's atoning death, bears out this meaning. When Margarita refers to the Master as "my poor suffering head" (p. 364), she again underlines the relationship between the Church, which is the Body of Christ, and the Head of the Body, Christ himself. When she says, "I'm the only one who knows how much you've suffered" (p. 363), she speaks symbolically for the Church, which figuratively suffered with Christ and thus is "the only one" who knows experientially how much Christ suffered.

There are two main metaphors in the Bible for the Church; the Body of Christ and the Bride of Christ. These refer to two aspects of the Church's relationship to Christ, the first to redemption and the second to discipleship. In both cases, "One who loves must share the fate of his loved one" (p. 378). So

Margarita is not free until the Master is free. Through the suffering of the Master, Margarita grows thinner and paler and more unhappy. She likens herself to Matthew; both return to their masters too late to be of help. Christ dies and descends into hell; the Master enters hell as symbolized by the insane asylum. Margarita enters hell too, as symbolized by Satan's Rout. We see here the sharing by the disciple of the fate of the master in a general way and the suffering of the Russian Orthodox Church at the hand of the Communists in particular.

Margarita is also the active agent seeking the redemption of the Master. On this level she acts as the Church, which lovingly seeks to save fallen man, represented by the Master. As always, the parallels in the novel shift kaleidoscopically and resist neat allegorical schematizing. When she says that she will save him and do his thinking for him, her assertion is in the context of her faith in providence. "I swear to you that everything is going to be perfect!" (p. 363). On the next page she repeats her claim of faith, adding a parallel between the Master's novel and *his* life. (Earlier she had paralleled it to *her* life, but their two lives are ultimately one, as Christ and his Bride are one or as Head and Body are one.) "I swear by your life, I swear by the astrologer's son you created that all will be well!" (p. 364). Milne sees in Margarita's compassion "a dim figural reflection of the compassion and love of Yeshua for mankind."[29] One could substitute *Church* for *Yeshua* with no loss—indeed, with some gain. For the Church is doing the Lord's work, as it brings lost souls to salvation. But the Church, as God's agent on earth, is not able to complete the work of salvation; God's personal intervention is needed. So the Church is "a dim figural reflection" of God. Margarita, while she is a compassionate agent of healing, cannot rid the Master of his disease, and his freeing comes only when Yeshua himself intervenes and ransoms the Master from the power of Woland.

Several things that happen to Margarita can best be explained in terms of the sacraments of the Orthodox Church and further define her as a symbol of the Church. Each in its own way illustrates what Le Guillou, quoting an eighth-century writer, sees as the "master-idea" of all Eastern typology: "The Heaven wherein the Triune God lives and moves on earth is the Christian holy place, the church, the bride of Christ arrayed in her wedding garments and sealed with the holy chrism, the irrefragable seal of the Spirit."[30] The most highly charged and important symbolic occasion among Margarita's activities is Satan's Rout, which is a Satanic parody of the Eucharistic celebration, as the Black Mass always is. But three events preliminary to the Rout are also parodies of ecclesiastical offices: Margarita has Azazello's Cream rubbed all over her body, she is washed in blood, and she is anointed with rose oil. The symbolic significances are, respectively, baptism and confirmation (linked in Orthodox liturgy), salvation, and sanctification. The greatest space is devoted to the first of these three.

The latter two occur in a brief passage on page 260. The washing in blood is a clear parody of the salvation imagery of the Bible, in which the believer is washed clean of his sins by the shed blood of Jesus Christ. The Book of the Revelation, from which Bulgakov drew heavily for *The Master and Margarita* (and which will be the focus of the Chapter Nine), praises Christ in the following words: "Unto him that loved us, and washed us from our sins in his own blood" (Rev. 1:5). The old hymn "Are You Washed in the Blood?" is a familiar evocation of this imagery and is but one of many on the subject. Blood, we shall see, also is an important element at Satan's Ball. For instance, when Margarita's strength flags during the Ball, she is "doused...with blood" (p. 270), and she revives.

Margarita's "bath of blood" is followed immediately by the application of "another liquid—dense, translucent and pink": "attar of roses" (p. 260). Then she is "laid on a crystal couch and rubbed with large green leaves until she glowed" (p. 260). We are reminded that Pilate hated the smell of roses, though the Master loves roses. Those who are sanctified by the Holy Spirit and given a ministry of loving witness are the aroma of Christ. II Corinthians 2:15-16, the passage which inspired George Herbert's poem "The Odour," says, "For we are unto God a sweet savour of Christ, in them that are saved, and in them that perish: To the one we are a savour of death unto death; and to the other the savour of life unto life." This Bible passage is interesting in relation to Margarita. She bears the odor of sanctity at that parody of the Eucharist which is staged by and for those to whom she can be only the odor of death unto death. However, she is the odor of life unto life for some—Frieda, Natasha, and especially the Master.

The rubbing of the cream is the topic of a whole chapter of the novel, Chapter Twenty, "Azazello's Cream." Azazello instructs Margarita to rub the cream over her whole body. When she does so, "she immediately glowed and turned a healthy pink" (p. 229). Her day-long headache (on the day of death, Good Friday), disappears, her muscles grow firmer, she loses weight, and she looks ten years younger. The restorative power of the cream in the physical realm is analogous to spiritual health as induced through the sacraments. Margarita now shouts, "Hurray for the cream!" (p. 229), as later she will cry, "Hurrah for the Devil" (p. 362), when Woland serves as the agent of deliverance for her beloved and her. She eagerly accepts cream from Azazello, despite its giver, just as she accepts release from Woland. The application of the cream is strikingly parallel (in parody form, of course) to the chrismation which in church ritual is one of the Orthodox sacraments. Chrism and Holy Cream are synonymous; so an Orthodox reader looking for symbolism in the novel would likely catch the parallel here because of the ecclesiastical associations of the word *cream*.

In the chrismation, which in church ritual follows immediately after one's baptism, "the whole body is anointed with chrism, and the priest says the form: 'The seal of the gift of the Holy Ghost. Amen'"[31] The whole body is anointed "in sign of spiritual baptism."[32] The composition of the Holy Cream

is enormously complicated, and certain chemists of Constantinople are officially appointed to prepare it. Besides olive oil and balsam, fifty-five other substances are put into it, among which are red wine, orange and rose-water, mastic, various gums, nuts, pepper, flowers, and ginger. It is made in huge vats and blessed on Maundy Thursday.[33]

It has been noted that Azazello's Cream is part of witchcraft and that the application of such oil allows witches to fly.[34] J. B. Russell reports that witches "who live inconveniently far away rub their bodies with an ointment that enables them to fly off in the shape of animals, or else astride broomsticks or fences."[35] It is in Chapter Twenty, "Azazello's Cream," that Margarita becomes a witch and flies off to meet Woland to prepare for Satan's Ball. What has not been noted is that Margarita's rite of initiation in applying the cream is a parody of the service of chrismation.

Azazello's Cream, as the parody, has a composition different from that of the Church's chrism. It smells of swamp mud and of marsh and forest, those locales traditionally associated with the gatherings of witches and with ever-lurking evil. In witchcraft, "Various recipes are given for the ointment, and it is interesting to note that they contain deadly poisons: aconite, belladonna, and hemlock."[36] Margarita uses the cream on Good Friday, the day after Maundy Thursday, when chrism is made. Following chrismation, the priest and the chrismated person walk around the baptistry, singing, "You who have been baptized in Christ have put on the garment of Christ. Amen."[37] Margarita, in the Satanic parody, appears naked at the Rout. Yet she "wears" the cream; it is her "garment." And thus she is protected from those sexual trespasses which her nakedness might invite and which are a standard part of witches' sabbaths. The Holy Spirit guards her even in hell.

The Orthodox Church links confirmation (chrismation) and baptism so closely that they merge into one service. According to Orthodoxy, baptism itself is by complete immersion in water, "which signifies the death unto sin, and the resurrection of every Christian into a new life."[38] It may be this total immersion which is being referred to in parodied form when Margarita interrupts her broomstick ride to the Ball and "[dives] head first into the water" and "[throws] up a column of spray almost to the moon" (p. 244). As both chrismation and baptism are necessary preliminaries to the partaking of the Eucharist, so these events in Margarita's life immediately precede her attendance at Satan's Rout.

It is virtually unavoidable to see Satan's Rout as a parody of the Eucharist and all that it typifies, since the Black Mass, of which this occasion is a variant, has always been a parody of the Christian Mass. Once again, as at various other points in the novel, Bulgakov does complex things in symbolism in the extended treatment which he gives to the preparations for and observance of Satan's Rout. On one level it is simply the antitype of a divinely inspired Christian observance. However, Bulgakov carefully develops many of the details so that they point to the true celebration. Since the Satanic incarnation is not just the opposite of the divine Incarnation but in this novel is also the seventh proof, so that faith in it implies faith in its counterpart, we are justified in seeing not only the antitype but the type, not only the shadow but the substance.

The Rout begins exactly at midnight. The guests keep arriving for three hours, after which a bell tolls twelve. It is still midnight; Satan has stopped the clock. We are now outside the realm of time and space. We are, in fact, in hell; the affair is held in Apartment 50, one of Bulgakov's symbols of hell. Earthly time does not apply. The midnight hour, the traditional time for witches to meet, is especially appropriate in this novel, with all of its emphasis on imagery of light and dark, day and night, sun and moon. Witches' sabbaths traditionally lasted from midnight until cockcrow; and, though the clock stands still in this case, the elapsed time is about right. Bulgakov does employ the notion of cockcrow as the ending of demonic powers in Chapter Fourteen, "Saved by Cockcrow." Hella the witch is about to kill Rimsky when the cock crows and destroys her power over men.

Satan's Ball is not the only occasion in the novel when time stands still. Pilate's interrogation of Yeshua is another one. As Proffer remarks, the interrogation occurs "around ten in the morning," is followed by "a lengthy process of consultation," so that "by all internal markers it is noon when Pilate pronounces sentence—yet the chapter ends with the set-off words 'It was ten in the morning.' Time has not passed since Pilate first sets eyes on Yeshua."[39] Though Pilate is unaware of the full import of the occasion, he is having his first direct contact with the supernatural realm. Beatie and Powell comment on these and other distortions of normal time and space, though some of their explanations, such as their reliance on Florensky's concepts, are extraneous.[40]

Orthodox readers would be in a position to intuit significance in the midnight hour of the Ball in addition to the one from demonology. The greatest celebration of the ecclesiastical year, Easter, is held not at dawn, as in the West, but at midnight as Easter Sunday begins. Satan's Rout parodies several details of this service, always in the slant way of the parallels in the novel, just as the scene at Griboyedov is the infernal parody of the Last Supper. The mood for Orthodoxy's midnight Easter service is one of joyous celebration. Woland explains to Margarita that "the night of the full moon is a night of celebration" (p. 275). An authority on Orthodoxy, Nicolas Zernov, says:

> The Russian Church celebrates Easter Matins at midnight, and the special atmosphere of jubilation created on that occasion has no parallel in the experience of other Christians. To be present at this service is to realize why the Orthodox Church is sometimes described as the Church of the Resurrection.[41]

The Easter celebration, even in parodied form, is crucial to the coherence of the novel. The Master's novel, since its viewpoint is sublunary, ends with Yeshua's burial. But, at the end of Bulgakov's novel, Yeshua is alive again in a state of transfiguration and glorification. Satan's Ball provides, by parody, the intermediate link of descent into hell and consequent resurrection to carry the story of Christ from burial to ascension.

Satan's Ball occurs on Good Friday, when Christ is in hell and the evil powers seem to have scored a temporary victory. Thus, Friday is an appropriate night for the festivities. Although a Saturday-night setting would be better for the Eucharistic parallels, that timing is impossible, because that night must be reserved for events of the conclusion, culminating in the breaking of the dawn of Easter Sunday, Resurrection Day, the beginning of the eternal day. Also, works on demonology indicate that Saturday is seldom the time setting for witches' sabbaths, because in the church week it is a day sacred to the Virgin

Mary.[42] And Wedeck notes that Good Friday was a common time for the witches' sabbath.[43] In regard to the Orthodox calendar, John Meyendorff, an Orthodox theologian, writes, "...the mystery of Holy Saturday starts on the afternoon of Holy Friday. The office of Vespers for Holy Friday—beginning at the ninth hour, i.e., 3:00 p.m., the very time that Jesus died on the cross—also inaugurates the 'Great sabbath.'"[44] Satan throws his "springtime ball of the full moon" (p. 250) annually, just as Easter is celebrated annually and in the spring.

Donald Fiene has gone to great lengths to discover if there is a year in which Easter Sunday and May Day Eve (Walpurgis Night) coincide in a way which would fit the events of the novel. "And the greatest satisfaction is achieved if Friday in Moscow occurs on April 30, with Easter the next Sunday."[45] Since a late date for Easter is allowed by Eastern Orthodoxy's use of the Julian calendar, Fiene find 1926 "the best 'astronomical' year," though not a perfect one.[46] This is an interesting speculation, and it suggests that, from the beginning of his thinking about the novel, Bulgakov had in mind bringing together the story of Woland and the events of the Passion Week. However, the novel is so rife with parallels which are intentionally inexact that we do best to conclude, with Fiene, "Perhaps it is finally better to state that it is 'satisfying' to observe the major Jewish, Christian, Communist and pagan spring holidays coalescing at the time center of Bulgakov's extraordinary novel."[47]

Satan's Rout is known also as "the ball of the hundred kings" (p. 250). Koroviev tells Margarita what to expect on that score: "We shall see people who in their time wielded enormous power. But when one recalls how microscopic their influence really was in comparison with the powers of the one in whose retinue I have the honor to serve, they become quite laughable, even pathetic..." (p. 251). The cross is God's judgment on sinful human power. As power puts others in bondage, so these once-powerful are now held captive by Satan. The theme of freedom versus bondage is a prominent one in the novel. The cross brings freedom to those who are believers; it liberates enslaved humanity. In the same way, Margarita's role at the Ball is for the ultimate purpose of freeing the Master. The preceding passage also underlines that the Devil's power is real. However, his power brings about war and bondage, not peace and liberty. So at the Ball we see the live chessmen at war. There is also a war occurring on the globe which Woland has in his possession. "The whole world lies in the hands of the wicked one" (I John 5:19, New English Bible).

Koroviev also tells Margarita "to be afraid of nothing you may see. There's no cause for fear" (p. 251). He need not have bothered; she already knows. But his words provide confirmation from a supernatural source of what she has intuited by faith. "Yea, though I walk through the valley of the shadow of death, I will fear no evil" (Psalm 23:4). Margarita is in the valley of death itself, since Abadonna is present and active. But she need not fear even him, for divine justice prevails even in hell, and he cannot in justice claim her. However, others present at the Ball—Baron Maigel, for instance—have good reason to fear, for in justice Abadonna can claim them. They cannot walk through hell unscathed, as can Margarita, who is protected by the chrism and blood. The vast hall, itself an image of hell since it is also Apartment 50, has an immense fireplace, and those already dead who attend the Rout issue forth from this mouth of hell. This detail is a neat inversion on the popular hell-mouth image of medieval literature and iconography, since the human denizens of hell now issue forth from it, rather than going into it.

Of the many guests who appear at Satan's Ball, one who is singled out for special attention by Bulgakov and, indeed, is given the climactic position at the end of the chapter on the Rout is Baron Maigel. A page and a half are devoted to his appearance. He is unlike the others in that he does not come forth from the mouth of hell in the train of the multitude who do, for he is not yet dead. Rather, he comes from the streets of Moscow, and the Rout is the occasion of his death. Margarita, with a shock, recognizes him; she had seen him many times in Moscow theaters and restaurants. It turns out that he is an informer: an "eavesdropper," a "spy" (p. 273). His job was as a guide to Moscow for foreign tourists, and in that capacity he had wanted to visit Woland in order to inform on him. Now Woland brings the Baron into his presence and inflicts upon the villain a deserved punishment. Abadonna takes off his glasses, Azazello shoots Baron Maigel, and the man dies. As his lifeblood spurts out, Koroviev catches it in the goblet which is the skull of Berlioz and presents the blood-filled skull to Woland. Woland offers a toast, drinks from the goblet, and then commands Margarita to do the same, which she does.

Several critics have observed that Baron Maigel is based on a real-life spy, Baron Shteiger, "whose job was to listen in to social conversations of foreign diplomats."[48] Milne appropriately calls the Baron a "judas figure," who "is killed by order of Woland at his Great Ball—as Judas was killed on Pilate's instructions."[49] We see in the killing of this state informer another instance of Bulgakov's intermittent satire of Soviet society.

However, more important than the discovery of the literary prototype for a fictional character is the symbolic significance of the occasion. As Margarita, upon Woland's command, approaches to drink the blood, a voice (Koroviev's?) whispers, "Don't be afraid, your majesty...the blood has long since drained away into the earth and grapes have grown on the spot" (p. 274). And what she tastes is "sweet juice." Deck is on the right track when she declares that this event "can be seen both as an inversion of communion, in which the juice of grapes is transubstantiated into the blood of Jesus, and as an affirmation of the Easter message."[50] There is, of course, an inversion, since the Eucharistic service is parodied in this hellish setting. But the matter is even easier than she suggests. For, if the Church's ritual signifies wine turning into blood, the historical order has the blood of Christ first, with the tasting of it by the communicant members of the Church (Margarita) being that of wine. Blood is shed; then wine is tasted. An exact parallel may be found in a poem by George Herbert of the seventeenth century:

> Love is that liquour sweet and most divine,
> Which my God feels as bloude; but I, as wine.
> ("The Agonie," ll. 17-18)

This transmutation of blood into wine is but one of many elements of the Eucharist which can be discerned in parodied form during Satan's Ball. There is, first, the parody of the Eucharistic altar. Seven fat wax candles burn in a candelabrum "with arms fashioned like snakes" standing on an oak table (p. 252). There is also a low bench. The candles cast shadows; their casting of light is not the detail mentioned, for we are in the medium of parody at Satan's Ball. The Orthodox Easter service at midnight features the carrying of candles by those in attendance. The chapter in which Margarita arrives at the site of the Ball and which immediately precedes the chapter devoted to "Satan's Rout" is entitled "By Candlelight." G. V. Shann, in his work on Orthodox euchology, notes, "Lamps and tapers burn about the Altar and before the Icons and Shrines, and on certain occasions, for example at the Easter Matins and during the reading of the Gospels of the Passion on Good Friday, all the worshippers hold lighted candles."[51]

For this grand occasion Woland is wearing a scarab on a gold chain on his bare chest, and it is carved of black stone and engraved with arcane script. This detail seems to be a parody of the crucifix worn by the presiding priest. Margarita wears on her breast "a picture of a black poodle in a heavy oval frame with a massive chain" (p. 260). This, too, seems to be a parody of a crucifix; the dog calls up associations with Goethe's Mephistopheles. Satan's bare chest reminds us of Margarita's nakedness. It is only after Satan's Rout that she is again clothed—in a black gown, perhaps symbolic of the black robes of the Orthodox priesthood, or perhaps symbolic of her still being in Satan's presence and not yet ready for the white robes of the redeemed in the Book of the Revelation. Sergius Bulgakov explains that the priests are still wearing black on Holy Saturday but change to white for the commemoration of the Resurrection.[52]

As the Rout commences, parrots shriek, "Ecstasy! Ecstasy!" (p. 261). This cry may be a parody of the joyous shouts of "Christ Is Risen," which resound at the Orthodox midnight Easter service. An "unbearably loud jazz band" strikes up; and, when Margarita passes by, the conductor yells, "Alleluia!" (p. 262). Then wild dancing begins. All three of these items—the loud jazz, the cries of "alleluia," and the dancing—were included in the account of the affair at Griboyedov the night before. In both cases, we have symbols of hell. Both parties break up with the news of a death. The music and dancing seem also to be parodies of Christian songs of praise and especially of the exuberant tone of the Easter service. Cries of "Alleluia, alleluia, alleluia" reverberate through Orthodox liturgy, especially that pertaining to Easter. Light streams from crystal grapes, and wine foams out of a marble wall into a basin of ice. Though these details of description, along with others, seem to be designed principally to add color and exotic dash to the scene, they may also be intended as a parodying of the richly colorful pageantry which accompanies the Eucharist in the Orthodox Church. Sergius Bulgakov observes, "The use of incense, of lighted candles, of silver and gold as ornaments of the temple, of vestments, of icons, etc.; all this is directly connected with the mystic side of the Office, with the sense of the real presence of God in the Church."[53] In the parody we have the real presence of Satan instead of Christ, but the trappings are similar, presumably intentionally so.

Many of the details at Satan's Rout are readily recognizable as direct borrowings from witches' sabbaths. Those devoted to the evil powers are assembled; they pay homage to the Devil; they engage in festivities, usually including a banquet; a woman plays the role of the Queen of the Sabbath, welcoming the guests; the Devil is believed to be present in person in one of various disguises sometimes as a huge black cat[54] (Behemoth is present), sometimes as a tall, black man[55] (similar to Woland's appearance); Satan reads the roll of those present, and they report their activities (Koroviev explains to Margarita who the guests are and what they have done). Also, Margarita rides part way to the Ball on the traditional broomstick. On her way she visits the rural locales traditionally suited for gatherings of witches. Then, the "naked Natasha riding a fat pig comes straight out of Goethe's Walpurgis Night...."[56] And, of course, "[t]he sabbath always took place at night, usually on Good Friday."[57] Although a witches' sabbath, often including the celebration of a Black Mass, was usually held outdoors in the woods, sometimes it was held indoors, even in "a great hall, brilliantly lighted, where men and women were feasting."[58]

However, Bulgakov's deviations from the traditional witches' sabbath and Black Mass (the two are not the same, but they are definitely related in this novel) are more striking than his direct appropriations from those sources. Just as he deftly manipulates the parodies of the sublunary Gospel account so that what is included is compatible with a Christian understanding of the significance of the events of Passion Week, so he retouches standard demonologies so that nothing occurs on this night which violates the Christian symbolism evoked, particularly the symbolism attaching to the character of Margarita. Anything that would be considered blasphemous is toned down or eliminated. These revisions and deletions are handled so as not to lose the sacred parallels which Bulgakov intends.

Throughout the Ball the role of Woland remains that of being the agent for dispensing cosmic justice. He does not inflict suffering according to his whims or desires. Berlioz, Baron Maigel, and the other personages attending the Ball receive only what their unbelief deserves. More important than these recipients, though, is Margarita, who is in attendance but who is a believer in spiritual reality. Woland and his company treat her with appropriate respect.

Thus, in Bulgakov's account the quality of licentiousness of sexual orgies is missing—surely not because of any squeamishness of the part of the author but because it would reflect badly on the presence of the naked Margarita. Further, "[w]omen attending sabbaths always had sexual intercourse with the devil,"[59] most notably the presiding hostess. But for Margarita to engage in such activity would obviously violate her symbolic significance as the Bride of Christ and as the Virgin Mary, and Bulgakov bypasses it. Finally, a witch ordinarily made a pact with the Devil, which "was usually for the term of her life, but sometimes...only for a number of years, at the end of which period the Devil was supposed to kill his votary."[60]

Margarita does make a pact of sorts with the Devil, but it is not one in which she delivers herself over to his power. Rather, something like the reverse is true. He pledges to her that she can have any one request—an extraordinary reworking of the Faust legend. Whereas writers on witchcraft refer frequently to the greater susceptibility of women than of men, Margarita is just the opposite of this generalization. Witches "had to make an explicit disavowal of the Christian faith,"[61] but nothing of the sort occurs in Margarita's case. Witches also promised "never to adore the Blessed Sacrament, always to abuse the Virgin and the saints, spit on and destroy holy relics as much as possible, not to use holy water or holy candles, never to make full confession of all their sins, and finally to maintain the strictest silence about their traffic with the Devil."[62] Not only does Margarita make none of these promises, but she violates the last phrase as totally as could be imagined. In addition, initiates into Satan worship were symbolically to remove the baptismal chrism, request the Devil to write their names in the Book of Death, and promise to sacrifice children to the Devil.[63] Margarita's role keeps her at a far remove from such blasphemous actions. So we see Bulgakov tailoring his borrowings from demonological sources in order to preserve the integrity of Margarita's symbolic functions. Though it is Satan's Rout, Margarita is the main character in this part of the novel, and Bulgakov is careful to insure that she escapes unblemished from her trip to hell.

The Easter symbolism seems to continue beyond the parodying of it at Satan's Rout to the events of the next night, Holy Saturday. The Master and Margarita, "having slept until Saturday evening" (p. 362)—a parallel to Christ's state of "sleep" between his death and resurrection—awake to find a table laid for their supper. They "had no idea where all this food and drink had come from—it had simply been there on the table when they woke up" (p. 362). After all of the other miraculous interventions of Woland, we can safely ascribe this meal to his doing as well. As is always the case in Bulgakov's novel, implied is the direct intervention of God; so it is really God who supplies the supper. And it, too, has symbolic value.

For the feast on Easter Eve is a standard part of Orthodox worship. "The Easter Feast is in fact the beginning of this unending day, and the joy of Easter is related to the joy of Communion."[64] Communion itself, with its elements of bread and wine, is understood in terms of a meal.

> The Communion service is understood in the East primarily as a corporate meal, and like all meals it reminds man of the interdependence of the whole creation. Men need to eat and to drink like all other animals and plants, and not only for the maintenance of their well-being, but also for their creative activities. So the Eucharistic feast teaches man that material elements of food can be transformed by them into higher forms of energy such as prayer, thought and charity.[65]

A relevant passage from the liturgy is this: "Ye that have fasted and ye that have not fasted, rejoice this day. The table is full, enjoy it all of you. The calf is a fattened one, let no one depart ahungered. Enjoy ye all the Feast of the faith."[66] That both the Master and Margarita are present at the meal is fitting, for

> the Messianic meal may be likened to a wedding supper...[where] the bringer of the heavenly kingdom appears as the celestial bridegroom, the

> chosen of the kingdom of God are the invited guests, and the congregation itself is the bride.... He initiates here on earth a fellowship of the table that extends over into the celestial kingdom.[67]

On their fateful Saturday evening, the Master and Margarita wake up to their supper feeling "completely revived" (p. 362) and ready for the momentous events about to befall them in a few hours, as the Day of Resurrection arrives. The Master looks "just as he had when he had created that world he had never seen yet knew to be true" (p. 363). That is to say, his appearance now, which contrasts sharply with his previous look of bedragglement, shows him as a man of faith, for "faith is the substance of things hoped for, the evidence of things not seen" (Hebrews 11:1). Both still feel "a slight ache in the left temple" (p. 362) as a reminder of the past night's visit with the Devil, this residual effect of schizophrenia serving to indicate that their transfiguration has not happened yet. Thus, this scene in the basement apartment, the Master's earthly abode, may refer to the state of the believer in time, after salvation and before transfiguration. For, following this interlude, the Master and Margarita move from this earthly dwelling place to the transfigured, heavenly cottage, which is far better.

In jubilation over the recovery of her beloved, Margarita kisses the Master. "She flung herself at the master, clasped him round the neck and began kissing his lips, his nose, his cheeks. Floods of unkempt black hair caressed the master's neck and shoulders while his face burned with kisses" (p. 363). The ancient Christian salutation of the Kiss of Peace is still exchanged by the Orthodox at the Easter midnight service. It expresses the "idea of fraternity" and the mutual forgiveness of sins in the community of love.[68] Margarita's exuberance, in anticipation of the entry into the realm of peace, accords well with the mood of ecstatic joy which characterizes the Orthodox celebration of Easter.

If Margarita is a symbol of the Church, she is equally, and as easily, a symbol of the Virgin Mary. As Eve is the mother of fallen humanity, man belonging to the earth, so Mary is generally viewed as not only the Mother of God but also the Queen of Heaven and thereby the Mother of redeemed humanity, of man belonging to heaven. As the mystical marriage of the fifth chapter of Ephesians is shown to be a mystery which is concerned with Christ and the Church, so also "it is applied to the Incarnation; directly to the mutual relation between Christ and his mother, the 'unwedded Bride'; more remotely in general to the soul of every man."[69] Mary is also viewed as the head of the Church: "...we have Church, with the Virgin of course at its head, symbolized chiefly by feminine figures, as in the Song of Songs, in the Apocalypse, and in Ephesians."[70]

We may note here, again, that the kind of imprecision of symbolic correspondences which we find in *The Master and Margarita* characterizes the mystical theology of Orthodoxy, especially as enunciated by Sergius Bulgakov, our author's older second cousin. The Head of the Church is Christ; yet in the preceding citation Sergius Bulgakov has Mary as the head. Elsewhere he calls Mary "the personal embodiment of the Church."[71] He goes on, "Mary as the personal habitation of the Holy Spirit is in truth the true personal expression of the Church, the heart of the Church of which Christ is the Head."[72] Carrying the equation one step further, he flatly asserts, "The Church is the Holy Spirit, the giver of life...."[73] Shifting equations such as these may discomfit those raised on a rational theology, but the mystical theology of the Eastern Orthodox Church is an especially suitable matrix for such switchings of symbolic parallels. Between Sergius and Mikhail Bulgakov, there is shared a certain habit of mind.

Although the Orthodox do not adhere to the doctrine of the Immaculate Conception of Mary, they do see in her "the goal and perfection of all creation, ready at last to receive the Savior...."[74] She is both the Mother of Christ and the Mother of mankind.

> By their association of the Divine Wisdom with the God-Bearer, the Russians manifested their search for the link between the Mother of the Incarnate Lord and Mother Earth whose chosen daughter was the Virgin Mary. To the Russians, she appeared to be the purest and most holy of all human beings, the person in whom the entire creation found its perfect representative and authentic spokesman. In her the fallen universe recovered its true image and was reconciled with its Lord and Master.[75]

With these references in mind, we can readily see why Bulgakov thought to use Margarita as a representative of both the Church (redeemed mankind) and the Virgin Mary.

The Annunciation of Mary is celebrated in the Orthodox Church on March 25, nine months before the traditional date of Christmas and four days after spring begins. "According to Orthodox tradition, it was on March 25 that Adam fell, so on this day Christ, the second Adam, was Incarnated to raise fallen man."[76] Easter is celebrated the first Sunday after the beginning of spring. (Eastern Orthodox Easter does not coincide with the Easter of Western churches.) Yet another conjunction of springtime events manifests itself.

When Azazello comes to Margarita to announce her salvific role, we seem to have a parallel, via parody of course, to Mary's Annunciation, when Gabriel, an unfallen angel, informs her of her vocation to bear the Savior of mankind. Mary "accepts the Annunciation as a call to suffering and service."[77] Margarita "had a look of suffering," and the Master is "struck less by her beauty than by the extraordinary loneliness in her eyes" (p. 138). Her attendance at Satan's Ball is the epitome of her suffering for the sake of the Master (mankind).

Woland and company have chosen carefully in their selection of Margarita as the hostess of the Ball. As we have noted earlier, tradition demands that the hostess "must be called Margarita and, second, she must be a native of the place where the ball is held" (p. 250). Margarita fulfills both prerequisites. (Mary was a native of the land in which occurred the events of Passion Week, the prototype of all Masses, white or black.)

Koroviev proceeds to tie these requirements to the issue of royal blood. Margarita is of royal blood, though the news surprises her. Koroviev explains, "...the question of blood is the most complicated problem in the world!" (p. 251). And he informs her that she is a descendant of a French king and queen of four hundred years earlier. Milne is one of several critics who have found in this passage a reference to

> Marguerite de Valois, wife of Henry of Navarre, later Henry IV of France. Queen Margot (heroine of Dumas' novel *La reine Margot*), during the blood-bath of the St. Bartholomew Massacre, displayed both courage and compassion and saved her husband's life. Her courage and compassion are a prefigurement of Margarita's—Margarita being, according to Koroviev, a distant descendant of the French queen.[78]

Two pages later, Azazello, with Margarita still in mind, says, "Blood will tell" (p. 253).

Blood, we have seen, is a major motif in this novel, especially in the chapter about Satan's Rout. The most important signification of blood in Christian understanding is that Christ shed his blood on the cross for the remission of the sins of men. In strict theological terms, blood *is* the most important of matters. But another biblical signification of blood has to do with Mary. She traces her lineage, according to the genealogies given by St. Luke and St. Matthew, back to the Israelites' royal house of King David and Father Abraham and the others. It is Mary, the earthly mother, who connects the Son of the King of Heaven to the earthly royal family. As in the Bible with Mary, so in this novel with Margarita, a point is made of the fact that they are of royal blood.

Her blood line makes appropriate Margarita's role at Satan's Rout as queen. Her being Queen of the Ball, wearing her diamond crown, makes her, in symbolic terms, Queen of Hell. Mary is the Queen of Heaven, and the parallelism between them is perfectly congruent with the Satanic incarnation of the novel and the divine Incarnation of the New Testament. An unknown (evil) man recognizes Margarita as "Your Majesty, Queen Margot" (p. 245). When she offers him her forgiveness for his lecherous advances, he expresses "cheerful devotion" (p. 245) to her. Woland himself addresses her as "madonna" (p. 289). Koroviev calls her *"Madonna bellissima"* (p. 283). These appellations are bestowed after she has completed her stint in hell and is in the position to have any request granted her.

This visit by Margarita to hell has symbolic significance which Westerners might well not see at first glance but which an informed Eastern Christian would understand. Eastern Orthodox tradition envisioned not only Christ but also the Virgin Mary paying a visit to hell and being involved in the harrowing of hell. Sergius Bulgakov contributes this comment about the mystical unity of Mary and Christ:

> The end was not yet, however: she had soon, in company with her son, and treading in his footsteps, to travel the road of his earthly ministry, to receive the sword in her heart: all the way to the station by the cross on Golgotha, where she had to suffer a spiritual death with him upon the cross, in order, with him, to enter into his glory.[79]

Mary's accompaniment of her Son extends beyond the stations on the way to the cross; it includes his descent into hell. This visit to hell by Mary is the substance of a popular Orthodox medieval apocryphal text entitled "The Descent of the Virgin into Hell," also known by the Russians as "The Visitation to the Torments by the Mother of God."[80] It is a story unknown in the Western Church. Her visit occurs between Christ's death and resurrection, as does Christ's. She travels in the company of an angel, Archangel Michael—thus providing yet another parallel for Woland/Satan. It is a confused and primitive account. The Holy Virgin sees all sorts of sufferings of the damned, and she is moved to pity. Among the damned are those "who strangled their children,"[81] as Frieda had done in the novel. Eventually, God the Father grants a temporary respite to the suffering. In the novel just such a brief reprieve is given to the hellions who issue forth from the mouth of the mammoth fireplace into the hall for the festivities of the Rout.

When Margarita says that she will come to live with the Master, his reply is, "It will be hell living with me, and I don't want you to perish here as I shall perish" (p. 146). (His abode is, we recall, one of the novel's images of hell.) This remark, which seems hyperbolic at the time, is fulfilled symbolically when Margarita, paralleling Mary, visits hell for (and, in a mystical sense, with) the Master at Satan's Ball. In her dream Margarita had seen the Master in a cabin by a bridge—"in short—hell" (p. 217). All of the passages which refer metaphorically to the Master's being in hell are enhanced by the parallelism between Margarita and Mary as visitors temporarily to hell.

Margarita's visit to hell is for the purpose of seeking the redemption of the Master. She is the active agent in salvaging his (man's) hopeless life. Like Mary, she plays the role of intercessor and mediatrix. Indeed, the whole matter of her activity versus the Master's passivity is greatly illumined by the correspondence between her and Mother Mary. As Mary is to sinful humans, so on one level Margarita is to the Master. As Mary can intercede in heaven, so Margarita can intercede in hell. "You have the power to ask for whatever you like and they'll do it for you," says Natasha, her maid, who also now calls her "Queen Margarita" (p. 243).

The intercessory role of the Virgin Mary receives considerable attention from the Orthodox:

> The Church sees in her the Mother of God, who, without being a substitute for the One Mediator, intercedes before her Son for all humanity. We ceaselessly pray her to intercede for us. Love and veneration for the Virgin is the soul of Orthodox piety, its heart, that which warms and animates its entire body.... She covers the world with her veil, praying, weeping for the sins of the world; at the Last Judgment she will intercede before her Son and ask pardon from Him. She sanctifies the whole natural world; in her and by her the world attains transfiguration. In a word, the veneration of the Virgin marks with its imprint all Christian anthropology and cosmology, and all the life of prayer and piety.[82]

Similar references abound in Orthodox liturgy. And the conscious linkage of Mary and the Church is a commonplace: "...the Mother of God personifies the Church itself, because She contained in Herself the creator of the world whom the whole world cannot contain."[83]

In *The White Guard* Elena Turbin prays to the Virgin to intercede before Christ for her family. This is fully and conventionally Orthodox, and Bulgakov presents the scene movingly. There is no textual reason to think that he is standing apart from this expression of piety by a character based on his own family membership. Margarita was introduced in the novel as the representative of "real, true, eternal love" (p. 215), and this description, too, is clarified by her symbolizing of Mary the mediatrix. Early in the novel, Margarita tells the Master, "I'm going to save you" (p. 145), a theological turn of phrase which echoes Mary's role. Margarita's relationship with the Master is described by Matthew, Yeshua's messenger to Woland, as that of "the woman who loved him and who has suffered for him" (p. 358).

It is particularly compassion, and of a peculiarly maternal kind, which is Margarita's (and Mary's) leading trait. It is a Godlike quality which can be reproduced by the image of God (mankind) and is most appropriately expressed by a female figure. Sergius Bulgakov writes, "Can those who love fail to forgive, and is not forgiveness the highest joy of love? It likens us to God...."[84] The passage fits Margarita perfectly. During Margarita's broomstick ride she temporarily acts the role of an avenging angel as she ravages the apartment of Latunsky, the vicious critic of the Master's novel. She wields a hammer, called Margarita's hammer, as she wreaks the justly deserved damage. *The Hammer of Witches* (*Malleus Maleficarum*) was the title of a fifteenth-century treatise on magic;[85] there may or may not be a connection here. But even at Dramlit House, where Latunsky and other hated critics reside, Margarita turns quickly from a minister of justice to a minister of mercy, her more natural role, when an innocent boy living in the building is frightened by the commotion which she has caused. She stops her vengeance long enough to tell him a pleasant story which returns him to his peaceful sleep. She exhibits the same quality of maternal love as she caresses and soothes the distraught Master.

Margarita has been promised the fulfillment of any one request as her payment for serving as Satan's hostess. When the Ball is over and Satan does not immediately bring up the subject, she is depressed, fearing that her labor was in vain. Still, with demureness but mainly with self-possession, she resists taking the initiative of asking Woland for anything. He compliments her for this attitude: "We have put you to the test.... You should never ask anyone for anything. Never—and especially from those who are more powerful than yourself. They will make the offer and they will give of their own accord" (p. 281). Whereas one may suspect an autobiographical echo here from Bulgakov's life, perhaps even a veiled allusion to his request to Stalin to be allowed to emigrate, on the symbolic level the meaning seems to be that salvation is a free gift bestowed by supernatural power and beyond the attainment of mortals in their own strength.

When Woland does invite Margarita to make her request, thoughts of the suffering Frieda, whom she had met at the Ball, so flood her mind that she fails to ask for herself (or for the Master, which is the same thing). She asks instead for Frieda's release from her terrible torment: "I want them to stop giving Frieda back the handkerchief she used to stifle her baby" (p. 282). As in Dante's *Inferno*, the punishment always suits the crime and is even an extension of it. This selfless request impresses Woland, because it is foreign to his nature, and he says to Margarita, "...you seem to be a good person. Am I right?" (p. 282). But she forcefully replies, "No." All have sinned. Woland says that he cannot grant that request, since it lies outside his department, as wide as that is. He tells her, "...you must do it yourself" (p. 283). When she asks whether she has the power to do it, Woland assures her that she does; so she forgives Frieda. It was right for Margarita to doubt her power to forgive one in hell, because no ordinary mortal has such power. However, as the symbol for Mary, Margarita does have supernatural power, and specifically of a kind belonging to a department other than Satan's. It is "real, true, eternal love" in action.

It turns out, after the fact, that Margarita's selfless request for Frieda does not count as the fulfillment of the one request promised her by Woland for her services at the Ball and that she can still make one request for herself, though of course she could not have foreseen that turn of events and her compassion is in no way minimized but, rather, highlighted. Her next, and her real, request is for herself in one sense—but only because what she most deeply desires is not something which could be described in terms of selfishness. She pleads, "I want you to give me back instantly, this minute, my beloved—the master" (p. 283). The work of the mediatrix succeeds; the Master is about to be released from his hell. Sinful man ascends. Christ, too, ascends from hell and joins his "unwedded Bride."

And so the Master "is released," as the title of Chapter Twenty-four says. Woland, the supernatural power present in this scene, is not said to have done the releasing. Rather, divine power, represented in part by Margarita's symbolizing of Mary, accomplishes it. Margarita's request is concluded as she asks that she and her beloved be returned to his basement apartment. This part of the request, too, is fulfilled—but in the transfigured form of their eternal abode, which is a far better final fate than this woman had imagined to ask for. Later, when Margarita explains to the Master that she virtually went through hell for him, Bulgakov again invokes the legend of the Virgin's visit to hell.

A few other minor elements are illumined by the correspondence between Margarita and Mary. One is the role of Hella. This vampire is a real witch, a female who dwells with Satan in hell as Mary does with God in heaven. Her acts of judgment are the counterparts of Margarita's acts of love. She is a hellish parody of Margarita, particularly in the latter's role as the madonna. Another has to do with the "enormous, invisible but undeniably real and apparently unending staircase" (p. 148) which Margarita walks up in the hall of Satan's Rout. It seems to be a diabolical parallel to Jacob's Ladder, which reached up to heaven.

Jacob's ladder, set up between heaven and earth, was a figure of our Lady. The complete manifestation of the mother of God to the world will only be possible when the world itself enters into the kingdom of glory in virtue of the general resurrection and all creation is transfigured.[86]

Yet another is the role of Natasha, Margarita's maid. In imitation of Margarita, she rubs the leftovers of Azazello's Cream on herself and becomes a witch, riding to Satan's Rout on her lecherous neighbor, Nikolai Ivanovich Bosoi, who has been appropriately (according to standard witchcraft) turned into a pig. In her intercession for Nikolai Ivanovich, Natasha dimly reflects Margarita's own intercessory role as the symbolic Mother Mary.

We have already, in the preceding chapter, examined the conclusion of the Master's story; now we return to this matter in the light of what this chapter has had to say about Margarita. Both the Master and Margarita, after the events of Good Friday night, reaffirm their belief in the supernatural by declaring without hesitation that they have been with the Devil. They call themselves "husband and wife" (p. 362). Although this marital relationship is not literally true on the physical level, as we have seen, it is true in several ways on the spiritual level (Christ and the Church, Christ and man, God and Mary, believing man and believing woman, the new Adam and the new Eve), as we have seen. Woland, as the shadow of God in this novel, assures them that the peace and eternal refuge which they are about to enjoy is the work of the risen Yeshua, not the Devil himself, and is better than anything which Margarita could have imagined on her own.

In this novel of beliefs, it is the faith of the Master and Margarita, albeit halting and unsteady at times, which is being honored. Matthew, as Yeshua's messenger, tells Woland what state his Lord has chosen for the Master. Woland, knowingly, treats Yeshua's request as a command and complies. Margarita, as she wished, shares the Master's fate—on the principle that a disciple should share the fate of the one to whom the disciple is loyal. Satan always obeys God, perforce. Even as their fate is being worked out, the Master demonstrates his faith by his "premonition that some more nonsense might be on the way" (p. 361). *Nonsense*: literally *not sense*. Yet what happens makes full sense on the spiritual level and is nonsense only on the sensory level. Woland has promised him, "Believe me—your novel has some more surprises in store for you" (p. 291). And now these surprises are about to be demonstrated in fact. It was at the time of this promise that the Master had cried, "I'm finished" (p. 291), corresponding to Christ's cry of "It is finished" on the cross. The promise is to be fulfilled—surprisingly to the Master—at the time of resurrection and transfiguration. The fulfillment comes on Easter Sunday, the Day of Resurrection.

All of the events of Chapters Twenty-nine through Thiry-two occur on Easter Sunday. As has been noted earlier, Easter Sunday begins, according to ancient Jewish calculation, at sunset of Holy Saturday, and it is that Saturday sunset when Chapter Twenty-nine opens. Bulgakov's handling of time here is done carefully and exactly. His characters at this point leave behind all earthly reality and enter into the new eternal day, the eighth day, the Day of Resurrection.

The Master and Margarita enter the state of the dead (that is, the eternally alive) through the agency of the murderer-demon, Azazello. His greeting to them, "Peace be with you" (p. 365), is, as we have seen, pregnant with spiritual meaning. Although it may seem that Azazello's killing of the man and woman is an evil deed, in fact it is God's plan being worked out, as usual in this novel, through the agency of the dark powers. The "crime" is due to divine providence, as Azazello well knows. It is done at the behest of Yeshua, as relayed via Matthew to Woland, who directly commands Azazello.

Azazello kills the Master and Margarita by giving them poisoned wine, the same Falernian wine, he makes a point of saying, which Pilate drank. They and Pilate, whose eternal destiny is also about to be decided and whose life story is also their life story, are again linked. The wine turns everything seen through it "to the color of blood" (p. 367). Again, we have the conjunction of wine and blood, as in the Eucharist itself. Blood is the most important of all questions, and Christ's shed blood, which communicants taste as wine, is destiny-deciding. The Master and Margarita are now dead to their old selves and alive to their new selves. There is no (permanent) death—only life everlasting. As Azazello remarks when the Master complains that he has killed them, "Your beloved calls you the master, you're an intelligent being—how can you be dead? It's ridiculous" (p. 368). The Master, concurring in this viewpoint and accepting his fate, replies to Azazello, "I understand what you mean...don't go on! You're right—a thousand times right!" (p. 368). Thus, there is no horror in their deaths. Bulgakov's view of death is strikingly similar to that expressed by Andrei Sinyavsky in his confession of faith, "Thought Unaware"—death is a completion and fulfillment of life, not its antithesis.[87]

Azazello's murder of the Master and Margarita takes place in the Master's basement apartment. Four pages later we learn that the Master died in the insane asylum, as the nurse tells Bezdomny in honest response to his probing. Bezdomny then tells the nurse that another person in Moscow also has died at the same time, a woman. He means Margarita, of course. For the Master and Margarita, after their poisoning by Azazello, had visited Bezdomny. These two title characters have, it seems, died twice.

What are we to make of these "double deaths"? Johnson sees them as an example of "apparent plot inconsistencies."[88] However, if we keep distinct the literal and symbolic levels, there is no inconsistency. In real life the Master and Margarita never meet; they die apart, the Master in the asylum and Margarita in her apartment. Only on the symbolic level do they get together, experience the various events of Book Two of the novel, die together, and go off into eternity together. It does of course seem to readers that in real life these two did meet and love. Bulgakov laces their plot with many ostensibly realistic episodes, and thus he invites us to revel imaginatively in their relationship. However, in calling attention to the "double deaths," the author underscores the essentially symbolic character of his novel and its title characters.

There is a precedent for this idea of "double deaths" in Norse mythology, if not elsewhere. According to the old Norsemen, souls were "able to leave the body and lead a semi-independent existence."[89] Body and soul could function apart from each other, and the soul could even act bodily. If, however, one of the two selves was killed, the other shared in that fate. By the time of the Christian Middle Ages, it was believed that only witches had the power to separate soul and body.[90] Thus, Margarita, when she applies Azazello's Cream, enters into the soulish state appropriate to her involvement with the supernatural forces with which she interacts for the rest of the novel. The Master and she share the same fate. However, their bodies also must die, and thus we can account for the "double deaths."

The story of the Master and Margarita concludes with the chapter "Absolution and Eternal Refuge," the final chapter of the novel. Absolution is a technical theological term with a clear meaning in Orthodoxy theology.

> Absolution is the forgiveness of sins. It is given when the priest, using the authority he has received through the Apostolic Succession which Christ instituted, lays his hands on the penitent and reads the prayer of Absolution; Absolution literally means to "unbind" or "unloose." In the Sacrament of Confession Christ, through the priest, forgives the confessed sins according to the words to His Apostles: "Whose sins you loose will be loosed in heaven."[91]

Of course, in this chapter we have not the mere prefiguring of absolution through the priestly prayer but the consummation itself, the loosing in heaven. The time is "the night of Sunday" (p. 381), the time of Orthodoxy's Easter midnight service.

The fate assigned to Margarita, just as much as to the Master, is peace and eternal refuge. Precisely what this means Bulgakov does not make clear. Orthodox beliefs explain this lack of clarity.

> ...the Eastern Church has never thought of Judgment Day in the strictly juristic terms customary in the West. It does not haggle over anyone's right to salvation or insist upon an individual's achieve-ments.... There is only confidence in grace and the "love of man—philanthropia," which is an attribute of the divine Logos.[92]

Nicolas Zernov expands on this doctrinal matter:

> Eastern Christians have never been attracted to...clear-cut answers to the mystery of death. Their underlying conviction is that the end of physical existence closes only one stage in human ascent toward God, and that the seeds of good and evil sown on earth continue to bring forth fruit long after the death of the individual. The final reckoning can be made only at the end of history. So even the blessed do not reach their full glory immediately after death and those who failed to learn how to love in freedom are not deprived of the possibility of improvement in their position....[93]

The theme of discipleship has been mentioned frequently throughout this study, and we can now recapitulate it and pull together its diverse strands. Both

Woland and Yeshua are masters who have their followers, and it is as a type of Christ that the Master has his disciples, Margarita and Bezdomny. Satan's disciples are comprised of both the fallen angels and the unbelieving Muscovites, who, from the vantage point of eternity, follow Satan even while they deny his reality. Yeshua's disciples are Matthew, Pilate, the Master, and Margarita—and, in his unfaithful way, Judas. The theme of discipleship is echoed in Banga's faithful loyalty to Pilate. It is in specific reference to Banga that Woland reiterates, "...one who loves must share the fate of his loved one" (p. 378).

We may classify these disciples into three groups: the stupid and ignorant but faithful (Matthew and Banga), the intellectual but doubting and wavering (Pilate, the Master, and Bezdomny), and the intelligently faithful (Margarita). Matthew is ignorant of Yeshua's real mission and at one point despairs to the point of denial. Nor does Banga understand who his master is; his loyalty is instinctive, not intelligent. Margarita's loyalty is far different from theirs. She understands, to the extent that mortals can, the spiritual realities which confront her, and still she chooses to remain faithful. In the middle are Pilate, the Master, and Bezdomny. They have a knowledge of the "enlightened" man's view of the world and its ways, and this knowledge causes them to doubt or, at best, to waver in their faith. All three suffer spiritual torment under the full moon. All three talk to themselves. It is these disciples, the ones who find faith hard to come by, who seem to fascinate Bulgakov most. Matthew, Banga, and Margarita are disciples who follow willingly, whether blindly or not. Pilate, the Master, and Bezdomny find the cost of discipleship so great that, if they are to enter the Kingdom of God at all, they will do so kicking and screaming. Yet they are pursued by Christ, that Hound of Heaven (to borrow the title image from Francis Thompson's famous poem), until he finally secures them. At least, that is the case for Pilate and the Master.

With Bezdomny we have quite a different, and very puzzling, situation. He is an important enough character to require that a full chapter, the next one, be devoted to him.

Chapter Eight

Homeless

❖ ❖

Of the various characters in the novel who qualify in one way or another as disciples, no other character is as important to the theme of discipleship as Bezdomny, or "Homeless." The Master explicitly calls Bezdomny his disciple; and, as the Master is about to leave this world, he pays a final visit to him and instructs him, "You must write a sequel to it" (the Master's novel about Pontius Pilate).[1] The central question about Bezdomny, as we shall see, is what kind of disciple he is, faithful or failed.

However, of his importance to the novel there can be no question. Only five characters—Woland, Pilate, Yeshua, the Master, and Margarita—have greater significance in thematic and symbolic terms. And in structural terms he is the most important character of all, for he is the only one who appears both at the opening and at the closing (the Epilogue) of the novel. Although he may not grab the first-time reader's imagination as do the above-listed five characters, a careful study of the novel indicates his importance, if only by the frequency of his appearances. He is a major figure in eight of the eighteen chapters of Book One—or eight of the sixteen, fully half, of the Moscow chapters. Then he reappears, after a considerable absence in which the Master and Margarita hold center stage, in two chapters of Book Two, strategically placed toward the end of the novel (Chapters Twenty-seven and Thirty). Finally, he is the chief character in the Epilogue. By then the above-listed five characters have all left this world for the next; Bezdomny remains, serving as the focus for the denouement.

Bezdomny enters the novel on its very first page. In this appearance the rather obtuse young Soviet intellectual is being scolded by his superior, Berlioz, head of the Writer's Union and keeper of the atheists' faith. The young poet, a self-avowed atheist but a superficial thinker and person, had just written a poem about Jesus Christ, one which he intended to be antireligious. Berlioz lectures him on his "fundamental error": that "his Jesus had come out...well, completely alive, a Jesus who had really existed, although admittedly a Jesus who had every possible fault"—whereas all good Soviets knew that "as a person Jesus had never existed at all and that all the stories about him were mere invention, pure myth" (p. 5). From the start, then, Bezdomny, while intellectually committed to a position of atheism, shows an interest in the story of Jesus Christ and perhaps has an unconscious recognition that his story has significance, possibly even a germ of spiritual truth.

It is during this discussion that the two men meet Woland. This meeting and its consequences have a profound effect upon Bezdomny. As we shall see in some detail, he does some things which suggest that he believes, at least to some extent, that Woland really is Satan, is therefore placed in an insane asylum for his ostensible schizophrenia, meets the Master and comes under his spell, and finally turns away from poetry to become a respected professor at the Institute of History and Philosophy, in which role he appears in the Epilogue. In that final appearance he concludes that he once met some hypnotists (Woland and company), through them became mentally ill, and now is cured; nevertheless, glimmerings of spiritual insight recur annually, at every springtime anniversary of the events of the novel proper. Thus, the Epilogue apparently leaves the character of Bezdomny somewhat ambiguous.

Just what are we to make of Bezdomny? What is his role in the novel? Several critics have paid him considerable attention, and they are sharply divided in their analyses. For some he is emphatically a spiritual failure; for others—and there are more of these—he is a spiritual success.

For both groups the key issue is Bezdomny's fidelity to the Master. This young poet, who indubitably has had his atheistic convictions unsettled by meeting first Woland and then the Master and Margarita, has been attracted to the Master and his way of thinking. Eventually, the Master commissions him to carry on that vision of reality by writing the sequel to the Master's novel. The question is whether Bezdomny remains faithful to this calling or backslides away from it.

Ellendea Proffer is a leading voice among those who evaluate Bezdomny negatively. She concludes that "Bezdomny has renounced his belief in the Master and the events connected to him" and that he is therefore to be viewed as "a disciple who has not learned from his teacher."[2] Carol Avins joins in this assessment: "Unable to meet the demands of discipleship, he fails not only to carry on the work of the Master, but even fully to grasp the lessons of his life and word, and to transmit them to others."[3]

Among the many who judge Bezdomny positively, Val Bolen says, "...Bezdomnyj, who starts as a disciple of Berlioz, becomes the Master's disciple.... The novel contains enough support for the assumption that Bezdomnyj will be successful in the search for truth begun by the Master."[4] Judy Ullman thinks that Bezdomny "has found a new meaning in life, *i.e.*, a spiritual home," and that each springtime full moon, when he experiences agitation, is "the anniversary of his personal rebirth."[5] Carol Arenberg finds Bezdomny "ready to assume the task the master assigns to him," as he "promises" to do.[6] Lewis Bagby is similarly confident that "the naive and innocent Ivan, who acquires the prophetic vision of the master, will continue the master's work."[7] Pierre Hart sees Bezdomny as "a man whose basic integrity remains uncorrupted," one whose "vaguely felt impulses which led to the first, ideologically unacceptable portrayal of Christ have been appreciably quickened by his direct experiences of the supernatural...."[8] Sharratt and Pearce are among others who find Bezdomny sympathetically treated.[9] Richard Pope presents the positive view well and indicates its logical culmination:

> Ivan Bezdomnij, who at the end of the novel is a new Ivan, Professor Ivan Nikolaich Ponirev, and no longer "Homeless," and who is now presumably living out his life in an exemplary manner, honestly and without ever compromising his integrity, will doubtless be taken unto Yeshua in the Kingdom of Light when he dies, just like that other reformed sinner Matthew the Levite.[10]

By far, the best and most thorough commentator on Bezdomny is Laura Weeks, who joins in the affirming chorus and also carries the argument further than anyone else. In her essay "In Defense of the Homeless," she notes that "his significance for the *structure* of the novel is indisputable," but also that he "remains one of Bulgakov's most controversial characters."[11] Her thesis, "that his structural significance is inseparable from his thematic significance," leads her to cast him in a positive light.[12] Properly, Weeks sees Bezdomny as "a composite image of 'discipleship,'" and she points out parallels between him and John the Baptist, Matthew, Peter, and John the Apostle.[13] But, for her, the main function of Bezdomny—as she indicates in her subtitle, "On the Uses of History and the Role of Bezdomnyj in *The Master and Margarita*"— is to convey "Bulgakov's model of history," which she says "resembles the primitive Christian model in many respects."[14] This view of history features the intervention of God in human history; there is a nexus between Kairos and Chronos, "the Great Time and profane time," "profane history (history with a small 'h') and sacred, redemptive History (History with a capital 'H')."[15]

It is within this framework that Weeks finds Bezdomny to be "a model of Christian conversion," one whose "'baptism,' for all its parodic elements, is quite real."[16] He is the one who understands that "the Master and Margarita of necessity die twice, once on the literal level, once on the symbolic—once in history, once in History."[17] The Epilogue finds him, and him alone, "'stranded' at the intersection of History and history," now "ready to write" the sequel to the Master's novel.[18] His conversion results in his self-initiated change of status:

> He has, after all, given up a position of prominence with considerable material advantages to become a comparatively obscure professor of history. Ideologically speaking, he has moved from a position at the center of his culture (insofar as MASSOLIT can be included among those state-controlled organs which both disseminate and control ideology) to a position nearer the periphery.[19]

His commitment to History is complete. "As one of the elect, he also participates in the yearly renewal of the central event, that is, he *participates* in History.... Another way of viewing Ivan's final position is that he retreats from history to become the *chronicler* of History"[20] (emphasis added).

Weeks' argument culminates in her making the case that Bezdomny is the real author of *The Master and Margarita* and also of the novel about Pilate and Yeshua contained within it, both the outer novel and the inner novel (thus chronicler of, as well as participant in, History). Disputing Proffer's position that "the lost novel written by the Master is *The Master and Margarita*," she claims that "the case for Ivan's authorship...is fairly strong."[21] She explains that Bezdomny knew of events which the Master could not have known of firsthand and demonstrates how Bezdomny could have learned afterward of all other events, those which he had not experienced himself, including how he could have come into possession of the two chapters of the novel-within-the-novel unquestionably written by the Master.[22]

The case for Bezdomny's authorship rests on two assumptions. One is that a character within the action is the narrator, a point which I have disputed earlier. The other is that Bezdomny is a positive character. As the immediately preceding pages have shown, this is a hotly debated point, to which I now turn.

Wright is correct to see "Ivan Homeless" as "the third major hero in Moscow," as he is when he concludes, "All in all, Ivan is the personification of man's susceptibility to spiritual truth."[23] However, neither the strictly positive nor the strictly negative reading of Bezdomny gets his character quite right. From beginning to end, he demonstrates some degree of spiritual openness and awareness. In between, he manifests what seem like some steps of spiritual growth, however halting and incomplete. Yet his final state is more like his original state than it is like those interim stages where his spiritual intuitions have been heightened through contact with Woland, the Master, and Margarita. We have seen that the key question about a character, in regard to his redeemability, is whether he believes in the reality of Satan. Bezdomny does and does not. In this matter, of which his psychiatric diagnosis is a symbol, he is schizophrenic. Thus, on the spectrum of faith, he falls in a middle place, between Berlioz (and others) on one end and the Master and Margarita on the other. Though called by the Master to be his disciple, Bezdomny does not fully actualize this role; and even Weeks can say only that he is ready to do so. In the Epilogue, the interpretation of which is the central issue in assessing the spiritual status of Bezdomny, his divided soul remains on display. He is homeless to the end.

But of course Bezdomny is still alive at the end of the Epilogue. Thus, the novel leaves his story unfinished, open-ended. The possibility remains that sometime in the future, beyond the end of the novel, he might fulfill the role of the Master's disciple. The open-endedness provides a note of hope. Although this atheist, who has had a serious flirtation with religious faith and even has temporarily gained some spiritual insight, albeit holding it only tentatively, has eventually relapsed into his original state of unbelief, divine grace continues to force its presence upon him. Thus, my reading of Bezdomny, although it falls between the negative and positive poles offered by other critics, is somewhat closer to the positive reading—and precisely because of the note of hope. It comports with the spirit of Bulgakov's novel to hope, as do the many critics who interpret Bezdomny favorably, that his character will find the redemption that the Master and Margarita have found. Where there is life, there is hope; and this is a novel in which hopes are fulfilled more than they are dashed.

The open-endedness of the story of Bezdomny would remove him from consideration as the author of either the inner novel or the outer novel. But it positions him perfectly to stand in the place of the reader of *The Master and Margarita*. If, as I think, Bulgakov is ultimately trying to force upon the reader the question "What think ye of the Christ?", it would be fitting, albeit not required, to have a major character in the novel who stands where the reader does and with whom the reader can directly identify. The reader, too, is homeless until he answers the novel's central question for himself. He is susceptible to spiritual truth (to use Wright's phrasing) in just the way that Bezdomny is. With this understanding in mind, the structural significance of Bezdomny, including his providing the envelope effect by appearing at both the beginning and the ending of the novel, makes sense. The case for this understanding depends on a tracing of the story of Bezdomny throughout the novel, to which task I now turn, concluding with an extensive consideration of the Epilogue.

Before the novel opens, Bezdomny has already written his poem about Jesus Christ, in which, despite his antireligious intention, the young poet became caught up with the character to the point of depicting him as fully alive. Then in the opening chapter Bezdomny hears Woland's prediction of Berlioz's death, and in the third chapter he sees it fulfilled exactly in the manner foretold. He muses, "Did he arrange the whole thing himself?"—an implied naturalistic solution to the puzzle. Immediately he rejects his own hypothesis: "But how on earth could he?" (p. 46). As often happens in the novel, the naturalist speaks more truly than he knows. There is no way *on earth*—no naturalistic way—that Woland could have done this arranging.

Woland has demonstrated the "seventh proof," that the reality of the Devil proves the reality of God, primarily for Bezdomny's sake. And Bezdomny's response to this demonstration shows that, to some considerable extent, he has gotten the point, for he acts on the basis of believing that Woland is Satan incarnate. As Bezdomny pursues Woland, he enters into the supernatural realm, in which "for no apparent reason" he experiences "a sudden intuition" of where to look for the mysterious professor (p. 49). Along the way he inexplicably (from an atheist's point of view) steals a candle and a little paper icon to carry, because, as he later explains, "...an icon frightens them [devils] more than anything else" (p. 67). He pauses in the chase to take a swan dive into the water of the Moscow River, this act being a parodied form of baptism, as Ullman, for one, has noted.[24] Bezdomny's next intuition sends him to Griboyedov House, where he tells the twelve waiting for their leader, Berlioz, "He's [Satan has] come!" (p. 61). In this symbolic version of hell, Bezdomny says, "I can sense that he's here!" (p. 61).

Throughout, though he is now a searcher, the object of his search (Woland—but also the truth in general) eludes him, Yet in this endeavor he demonstrates a certain break with his naturalistic world view and thus shows himself to be a large cut above the other naturalists—his mentor Berlioz, for example. Some glimmer of the truth of supernatural reality has penetrated his soul.

His new outlook and irrational behavior can strike the habitues of Griboyedov House only as insane, for they are at odds with atheism. Thus, he is sent packing to the insane asylum, Satan's stronghold for those who perceive supernatural truth even fragmentarily. In this novel it is always a mark of honor to be considered insane by atheists. The diagnosis is schizophrenia. The condition of a divided mind is shared by the Master with his schizophrenia and Pilate with his hemicrania. However, to have a divided mind is not yet to have mental or spiritual health; rather, it is the first step toward it, a pre-condition for it. By the end of the novel, both the Master and Pilate move beyond this stage; there is no solid evidence that Bezdomny ever does.

The brief eleventh chapter of the novel, "The Two Ivans," is important for understanding Bezdomny's response to his inner conflict, as the "old Ivan" and the "new Ivan" argue. Some of those who interpret Bezdomny positively get these terms, old and new, reversed. Ullman, for example, asserts, "Once he is in the asylum, the new Ivan is born. He repudiates his past life."[25] Similarly, Hart declares that "...the 'new' Ivan must convince the 'old' one that it is necessary to assume a more positive attitude toward the realm of the supernatural."[26] Weeks follows suit: "Meanwhile, Ivan, who has been diagnosed as schizophrenic, is developing a new personality. As the new Ivan emerges, the old Ivan is laid to rest."[27]

Actually, it is the old Ivan, the one who entered the asylum, who is open to spiritual reality and the new Ivan, the one who is in the process of being "rehabilitated" back to sanity according to the lights of atheism so that he can leave the asylum, who seeks to check the impulses of the would-be believer. After receiving drug injections, Bezdomny wonders why he "got so excited about Berlioz falling under that streetcar" (p. 115). The old Ivan says, "Wait a moment, though! ...He [Woland] did know in advance that Berlioz was going to have his head cut off, didn't he? Isn't that something to get upset about?" (p. 115). The new Ivan, while not flatly denying the supernatural character of Woland, seeks to deflect the old Ivan's quest for spiritual truth:

> What do you mean? ...I quite agree that it's a nasty business.... But he's a mysterious, superior being—that's what makes it so interesting. Think of it—a man who knew Pontius Pilate! Instead of creating that ridiculous scene at Patriarch's, wouldn't it have been rather more intelligent to ask him politely what happened next to Pilate and that prisoner Ha-Notsri? And I had to behave like an idiot! Of course it's a serious matter to kill the editor of a magazine. But still—the magazine won't close down just because of that, will it? Man is mortal, and, as the professor so rightly said, mortality can come so suddenly. So God rest his soul and let's get ourselves another editor.... (pp. 115-16)

After a brief doze the new Ivan "spitefully" reproaches the old Ivan, "And how do I look after this affair?" (p. 116).

There are signs of hope and potential spiritual progress in Bezdomny's stay at the asylum. He "gaze[s] at the rainbow stretched across the sky" (p. 114), that archetypal biblical symbol of hope. He meets the Master and learns from him. Nevertheless, in this pivotal eleventh chapter the terms are set which leave him in that middle position between belief and disbelief. This man, who has some capacity for both thinking and believing, is wracked by indecision about eternal issues. The chapter records the inner struggle between the new (rehabilitated naturalist) Ivan and the old (quasi-believer) Ivan. As quasi-believer he intuits that there is something of eternal significance which is beyond his reason's and senses' ability to comprehend. As rehabilitated naturalist he refuses to follow the seventh proof to its logical conclusion. After this chapter, whenever Bezdomny appears, he is seen to be wavering between the two poles of belief and disbelief. On Good Friday he has a "half-waking dream" (p. 334) of Pontius Pilate, which epitomizes his position halfway between day and night, belief and disbelief.

The last of the eight chapters in Book One in which Bezdomny appears is Chapter 13, "Enter the Hero." Here, through the conversation with the Master, Bezdomny expresses his belief in the reality of the supernatural. When, after hearing Bezdomny's story, the Master asserts, "...you met Satan" (p. 134), Bezdomny replies, "It can't be! He doesn't exist!" (p. 134). This is the "new" Ivan speaking. After the Master presses his point, saying, "The man you were talking to *was* with Pontius Pilate, he did have breakfast with Kant and now he has paid a call on Moscow," we read this revealing brief paragraph: "'But God knows what he may do here! Shouldn't we try and catch him somehow?' The old Ivan raised his head, uncertain but not yet quite extinguished" (p. 135). Again, it is the "old" Ivan who is open to the motions of grace, but he is "uncertain," wavering, unable to commit himself to the kind of belief in the supernatural which the Master embraces. Even the Master's summary of his Pilate story, so consonant with Bezdomny's own version of the same story, does not avail to bring certainty to the young poet. The "old" Ivan may be "not yet quite extinguished," but he is far from being in the ascendancy over the "new" Ivan.

Bezdomny appears in only two chapters in Book Two, and here he continues to demonstrate the middle state at which he has arrived. As he is having his "half-waking dream" of Pilate, a detective arrives at the asylum to question him about Berlioz's death at Patriarch's Ponds. However, Bezdomny shows no interest in Berlioz's fate or in capturing Woland, as he had shown when he entered the asylum. "For Ivan, alas, had altogether changed since the night of Berlioz's death" (p. 334). The new, rehabilitated Ivan is now in the ascendancy.

In the second of his two appearances in Book Two, the "old" Ivan resurfaces. As the Master and Margarita are about to depart this world, they pay a farewell visit to Bezdomny at the asylum. Seeing the beautiful Margarita, Bezdomny says to the Master, "Everything has worked out wonderfully for you,

you lucky fellow. And here am I, sick.... Or perhaps I'm not so sick after all" (p. 371). Maybe sick, maybe not—the middle state. The next words are by Margarita, believer in providence: "That's right.... I'll kiss you and everything will be as it should be" (p. 371). After that Kiss of Peace, the Master says, "Farewell, disciple" (p. 371), and he and Margarita vanish. When Bezdomny coaxes the nurse into telling him that the Master has died, he tells her that "another person has just died in Moscow, too. I even know who.... It is a woman!" (p. 372). This affirmation of spiritual reality belongs of course to the "old," partly believing Ivan. The point is that in this chapter both Ivans are present; Bezdomny is a divided man, as he remains in the Epilogue.

Bezdomny is certainly the main character in the Epilogue, specifically, in the second half of it. Here his story is projected several years, maybe seven or eight, into the future, that is, several years beyond the year of the fateful events in Moscow during Holy Week. To the end of the Epilogue, however, both the "old" and the "new" Ivan are present; neither vanquishes the other. As the educated and cultured people of the first part of the Epilogue have come to accept naturalistic explanations, however implausible, for the strange events of those few days, so does Bezdomny. But, unlike them, he is ineluctably reminded every year at the time of the vernal full moon of those events, and they exercise a certain power over him annually.

> Ivan Nikolayich now knows and understands everything. He knows that as a young man he fell victim to some crooked hypnotists, went to the hospital and was cured. But he knows that there is still something that is beyond his control. He cannot control what happens at the springtime of the full moon. (p. 391)

Bezdomny has settled down as Professor Ivan Nikolayich Poniryov of the Institute of History and Philosophy, and he has gotten married. Now rehabilitated almost entirely, he functions within the Soviet intellectual establishment. Nevertheless, once a year he inexplicably "grows uneasy and irritable, loses his appetite, cannot sleep and waits for the moon to wax. When full moon comes, nothing can keep Ivan Nikolayich at home. Toward evening he leaves home and goes to Patriarch's Ponds" (p. 391). He finds it "useless to fight his instinct at full moon" (p. 391). After he returns home and falls asleep, he has a dream, which replays the execution on Bald Mountain. Waking up in agony, weeping and raving, he receives from his wife an injection from a hypodermic syringe, upon which he returns to sleep and now to happy dreams, which focus on Pilate, the Master, and Margarita—all in their final state. In the morning he returns to his normal life for another year.

Laura Weeks, with her positive reading of Bezdomny, says that in the Epilogue he has

> given up a position of prominence with considerable material advantages to become a comparatively obscure professor of history. Ideologically speaking, he has moved from a position at the center of his culture (insofar as MASSOLIT can be included among those state-

controlled organs which both disseminate and control ideology) to a position nearer the periphery.[28]

Furthermore, she finds that "the injection his wife gives him to enable him to carry on is no more sinister than the medicine given to the Master by Woland with Margarita's encouragement."[29] A similar positive reading of the Bezdomny of the Epilogue is offered by Barbara Kejna Sharratt: "Significantly Ivan discards his literary pseudonym 'Homeless' when he finally find a home (a wife and a new profession). Thus he stops being a wanderer, having discovered, through his meeting with the Master, a new purpose in life."[30]

There are problems with this line of approach. The text provides no evidence for considering a professorship at a Moscow institution of advanced learning to be an obscure position, one on the periphery of Soviet culture. The correct parallel to the injections administered by the wife is surely the injections administered in the insane asylum, for both serve the purpose of deflecting Bezdomny from his spiritual quest and returning him safely to the naturalistic outlook of established Soviet society. Also, to the extent that Bezdomny can be said to have found a home through his marriage and career, it is within that officially atheistic society; he does not operate with a new purpose in life which would place him outside the pale.

On the conscious level, then, the "new" Ivan has prevailed. The "old" Ivan shows up just one night per year, quickly to be subdued. It is within this framework that Bezdomny's annual dream should be interpreted. In the nightmarish first part, Bezdomny sees what really happened, the grisly execution. After the medication is administered, the dreaming turns happy but also false. Now comes a conversation between Yeshua and Pilate in which Pilate, referring to the execution on Bald Mountain, pleads, "...it did not take place, did it? I beg you—tell me that it never took place?" (p. 393). Yeshua replies, "No, of course it never took place.... It was merely your imagination" (p. 393). Pilate asks him to swear to that, and Yeshua does. The dream then switches to a scene featuring the Master and Margarita. When Bezdomny "asks greedily, 'So was that how it ended?'," the Master answers, "That is how it ended, disciple" (p. 393). Margarita concurs, adding, "I'll kiss you on the forehead and everything will be as it should be..." (p. 393). She then repeats her Kiss of Peace, "and Ivan strains toward her to look into her eyes, but she draws back, draws back and walks away toward the moon with her companion..." (pp. 393-94).

The drug-induced, happy second half of the dream is not to be interpreted as any sort of fulfillment of the spiritual quest upon which the "old," quasi-believing Ivan had once tentatively commenced. To the contrary, it is the nightmarish first half which belongs to the "old" Ivan. The Pilate who wishes to believe that the execution on Bald Mountain never took place and the Yeshua who denies that event are not the Pilate and Yeshua of either the inner novel, that by the Master, or the outer novel, that by Bulgakov. Rather, they are projections by the "new" Ivan. The dream as a whole serves as a transition out of the "old" Ivan's evening of wandering to Patriarch's Ponds and back into the "new" Ivan's return in the morning to his normal naturalistic style of life, with the dream's first half belonging to the "old" Ivan and its second half to the "new" Ivan. Thus, the reassurance by the Master that the story of Pilate and Yeshua is as Bezdomny has dreamed it is false. Bezdomny's desire to consider himself somehow a faithful disciple of the Master remains unfulfilled, for the would-be disciple does not now believe in the story that his master believes in. The same applies to the efficacy of Margarita's kiss and benediction. Whereas it is true that everything will be as it should be in the cosmic scheme of things, her words do not indicate that things are right in Bezdomny's life. It is very significant that the dream ends with Bezdomny's separation from Margarita (and the Master), rather than with union. The gulf between him and them remains fixed. He awakes in the morning not to follow his old spiritual intuitions but to deny them.

Nevertheless, the contents of the dream are indicative of something heartening about Bezdomny's spiritual condition. He may live as though the supernatural were not real, and he may wish for a naturalistic conclusion to the Pilate-Yeshua story; but he cannot entirely shake himself loose from its grip upon his imagination. He is never redeemed. He remains homeless to the end. Still, unlike Berlioz and some others, he is also never consigned to Woland's infernal realm. The Hound of Heaven continues to pursue this homeless one. Though Bezdomny strives to stifle his spiritual intuitions, willy-nilly he continues to demonstrate his openness to them. The most important thing about the Epilogue is that Bezdomny's story remains open-ended. He continues to live—and to have his capacity for belief prodded. Perhaps he will never believe; then again, perhaps one year he will believe. Thus, the final note of Bezdomny's story is one of hope, for certainly the reader wishes for this sympathetic character's ultimate redemption, wishes for him to join the Master and Margarita in eternal bliss. And of course, were he to believe, he would thereby be writing the sequel to the Master's novel—writing it in his own life. At this point, as at every other point in his saga, Bezdomny stands where the reader of *The Master and Margarita* stands.

A generally neglected fact about the Epilogue is that Bezdomny is not the only Moscow character to appear in it. George Bengalsky, the former master of ceremonies at the Variety Theater, and Nikanor (sometimes called Nikolai) Ivanovich Bosoi, chairman of the tenants' association at Berlioz's apartment building, also appear.

Though a few others do, too, these two, like Bezdomny, fall under the influence of the full moon every spring. Since they were never privy to the Pilate story, as Bezdomny was, their thoughts are limited to the visit to Moscow by Woland and company. Still, supernatural reality has impinged upon them. Bengalsky had denied the supernatural character of the tricks played by Woland's crew, and for his disbelief he experienced the seventh proof by being temporarily beheaded. Bosoi had had an encounter with Koroviev and had been exposed as one who would accept a bribe. Both were so shaken by their experiences with the Satanic forces that they were placed in the insane asylum, where they were neighbors of the Master and Bezdomny.

It is their institutionalization which makes Bengalsky and Bosoi appropriate candidates for reappearing in the Epilogue. They have demonstrated enough awareness of the reality of the supernatural to be judged insane by the naturalists of the Soviet establishment. Nevertheless, there is not the slightest hint, in the Epilogue or earlier, that either of these two men is redeemed. The vernal full moon can unsettle them out of their routines, but there is no suggestion that its effect on them is to move them toward spiritual illumination. They do not deny the events which resulted in their hospitalization, but neither do they follow their experiences of the seventh proof, namely, the reality of the Devil, to the logical conclusion of the reality of God. Thus, they serve as a warning not to conclude that Bezdomny's annual experiences of the springtime moon indicate that he is a successful character in spiritual terms. Because Bezdomny has more evidence of spiritual reality than Bengalsky and Bosoi do, a greater note of hope attaches to his story. But their presence in the Epilogue suggests that mere awareness that some things are beyond one's ability to comprehend is no guarantee of redemption.

At the same time, the note of hope in Bezdomny's story is enhanced by the strong parallels in the novel between Bezdomny and Pontius Pilate. Both have a split in sensibility, Bezdomny with his schizophrenia and Pilate with his hermicrania; they are divided men. Both have powerful evidence of supernatural reality, yet wander between belief and disbelief. Pilate shares that middle state with Bezdomny as no other character in the novel does. For their indecisiveness both suffer over a long period of time following the crucial events of their lives. As Pilate is representative of mankind in general, so is Bezdomny, particularly as he is representative of the readers of Bulgakov's novel.

The key difference between the two is that within the novel Pilate is redeemed and enters into the realm of eternal light and Bezdomny is not redeemed. Yet the very fact of the release of Pilate, which comes to him as a gift and is not of his own devising, serves to underline the note of hope which attaches to the story of Bezdomny. Grace can intervene in human affairs as God wills, as happens in Pilate's case. Sometime it could happen in Bezdomny's case, as well. Thus, if we must conclude that Bezdomny remains spiritually homeless to the end of the novel, the note of hope which marks the end of the Epilogue disallows any firm conclusion that a final negative judgment is to be cast on Bezdomny. Since the note of hope, however tenuous, is not required by what we know of Bezdomny, we do well to conclude that Bulgakov placed considerable importance on it by offering it as his final word. As St. Augustine understood, our hearts are restless until they find their rest in God.

Chapter Nine

The Apocalypse

❖ ❖

As we have traced the various characters of the three strands of plot of *The Master and Margarita*, there have been many occasions to refer to the end of the novel, comprised of Chapters Twenty-nine through Thirty-two. The final chapter of this study focuses on that concluding section. These four chapters of the novel, comprising merely some twenty-five pages, occur after sunset on Holy Saturday, as Easter begins. In other words, here the action moves outside of time and into the eternal day. The believing characters attain transfiguration in this section; they embark on their eternal destinies. Satan and the fallen angels conclude their visit to earth (Moscow) and return to their infernal abode.

The Christian character of the novel, which has been pervasive throughout, becomes even more apparent when we realize that the work ends with an extensive echoing of the last book of the Bible, the Book of the Revelation, or the Apocalypse. Since all four chapters occur after sunset, therefore under the light of the moon, we cannot expect to see the picture clearly and in full color. Bulgakov's borrowings from the Revelation are fragmentary and intentionally distorted. Thus, the apocalyptic conclusion to the novel stands in a relationship to St. John's Revelation that is parallel to the relationship between the Master's novel and the four Gospels of the New Testament.

The preceding chapters of this study have already treated some of the references to the Revelation, such as the passages regarding Abadonna and possibly Behemoth and Koroviev discussed in Chapter Four. Obviously, then, on occasion the Book of the Revelation illuminates aspects of the novel which appear prior to its final four chapters. But this concluding section of the novel forms the extended parody of the concluding book of the Bible.

Few critics have commented on Bulgakov's borrowings from the Book of the Revelation. One who has done good work on this subject is David M.

Bethea. Whereas he notes that some critics have observed that *The Master and Margarita* has something of the apocalyptic about it, he adds, "Only Edward Ericson has ventured further than casual allusion to claim, in the closing of his article, that 'the ending of the novel is an elaborate parody of the last book in the Bible, the Apocalypse of St. John.'"[1] He is referring to an article of mine,[2] and he agrees that Bulgakov uses the source which I identify. For reasons of space, I did not in that article expand upon the sentence which Bethea quoted. This chapter is that expansion.

The strength of Bethea's article is the illumination which he casts not on the final four chapters of the novel, which will be the focus of this chapter, but on the Pilate story. He sees in the imagery of the Four Horsemen, one of the best-known parts of the Revelation, a clue to the understanding of Pilate, who is a knight, a horseman, the Rider of the Golden Spear. Indeed, he sees "Pilate's chief function as apocalyptic horseman," who brings "judgment (both on others and, equally important, on himself) and death to Ershalaim [Jerusalem]."[3] Bethea associates Bulgakov's use of "equine and equestrian images" with "a rich, and so far virtually unstudied, tradition in Russian literature" which features "the horse as a mysterious agent of death,"[4] and his treatment of horse imagery in the novel is definitive.

Bethea says that the concluding chapters of the novel "contain not only the most 'elaborate' but the most *explicit* parody of the Book of Revelation in Russian literature," and he adds that with this novel we have "a broad application of the text of Revelation involving themes, characters, and the very climax of the novel."[5] However, Bethea hits only the highlights when he focuses on two elements of this borrowing, the storm-earthquake and the Four Horsemen. These elements are present—and prominent; there are yet more. He stops far short of the mark when he limits Bulgakov's use of the Revelation to "an artistic point of departure."[6] Further, his understanding of the message of the Revelation is somewhat faulty, in that he emphasizes the themes of retribution and vengeance, to the minimizing of the themes of compassion and bliss; this misplaced emphasis leads him to conclude that Bulgakov's parodic rendering of the Revelation is unorthodox.[7]

In broadest terms, the Revelation moves from the theme of judgment to that of bliss. So do the final two chapters, Thirty-one and Thirty-two, of *The Master and Margarita*. Still, there is a difference in the balance between the two themes. The bulk of the Revelation is devoted to judgment, with only the closing chapters devoted to bliss. In the novel, on the other hand, Chapter Thirty-two, featuring bliss, is twice as long as Chapter Thirty-one, featuring judgment. This difference in balance is simply explained. St. John focuses on divinely initiated activity; Bulgakov focuses in his closing chapters on the fate of human beings: the Master, Margarita, and Pontius Pilate.

Another critic who has remarked the significance for Bulgakov of the last book in the Bible is Laura D. Weeks. She notes that "the significance of the final two chapters of the novel (not including the epilogue) is intended to be understood in apocalyptic terms."[8] However, in her eagerness to locate Old Testament influences on *The Master and Margarita*, which is the subject of her essay, she does not give the Revelation its due. For instance, Zechariah mentions four horsemen, but there is no reason to think that Bulgakov went back any further than Revelation to find his four horsemen, especially since there are various other references to the Revelation, as we shall see. Still, she is certainly right in pointing to works of Jewish apocalyptic literature for material which Bulgakov used to fashion the conclusion to his novel.

The apocalyptic impulse is of greater importance to Eastern Orthodoxy than it is to any other branch of Christianity. The primacy of the apocalyptic vision in Orthodoxy has been alluded to early in this study and is confirmed by Nicolas Zernov:

> The Russian Church has always been deficient in discipline and organization, inarticulate in speech and logical thought, but captivated by the vision of the transfigured cosmos; confident of the resurrection of the dead, and expectant of the Second Coming.[9]

The apocalyptic aspect of Christianity emphasized by Orthodoxy is precisely the element which dominates *The Master and Margarita*.

One significant indication of Bulgakov's deep indebtedness to Jewish apocalyptic literature in general and to the Revelation in particular lies in the technique of the novel. Many critics have tried to locate the literary genre to which to assign *The Master and Margarita*, and the most frequently mentioned one is Menippean satire. But probably the most helpful clue concerning genre comes from the Revelation, the most famous and most influential of all works of Jewish apocalyptic literature. The Revelation is a heavily symbolic work which piles up correspondences in a chaotic pattern, thus making the task of interpretation exceptionally complex. Austin Farrer has commented, "An exposition of the Revelation is at the same time an argument. And it is one of those arguments in which nothing short of the whole story proves the case."[10] Exactly the same task faces the interpreter of *The Master and Margarita*. An exposition of it is an argument. Further, one must see all of the details of the story in relationship with one another and in the perspective of the whole before one can properly interpret the novel. To pull out from the fabric of the whole one theme or some elements is to handle this text inadequately.

The reason is clear why this situation is so, for both the Revelation and *The Master and Margarita*. The genius of both works is symbolic suggestiveness, not logical statement and not straightforward realistic narration. Nor are the symbols always natural or obvious ones; often they are, at least at first glance, arbitrary. Speaking of the details in the Revelation, Farrer says, "They are symbolical images, or mythic tales, casting a light of some kind (but of what kind?) on the expected future. Alternative images, different tales might have been put forward with the same general intent."[11] Not only is this statement equally applicable to Bulgakov's novel, but the novel is itself an example of one of those constructs of alternative images "put forward with the same general intent": to offer an apocalyptic vision of the human story. The story need not have featured the Master and Margarita. Using them as the microcosmic specific by which to tell the general story of mankind was only one alternative, but it was the one which Bulgakov chose.

It has also been observed that "Revelation is a book full of colours and sounds; it has in this respect the attractive simplicity of a child's picture-book, but it has also the cosmic range of *Prometheus Bound* or *King Lear*. John fairly throws colours and sounds at us."[12] This comment comports equally well with Bulgakov's book: the colors and sounds, the apparent simplicity of reading, the cosmic range. But that simplicity is only apparent. My students bear witness: they read the novel easily and with pleasure; but they, being no longer young children, know that they are missing much of the meaning. In actuality, as they sense, it is an extremely difficult book to interpret, because one cannot press too hard each of those seemingly simple elements in isolation—and for the same reason that one cannot do so with the Revelation offered by St. John: "...it is a mistake to press the details too closely and try to construct a precise visual impression of what he is describing. It is impossible to do so. Mortal man cannot describe heaven; the best he can do is to pile up visual metaphors from the language of the earth."[13]

The kaleidoscopically shifting arrangement of the images in *The Master and Margarita* we have already remarked. The same applies to the Revelation and, indeed, to all apocalyptic literature. "St. John follows the convention of vision; his story is presented in 'stills'—there is some simple movement within each visionary episode; but there is no continuous flow of movement from one to another."[14]

Not only Bulgakov's style but also his themes are drawn directly from apocalyptic literature and contribute to establishing the same mood. D. S. Russell takes notes of certain characteristics which, taken together,

> build up that varied "mood" which goes under the name of "apocalyptic." J. Lindblom, for example, suggests the following list: transcendentalism, mythology, cosmological survey, pessimistic historical surveys, dualism, division of time into periods, teaching of Two Ages, numerology, pseudo-ecstasy, artificial claims to inspiration, pseudonymity, and esoterism. To these might be added the idea of the unity of history and the conception of cosmic history which treats of earth and heaven; the notion of primordiality with its revelations concerning creation and the fall of men and angels; the source of evil in the universe and the part played in this by angelic powers; the conflict between light and darkness, good and evil, God and Satan; the emergence of a transcendent figure called "the Son of Man"; the development of beliefs in life after death with its various compartments of Hell, Gehenna, Paradise and Heaven and the increasing significance of the individual in resurrection, judgment and eternal bliss. These various "marks" belong to apocalyptic not in the sense that they are essential to it or are to be found in every apocalyptic writing, but rather in the sense that, in whole or in part, they build up an *impression* of a distinct kind which conveys a particular *mood* of thought and belief.[15]

Applying this list to *The Master and Margarita*, we cannot but be struck by how many of the items we find present in the novel. And these items combine to create the very same tone of apocalyptic which Russell is describing. Apocalyptic literature is not divorced from cosmology. Rather, the writers of such literature see the crisis which provides the impulse for apocalyptic literature as being set against the backdrop of the whole history of man and the world, and the given crisis takes on cosmic proportions. Indeed, all of history is interpreted in the light of that crisis.

> It is characteristic of these [Jewish apocalyptic] writings that they portray the present crisis...against a background of world history, the present struggle as part of an agelong struggle between the kingdom of light and the kingdom of darkness, and victory over the immediate enemy as the embodiment of the final victory of God. It is also characteristic of them that they are written in symbolic language. The writers believed that every earthly person, institution, and event had a heavenly equivalent, so that a seer, transported to heaven in an ecstatic rapture, could see enacted in the symbols of heavenly drama the counterpart of earthly events, past, present, and future.[16]

Sergius Bulgakov takes this same tack in his discussion of the history of the Church, thereby underlining Orthodoxy's intensely apocalyptic outlook:

> The history of the humanity of Christ is the history of the Church as it is figured in the Apocalypse. The apocalyptic content of history is the drama of the world conflict between the forces of Christ and those of Antichrist. And since Christ is conqueror, therefore it is the history of his victory and his conquest, the triumph of the kingdom of God. This can also be presented in the sense of a struggle between two rival principles; between the true Sophia which irradiates the world with wisdom, and the forces of evil, "Sophia fallen." The "woman clothed with the sun" and pursued by the dragon is opposed to "the great whore," "Babylon the great, the mother of harlots and abominations of the earth" (Rev. xvii.5).[17]

The parallel with *The Master and Margarita* is patent. Mikhail Bulgakov is concerned with the present; he sets the main line of his story in it. But his concern is not limited to the present; rather, he sees it as a manifestation of that perennial conflict between the kingdom of light and the kingdom of darkness. The present evil time sets the stage for and leads toward the apocalyptic consummation of history, and the novelist finds in the Revelation a framework within which to treat events set in the current period. It is the same framework which governs Bulgakov's novel on contemporary history, *The White Guard*.

It is likely that Bulgakov perceived in the Great Tribulation described in the Revelation an analogue for the period of Stalinist terror, with its persecution of goodness and the Orthodox Church. While it was to last seven years (a week of years), the deep agonies of the Great Tribulation were to occur in the second half of the week, corresponding to the suffering of Christ in the second half of

Holy Week. Farrer is one of many biblical commentators who have noticed this parallel between the Incarnation and the Consummation:

> ...the earliest Christian minds had their own strong reason for thinking of the terrible half-week as the end of the week, rather than the beginning. The reason lay in a parallel between Christ's coming in the flesh and his return in glory. The parallel was inescapable, and wherever it may or may not be found, its influence on the Revelation is evident. If there was to be an apparent triumph of Antichrist before Christ's victorious Advent, there had been an apparent triumph of Antichrist also before his victorious Resurrection, and it had filled the end of a week, not the beginning. Christ was seized on a Thursday, suffered on a Friday, and lay in the tomb until the dawn of Sunday.[18]

It is on Easter Eve that the Master explains why he is no longer afraid: "...I have been through everything that a man can go through. I've been so frightened that nothing frightens me any longer."[19]

However, the suffering of the Church, the Bride of Christ, was to pass away and to be replaced by joy, just as was the case with the Bridegroom as he moved through death and burial to resurrection. Again, the parallels abound in Christian thought, as they do in *The Master and Margarita.*

> In another aspect, the Eve who travails with the manchild is the people of God in the birthpangs of their messianic destiny. The travail of Mary at Bethlehem brought forth Jesus, the travail of the Church in the Great Tribulation brings forth the Messianic Advent. Similarly, according to the Gospel, the agony of Jesus's disciples in his Passion brought forth the Christ of the Resurrection but (says the Christ of John xvi. 19-22) the tribulation was to be blotted from memory by the joy to which it would give birth.[20]

When the Master and Margarita reach their destination for eternity, "...the master's memory, his accursed, needling memory, began to fade" (p. 381).

Although all four concluding chapters, Twenty-nine through Thirty-Two, happen after sunset on Easter Eve, therefore outside of time, the direct borrowings from the Revelation comes in Chapters Thirty-one and Thirty-Two. These very short chapters are, respectively, three and six pages long. Thus, there cannot be long stretches of parody of the Revelation; most of its details are absent. Nor is there any attempt to follow the outline of the organization of this last book of the Bible—except in the broadest terms of the movement from judgment to bliss. Rather, the borrowings are fleeting and truncated. They are mostly echoes of striking images. They are just enough to serve the purpose of bringing to mind the Book of the Revelation—and its apocalyptic theme.

When we reach the final chapter of Bulgakov's novel, we find that "all deception vanished and fell away..." (p. 377). The disguises in which Woland and his retinue traveled incognito during their visit to earth are now unmasked (p. 376). Now we see them no longer as through a glass, darkly. Now we have, stated explicitly, what we really knew from the first chapter of the novel: that Satan and his cohorts were in disguise during their visit to Moscow. Only now are their true natures revealed. That is to say, in all that has preceded this final section, deception has held sway. Nothing in the preceding chapters has been presented in its true aspect, free of distortion. Only those who have discerned the clues to reality as conveyed through symbolism will have seen what Bulgakov actually is doing. But now that deception-inducing moonlight turns "brilliant," "brighter than an arc light" (p. 378). The consummation is at hand.

The consummation is heralded by Woland's trumpet-like cry of "It is time!" (p. 375). Chapter Thirty is entitled "Time To Go" by Glenny, "Time! Time!" by Ginsburg.[21] Much earlier in the novel, Pilate had announced the crucifixion with, "It is time!" (p. 36). Christ's first advent, by which all time is marked, has determined human destiny and foreshadows the consummation of time, which is accomplished in his second advent. In Revelation 10:6 a mighty angel announces "that there should be time no longer." Woland, in his new aspect at the end of the novel, is a substitute for and parody of the mighty angel of Revelation 10, as elsewhere he had often been a parody of God. After all seven vials of God's wrath are poured out upon the world in judgment of sin, a great voice from the throne in the temple of heaven asserts, "It is done" (Rev. 16:17). This is the eschatological fulfillment of Christ's cry at Golgotha of "It is finished" as he judges sin through his death upon the cross.

Woland's "terrible" cry of "It is time!" rings out over the hills "like the blast of a trumpet" (p. 375). This simile calls to mind the seven trumpets of chapters 8, 9, and 11 of the Revelation, which herald the judgments on a wicked world at the end of time and the coming of the Kingdom of Christ. Bulgakov parodies the sounding of those trumpets with piercing whistles—whistles, by their nature, normally being of a lesser magnitude than trumpet sounds.

This is not the first time that whistles sound in the novel. Two whistles occurred back when Margarita flew off to Satan's Rout (pp. 245-46). And, away back when Pilate announced that Yeshua was to die, "the sharp, bright call of a trumpet" is "echoed by the piercing whistles of boys from the rooftops..." (p. 39). Horses and horsemen—including a black horse—also are present in this Jerusalem scene, as they are at the consummation, apparently hinting at the biblical parallelism between the Old Jerusalem and the New Jerusalem.

In the concluding section, several more whistles sound. They do not add up to the biblical number of seven for trumpet blasts, but by now we are accustomed to Bulgakov's truncations and irregularities in his deployment of symbolic correspondences for purposes of parody. The first of these whistles is Azazello's, as he leads the Master and Margarita, following their deaths, on to their final journey. As he whistles, a storm lashes Moscow; and a fire, the symbol of judgment, begins to destroy Griboyedov, one of the earthly symbols of hell. Bulgakov conjoins the whistles with storm and fire, those natural images of judgment, just as St. John does the trumpets.

As the storm over Moscow rages, "a distant whistle" sounds (p. 371). The Master, who has stopped for a last visit with Bezdomny but who also understands the fact of the impending apocalyptic consummation, tells him,

"...they're calling me, it's time for me to go" (p. 371). The Master does not know which devil issues the whistle, and neither do we; but he knows that it comes from Woland's company.

The third "farewell whistle call" (p. 374) comes from Behemoth. It has extraordinary effects:

> Margarita's ears sang. Her horse roared, twigs snapped off nearby trees, a flock of rooks and crows flew up, a cloud of dust billowed toward the river and several passengers on a river steamer below had their hats blown off. (p. 374)

Koroviev, a musician (choirmaster), is not to be outdone. The fourth whistle is his. Again, the effect is spectacular.

> Margarita did not hear this whistle, but she felt it, as she and her horse were picked up and thrown twenty yards sideways. Near her the bark was ripped off an oak tree and cracks opened in the ground as far as the river. The water in it boiled and heaved, and the river steamer, with all its passengers unharmed, was grounded on the far bank by the blast. A jackdaw, killed by Faggot's whistle, fell at the feet of Margarita's snorting horse. (p. 375)

Koroviev had asked permission of Woland to whistle "just for old times' sake" (p. 374). What did he mean? Perhaps, this ex-choirmaster was harking back to the days when he was an unfallen archangel and led the angelic choir in its songs of praise. Otherwise, this phrase is inexplicable, since there is no occasion within the novel which would serve as an antecedent.

Laura Weeks finds, correctly, a connection between the whistles and the four winds of Revelation 7:1. Referring to the whistling match between Behemoth and Koroviev, she states,

> It seems obvious that in this scene Behemoth and Korov'ev are the embodiments of winds, and destructive winds at that. In the scene immediately following they are transformed into the dark riders. Given the close proximity of these two scenes, it seems clear that Bulgakov evokes the association of winds with riders deliberately.[22]

Winds are, of course, destructive; and minor damage follows the whistles of Behemoth and Koroviev. But the emphasis in Revelation 7:1 is on the restraining of destruction. The four angels at the four corners of the earth are "holding the four winds of the earth, that the wind should not blow on the earth, nor on the sea, nor on any tree."

Similarly, when Koroviev asks for permission to whistle, Woland's permission has a qualifier. "'Very well,' said Woland sternly, 'but without endangering life or limb, please'" (p. 375). The instruction to the four angels who are holding the winds is, "Hurt not the earth, neither the sea, nor the trees, till we have sealed the servants of our God in their foreheads" (Rev. 7:3).

Two chapters later, that command is repeated (Rev. 9:4). In the Revelation the command is given by a heavenly angel, speaking for God. In Bulgakov's novel it is given by Woland, in parodied form. Specifically, it is those who are marked as God's own who are not to be harmed; in the novel they are represented by the Master and Margarita. Once again, the Devil and company must dispense judgment according to divine intent.

Following Koroviev's spectacular whistle comes Woland's voice, sounding "like the blast of a trumpet" (p. 375), then an echoing laugh and final whistle by Behemoth. With the final whistle come the storm and fire in Moscow below. This cataclysm is described in terms not unlike those employed in the description of the judgments of the seven trumpets in the Revelation. At just this point, in the final paragraph of Chapter Thirty-one, Woland's "terrible voice" cries out, "It is time!" (p. 375). It is when the seventh, and final, angel sounds his trumpet that "there were great voices in heaven, saying, The kingdoms of this world are become the kingdoms of our Lord, and of his Christ; and he shall reign for ever and ever" (Rev. 11:15). Immediately following in the novel is the chapter "Absolution and Eternal Refuge," in which only good things happen to the Master and Margarita. Revelation 11:18 reads:

> And the nations were angry, and thy wrath is come, and the time of the dead, that they should be judged, and that thou shouldest give reward unto thy servants the prophets, and to the saints, and them that fear thy name, small and great; and shouldest destroy them which destroy the earth.

The final paragraph of Chapter Thirty-one contains this initially puzzling but very vivid sentence: "Woland's cloak billowed out over the heads of the cavalcade, and as evening drew on, his cloak began to cover the whole vault of the sky" (p. 375). Only when this "black veil blew aside for a moment" (p. 375) could Margarita see the destruction wreaked upon the whole city of Moscow. This darkness has its parallels in the Revelation. In Revelation 6:12, "the sun became black as sackcloth of hair...." The sun, moon, and stars are smitten, "so as the third part of them was darkened..." (Rev. 8:12). And, when smoke ascends from the bottomless pit, "the sun and the air were darkened by reason of the smoke of the pit" (Rev. 9:12). Smoke is precisely one element which remains after Moscow is, on the symbolic level, destroyed. Why, one wonders, would Bulgakov make a point of mentioning the darkness caused by Woland's billowing cloak if he were not signaling some symbolic import?

As the trumpets in the Revelation are simultaneous with judgment through fire and earthquake and storm, so the whistles are in *The Master and Margarita*. Lightning, thunder, and earthquakes occur repeatedly throughout the Revelation, and their function is as the natural images of divine judgment. "The cosmic earthquake is indeed one of the most regular features of the Jewish apocalyptic tradition."[23] For instance, when the seventh vial is opened and a great voice says, "It is done," we read: "And there were voices, and thunders, and lightnings; and there was a great earthquake, such as was not since men were upon the earth, so mighty an earthquake, and so great" (Rev. 16:18).

Immediately preceding the seven trumpets, we read: "And the angel took the censer, and filled it with fire of the altar, and cast it into the earth: and there were voices, and thunderings, and lightnings, and an earthquake" (Rev. 8:5). At the very end of the sounding of the seventh trumpet, "there were lightnings, and voices, and thunderings, and an earthquake, and great hail" (Rev. 11:19). These passages are paralleled, in truncated and parodied form, in the final paragraph of Chapter Thirty-one.

The apocalyptic storm in Bulgakov's novel occurs during Saturday night as a prelude to Easter Sunday, the Day of Resurrection. As in the Revelation, destruction immediately precedes consummation; judgment of evil precedes bestowal of eternal bliss. The onset of the storm of judgment comes as early as Chapter Twenty-nine.

> The thunderstorm that Woland had predicted was already gathering on the horizon. A black cloud was rising in the west; first half and then all of the sun was blotted out. The wind on the terrace freshened. Soon it was quite dark.
> The cloud from the west enveloped the vast city. Bridges and buildings were all swallowed up. Everything vanished as though it had never been. A single whiplash of fire cracked across the sky, then the city rocked to a clap of thunder. There came another; the storm had begun. In the driving rain Woland was no more to be seen. (p. 360)

Simultaneous with this storm is the fire: "The fire—where it all began and where we shall end it" (p. 369). The fire combines with the storm and earthquake to bring the Final Judgment to Moscow.

As we have seen, the climax of this doom comes at the end of Chapter Thirty-one. As Margarita leaves the earth behind, she looks back and sees "that not only the many-colored towers but the whole city had long since vanished from sight, swallowed by the earth, leaving only mist and smoke where it had been" (p. 375). Along with the earthquake and the blotting out of the sun in the Revelation, "the moon became as blood" (Rev. 6:12). In the novel "a full purple moon rose toward them..." (p. 377).

It is important to note that Woland only foretells the storm which marks the judgment of the earth; he does not initiate it. The cause of the storm is not stated, nor is its "causer" named. When we read that "The Fate of the Master and Margarita Is Decided" (the title of Chapter Twenty-nine), we see an exact parallel. Ultimately, the same point pertains when "pardon had been granted" (p. 381) to Pilate. Woland is present within the novel; God is not directly and personally present. When the agency of a supernaturally directed event is not stated, as it is not in the passive constructions, we are to understand that the agent is God himself, not Woland, not even in the form of parody. Woland can serve as a parody of God on earth but not above it. When the apocalyptic storm had passed, "a rainbow had arched itself across the sky..." (p. 373). This famous biblical image, which descends through history all the way from the story of Noah and the flood, is a sign of promise and hope; it is a sure indication of divine benevolence at work.

In fact, the only earthquake to which agency is assigned is that initiated by the Master and Margarita, now in the process of being transfigured and glorified. As they seek to release Pilate from his long torment and into eternity, Margarita's piercing shout, like that which she gave when she became a witch, "shattered a rock on the mountainside, sending it bouncing down into the abyss with a deafening crash..." (p. 379). In his first advent, Jesus Christ had said, "If ye have faith as a grain of mustard seed, ye shall say unto this mountain, Remove hence to yonder place; and it shall remove..." (Matthew 17:20). Woland laughingly tells Margarita, "Shouting at the mountains will do no good. Landslides are common here..." (p. 379). Still, when the woman and the man of faith shout, respectively, "Let him go!" and "You are free! Free! He is waiting for you!", their cries are efficacious. With the Master's assertion of faith, the mountains vanish into the abyss (p. 380). Shouting through hands "cupped into a trumpet," he moves mountains. "The mountains turned the master's voice to thunder and the thunder destroyed them. The grim cliffside crumbled and fell" (p. 379). Revelation 6:14 provides similar imagery: "And the heaven departed as a scroll when it is rolled together, and every mountain and island were moved out of their places."

Just after Moscow vanishes, so, to fulfill the correspondence, does the Old Jerusalem. First, the New Jerusalem appears. Then, just afterwards, or virtually simultaneously, the Old Jerusalem disappears. "At this Woland waved his hand toward Jerusalem, which vanished" (p. 380). It is the earthquake initiated by the Master which brings about the manifestation of that New Jerusalem, the Heavenly City of Revelation 21. To make the parallelism clear, Bulgakov uses for the New Jerusalem the same terms employed for describing the Old Jerusalem:

> Above the black abyss into which the mountains had vanished glowed a great city topped by glittering idols above a garden overgrown with the luxuriance of two thousand years. Into the garden stretched the Procurator's long-awaited path of moonlight, and the first to bound along it was the dog with pointed ears. The man in the white cloak with the blood-red lining...could only be seen hurrying along the moonlight path after his faithful watchdog. (p. 380)

St. John likens the New Jerusalem to "the bride, the Lamb's wife" (Rev. 21:9). It descends out of heaven; thus, it settles in roughly the same place that the transfigured city of Bulgakov's novel does, which city glows above the abyss. St. John's vision includes "that great city, the holy Jerusalem, descending out of heaven from God, / Having the glory of God..." (Rev. 21:10-11; see also 21:2). This New Jerusalem is the appropriate eternal abode for the transfigured Pilate, that erstwhile resident of the Old Jerusalem.

Parallels between ancient Jerusalem and modern Moscow, the two settings of the novel, are obviously abundant. However, Jerusalem is transfigured, along with Pilate; and Moscow is not. In the Revelation there is a city which suffers outright destruction akin to that which befell Moscow: Babylon. St. John's vision of Babylon had frequently been interpreted as a reference to Rome (partly because of the city's seven mountains in Revelation 17:9), and Moscow has been known as the Third Rome. Immediately after the earthquake of Revelation 16:18 comes the first mention of the destruction of Babylon (16:19). It is elaborated in chapters 17 and 18 of the Revelation. David Bethea, too, takes note of the parallel between Bulgakov's Moscow and St. John's Babylon. "Like Ershalaim before it, Moscow is the city of the devil, a getting-and-spending world of petty Judases, the fallen Whore of Babylon with her 'merchants ...grown rich with the wealth of her wantonness' (Revelation 18:3)."[24]

In Revelation 18:2 an angel cries, "Babylon the great is fallen, is fallen, and is become the habitation of devils, and hold of every foul spirit...." The sentencing continues:

> Therefore shall her plagues come in one day; death, and mourning, and famine: and she shall be utterly burned with fire: for strong is the Lord God who judgeth her.... Alas, alas, that great city Babylon, that mighty city! for in one hour is thy judgment come.... Rejoice over her, thou heaven, and ye holy apostles and prophets; for God hath avenged you on her.... Thus with violence shall that great city Babylon be thrown down, and shall be found no more at all.... And in her was found the blood of prophets, and of saints, and of all that were slain upon the earth. (Rev. 18:8, 10, 20, 21, 24)

Many of the details mentioned in regard to Babylon fit Bulgakov's Moscow. Specifically, Moscow has, with the coming of Woland and company, become the habitation of devils. Followers of God, believers in the supernatural, are mistreated. Fire is the chief element of destruction, though there is also the earthquake. And the destruction is both immediate and entire. Everything that we know about Bulgakov's antagonism toward the capital of the Soviet state makes St. John's Babylon an appropriate symbol for Bulgakov's Moscow.

Another element of the Book of Revelation which it seems that Bulgakov used is the scroll, or book, of Revelation 5:17. A common view is that "it contains the full account of what God in his sovereign will has determined as the destiny of the world."[25] Another commentator elaborates:

> The easiest identification of John's scroll is that it contains the prophecy of the end events, including both the salvation of God's people and the judgment of the wicked. It is God's redemptive plan for the denouement of human history, the overthrow of evil, and the gathering of a redeemed people to enjoy the blessings of God's rule.[26]

R. H. Charles observes, "In apocalyptic literature we have conceptions closely related to that of the Book in our text," and he gives a series of examples.[27]

Of this book we read that "no man in heaven, nor in earth, neither under the earth, was able to open the book, neither to look thereon" (Rev. 5:3). But then the resurrected and ascended Christ—the Lion of the Tribe of Judah, the Root of David, the Lamb—offers himself as the agent to open the book and to bring about the final triumph of right over wrong.

Earlier it was suggested that the novels of the Master and of Bulgakov, which ultimately are one and the same, tell the story of man and his destiny. In both, suffering gives way to glory for the redeemed. It is the heavenly Lord, Matthew tells Woland, who "has read the master's writings" (p. 358). Only after the risen Christ has read the as-yet-incomplete novel does he announce the eternal destiny of the Master and Margarita; only then does the Master receive permission to finish his novel and thus to determine the final fate of his character Pilate. God's redemptive plan is brought to fruition only through the power of the glorified Yeshua. If Bulgakov's vision is an apocalyptic one and if the writing of a book is a central factor in his novel, it should not be surprising if he had Revelation 5 in mind.

Whereas the preceding linkage, that between books, is speculative, Bulgakov's borrowing of the Four Horsemen of the Apocalypse is not. This is the most readily identified element of the Revelation to appear in the final section of *The Master and Margarita*. The horsemen "are among the more widely recognized symbols of the book of Revelation."[28] They appear in Revelation 6 riding horses which are, respectively, white, red, black, and pale. (Zechariah, from whom St. John borrows, also has horses of various colors.) However, since in *The Master and Margarita* the horses are seen only by the dim light of the moon, even colored horses might well appear black. In fact, at one point they are seen only in silhouette (p. 373). But, of course, we have learned to expect inexact correspondences from Bulgakov. The four riders are Woland, Azazello, Koroviev, and Behemoth—Hella being conveniently omitted from the entourage.

Chariots and horses are frequently used in the imagery of biblical prophecy to refer to God's judgment upon the world. "'The four horsemen of the Apocalypse' stand for kinds of disasters which are to come on the earth in the immediate future."[29] The Four Horsemen represent invasion, rebellion, famine, and pestilence—or, in the words of Robert Mounce, "conquest (white), bloodshed (red), scarcity (black), death (pale, livid)."[30] Despite the dire symbols,

> [a]ll these happenings, John would have us understand, are the results of the working out of God's righteous laws for his universe. Things have not got out of control. God does not approve of death and hell and famine, but they are what must follow if men persist in opposing God's rule, and hence they are part of God's purpose.[31]

We would not expect Bulgakov to develop St. John's specific symbolisms of the Four Horsemen, and he does not. Rather, there is a blending together, as is indicated by the blackness of all of the horses when under the moonlight, to form a single symbol of judgment. But Bulgakov does retain the sense that God's purpose is being worked out at the end of the novel, which point can be seen by the fact that none of the righteous suffer from the judgment inflicted upon Moscow.[32] Bulgakov calls the carriers of the departing devils "the magic black horses" (p. 376), and indeed they appear here at the consummation of the novel when the natural order is left behind and all events take place in the supernatural realm. The devils who now become the riders of the magic horses had earlier, in those episodes which comprise most of the first half of the novel, brought the first installment of the disasters which are God's judgment upon a sinful world. They appear on horseback at just that point when the full force of God's wrath falls upon Moscow, as it disappears in the storm and the earthquake.

We saw earlier, as Bethea said, that horse imagery occurred in the Jerusalem chapters when Yeshua was sentenced by Pilate. Incidentally, it was a black horse which the commander of the Roman squadron rode (p. 39). At first glance, there seems to be no particular reason for Bulgakov to mention horses in that scene, unless they are present just to add local color and surface verisimilitude. However, when similar horse imagery appears at the end of the novel, the correspondence underlines the relationship between the two advents. For traditional Christian theology sees the first advent of Christ as not only providing redemption but also bringing judgment upon sin (and Satan), a judgment which will be consummated only with the second advent at the end of time.

So Bulgakov's borrowing of the imagery of the Four Horsemen of the Apocalypse fits with the general symbolic intent of St. John; they bring judgment. However, Bulgakov gives the horses a role which goes beyond anything mentioned in the Revelation. In *The Master and Margarita* they serve as the vehicles to transport characters to that realm beyond the earthly. Thus, the Master and Margarita also ride horses, though their appearance on horseback has nothing directly to do with the final judgment wreaked upon Moscow. Indeed, the matter of transportation is the main function of the magical horses in the novel, and the fact of the borrowing from the Revelation could therefore easily be missed by the reader who is not on the lookout for symbolic correspondences.

The destination of Woland and his three companions is the abyss, their proper eternal abode. It is while on horseback that the fallen angels lose their earthly disguises and are seen in their true aspect. Before the devils plunge into the abyss, Woland points the Master and Margarita along a different route. "The abyss was traditionally the element hostile to God, which he had to overcome before creating the world.... Hence it came to be looked on as the abode of God's enemies...."[33]

The "angel of the abyss," its keeper, is Abaddon, a synonym for the Destroyer, or Death.[34] He is mentioned in Revelation 9:11, and he is also called "the angel of the bottomless pit." Bulgakov describes him, as we have seen previously; he appears as a character within the novel, under the name Abadonna. Bringing this character into his novel is one of Bulgakov's more obvious clues pointing toward both the validity of a general theological interpretation of his work and a recognition of the importance of his borrowings from the Revelation as a key element in that interpretive scheme.

Satan's return to hell is described by Bulgakov as follows: "Then the black Woland, taking none of the paths, dived into the abyss, followed with a roar by his retinue. The mountains, the platform, the moonbeam pathway, Jerusalem—all were gone. The black horses, too, had vanished" (p. 381). Revelation 20:10 offers the biblical parallel: "And the devil that deceived them was cast into the lake of fire and brimstone...and shall be tormented day and night for ever and ever." That the Bible uses a passive construction but Bulgakov allows Woland to be the active agent in his "dive" is owing to the fact that God himself never appears in the novel, whereas Satan does. But, certainly, the contrast between the end of Woland and company and that of the Master and Margarita, and also Pilate, should lay to rest any notion of Satan as a "good guy" in this novel. Whatever good he has done has not been of his own will. He always willed evil, and his end is fitting.

There have been references in this chapter to the dual character of the Book of Revelation: that it contains both judgment and bliss. Sergius Bulgakov sets this duality in Eastern Orthodox terms: "The Russian Apocalypse has two aspects, just as have the apocalyptic prophecies themselves: a sad aspect and a joyous."[35] He elaborates, with an emphasis on the joyous aspect:

> The second coming of Christ is not only terrible for us (for He comes as Judge) but also glorious, for He comes in His Glory; and this glory is, at the same time, the glorification of the world and the fullness of all creation. The glorified state, inherent in the body of the risen Christ, will be communicated to the whole of creation; a new heaven and a new earth will appear, a transfigured earth, resurrected with the Christ and His Humanity. All this will be connected with the resurrection of the dead performed by Christ through His angels. This "fullness of completion" is represented in Scripture symbolically in the images of the Jewish apocalypse. In one way or another death is vanquished, and all mankind, freed from the power of death, appear, for the first time, entire and whole, forming a unity which is not weakened by the changing generations.[36]

The ideas in this quotation help clarify the end of the Master and his beloved Margarita. In their fates we see highlighted both the dual character of the apocalypse and the ultimate transfiguration of human beings and of the earth.

The duality of the apocalypse can be understood by referring to several details in the conclusion of the novel which bring judgment to sinful men but glory to the Master and Margarita. The storm which destroys Moscow has a different effect on these two. As it approaches, Margarita says, "I think it's going to rain soon. Can you feel how the air's growing *fresher*?" (p. 361, emphasis added). The storm's thunder is experienced by the Master and Margarita in terms different from those applicable to the Muscovites. For these two, "There was a short, *cheerful* clap of thunder" (p. 369, emphasis added). Thus, the storm is a symbol of judgment on the one hand but a symbol of the newness of life on the other. God sends the rain on the just and the unjust alike. But the same natural reality has different moral effects depending on the moral conditions of the individuals affected. The same elements are differently applied, and each receives what he deserves. After the storm comes the rainbow, that ancient symbol for the promise of God's providence and care. After life on the sinful earth comes the glorious eternal life.

The same principle which applies to the apocalyptic storm applies equally to the apocalyptic fire. While it is destructive for the unbelieving Muscovites, it is purgative for the Master and Margarita. As the Master's old basement room bursts into flames, the Master cries, "Burn away, past!" and Margarita echoes, "Burn, suffering" (p. 369). The storm and the fire both destroy the old and prepare for and herald the new.

Also, the same principle applies to the black horses. While Satan and his host are taken by them back into the abyss, the Master and Margarita are transported on black horses as they journey to their happy eternal destiny (p. 369). The black horses may be linked to the black Woland, but Woland does the title characters only good, never harm, whatever he may have generally willed.

On the last page of the final chapter, we find analogues to, or borrowings from, the concluding two chapters, 21 and 22, of the final book of the Bible. The transfiguration of the Master and Margarita is completed, and they enter upon their eternal life. They do not gain it by their own merits. It is offered them by Woland (the shadow of God and his agent for justice); but, more important, it is "what Yeshua has begged to be given to you..." (p. 380). Woland describes their new dwelling place and tells them, "...you will arrive at dawn" (p. 381). It is the dawn of Easter Sunday, that unending "day of the Resurrection" (p. 381). Now, for the first time, they are beyond the moon and out of Satan's sphere of power. "And there shall be no night there...for the Lord God giveth them light..." (Rev. 22:5). Only on the final page of the novel (always, in this chapter, excepting the Epilogue) do the human characters move beyond that realm over which Satan has immediate (albeit not ultimate) control.

Also on this final page, and in its last paragraph, Pontius Pilate receives pardon. Although he has been cruel, he, too, enters into the light of the day of the Resurrection. It is mentioned once again, at the conclusion of the novel, that he is garbed in "the white cloak with the blood-red lining" (p. 380). Although it is not clear what, if any, symbolic significance attaches to this garment in the Jerusalem chapters, the Book of the Revelation has a sustained reference to white robes. They are worn by those who stand before the throne of the Lamb of God and sing his praises (Rev. 7:9-12). An elder at the scene asks St. John, "What are these which are arrayed in white robes? and whence came they?" (Rev. 7:13). The elder then answers his own question: "These are they which came out of great tribulation, and have washed their robes, and made them white in the blood of the Lamb" (Rev. 7:14). As with Pilate's cloak, here there is a linkage between whiteness and the red of blood. Indubitably, Pilate has endured great tribulation, as he has waited for 24,000 moons until he could embark upon his "long-awaited path of moonlight" (p. 380) to his eternal destiny. And his destiny is to enter the realm of light itself, not just that of peace. It is of those clad in white robes that the elder of Revelation 7 says, "Therefore are they before the throne of God...and he that sitteth on the throne shall dwell among them" (v. 15).

The entry of the Master and Margarita into the realm of bliss is described in terms of crossing a river. "In the first rays of the morning the master and his beloved crossed a little moss-grown bridge. They left the stream behind them and followed a sandy path" (p. 381). There is here an echo of the familiar "crossing over Jordan," as the children of Israel did in the Old Testament when they ended their wanderings and entered the Promised Land. A traditional understanding is that their passage across the river is an Old Testament type and symbol of the New Testament believer's passage through death into eternal life. Revelation 22:1-2 speaks of the river of life, and these verses were probably in Bulgakov's mind as he wrote the final page of his novel: "And he shewed me a pure river of water of life, clear as crystal, proceeding out of the throne of God and of the Lamb."

Margarita describes their new abode in very homey terms:

> Listen to the silence and enjoy it. Here is the peace that you never knew in your lifetime. Look, there is your home for eternity, which is your reward. I can already see a Venetian window and a climbing vine which grows right up to the roof. It's your home, your home forever. In the evenings people will come to see you, people who interest you, people who will never upset you. They will play to you and sing to you, and you will see how beautiful the room is by candlelight. You shall go to sleep with your dirty old cap on, you shall go to sleep with a smile on your lips. Sleep will give you strength and make you wise. And you can never send me away—I shall watch over your sleep. (p. 381)

This, "their everlasting home" (p. 381), is described in terms of domesticity, perhaps for the sake of bringing to mind the Revelation's concept of a new earth, along with a new heaven. The abode is the Master's old apartment in transfigured form. Going to sleep "with a smile on your lips" corresponds to Revelation 21:4: "And God shall wipe away all tears from their eyes; and there shall be no more death, neither sorrow, nor crying, neither shall there be any more pain: for the former things are passed away." Finding peace which follows the surcease of pain is one of the happy fates assigned to believers in the Revelation; and peace, or rest, is the Master's fate. A voice from heaven said that those who "die in the Lord" are "blessed," because "they may rest from their labours; and their works do follow them" (Rev. 14:13). This verse seems especially applicable to the Master—not only in regard to his reward of peace but even in regard to the detail of his work (the Pilate of his novel) following him.

It is with such consolation at hand that "the master's memory, his accursed, needling memory, began to fade" (p. 381). The new heaven and new earth of the Book of Revelation appears as the consolation for man at the conclusion of Bulgakov's *The White Guard*, also. As Bulgakov closes that novel, he quotes Revelation 21:4 in its entirety.[37] It was a verse—and a concept—which fired his imagination.

NOTES TO CHAPTER ONE

1. A. Colin Wright, *Mikhail Bulgakov: Life and Interpretations* (Toronto: University of Toronto Press, 1978), p. 261.

2. A. Colin Wright, "Mikhail Bulgakov's Developing World View," *Canadian-American Slavic Studies* 15 (Summer-Fall 1981), 159.

3. For a history of the composition of this novel, we may thank Marietta Chudakova, especially in her *"The Master and Margarita*: The Development of a Novel," *Russian Literature Quarterly* 15 (1978), 177-209.

4. A review which pinpoints some differences between the Glenny and Ginsburg translations is Ernest J. Simmons, "Out of the Drawer, Into the Light," *Saturday Review* (November 11, 1967), 36. He allows that "...both renderings are adequate...." A further stage in the tangled skein of the publication of the novel is traced by Donald M. Fiene in his "A Comparison of the Soviet and Possev Editions of *The Master and Margarita*, with a Note on Interpretation of the Novel," *Canadian-American Slavic Studies* 15 (Summer-Fall 1981), 330-54. Since my concern is to explain this novel mainly to English-speaking readers, my references are, unless otherwise specified, to the Glenny translation (New York: Harper & Row, 1967). Signet has published the paperbound version of this version; pagination does not match exactly. Except in quotations from others, where I do no transliterating, I adhere to Glenny's English spellings. On occasion, I refer to the Ginsburg translation for wording, and I so note (New York: Grove Press, 1967).

5. Simmons, p. 56.

6. Patricia Blake, "A Bargain with the Devil," *New York Times Book Review* (October 27, 1967), 1.

7. M. V. Glenny, "Mikhail Bulgakov," *Survey* (October 1967), 13.

8. Helen Muchnic, "Laughter in the Dark," *New York Review of Books* (July 11, 1968), 28.

9. Donald Fanger, "Rehabilitated Experimentalist," *Nation* (January 22, 1968), 117. Similar high praise came from other reviewers, for example: Irving Howe, "The Continuity of Russian Voices," *Harper's* (January 1968), 71; Ernst Pawel, "The Devil in Moscow," *Commentary* (March 1968), 92; Theodore Solotaroff, "Christ and the Commissars," *New Republic* (December 2, 1967), 27; Guy Davenport, "With a Long Spoon," *National Review* (January 30, 1968), 93; David Williams, "New Novels," *Punch* (December 20, 1967), 950; "Diabolical Experiment," *London Times Literary Supplement* (December 7, 1967), 1181.

10. David M. Bethea, *The Shape of Apocalypse in Modern Russian Fiction* (Princeton: Princeton University Press, 1989), p. 87

11. Wright, *Mikhail Bulgakov*, p. 261.

12. Wright, *Mikhail Bulgakov*, p. 278.

13. T. R. N. Edwards, *Three Russian Writers and the Irrational: Zamyatin, Pil'nyak, and Bulgakov* (Cambridge: Cambridge University Press, 1982), p. 137.

14. Edythe C. Haber, "The Mythic Structure of Bulgakov's *The Master and Margarita*," *Russian Review* 34 (October 1975), 382.

15. Nadine Natov, "Mikhail Bulgakov 1891-1981: Preface," *Canadian-American Slavic Studies* 15 (Summer-Fall 1981), 149.

16. Solotaroff, p. 27.

17. Muchnic, p. 28.

18. Howe, p. 72. Other reviewers were in substantial agreement. See Davenport, p. 94; Ian Hamilton, "Revenger," *Listener* (November 30, 1967), 727; "The Devil in Moscow," *Time* (October 27, 1967), 106; Simmons, p. 56.

19. Val Bolen, "Theme and Coherence in Bulgakov's *The Master and Margarita,*" *Slavic and East European Journal* 16 (Winter 1972), 427.

20. Lesley Milne, *The Master and Margarita: A Comedy of Victory* (Birmingham, England: Birmingham Slavonic Monographs, 1977), p. 16.

21. Bruce A. Beatie and Phyllis W. Powell, "Bulgakov, Dante, and Relativity," *Canadian-American Slavic Studies* 15 (Summer-Fall 1981), 267.

22. D. G. B. Piper, "An Approach to Bulgakov's *The Master and Margarita,*" *Forum for Modern Language Studies* 7 (April 1971), 134.

23. Wright, "Mikhail Bulgakov's Developing World View," p. 151.

24. Donald M. Fiene, "Further Elucidation of the Pilate Theme in Bulgakov's *The Master and Margarita,* with a Note on May Eve, Good Friday and the Full Moon," p. 16. Unpublished paper presented at Southern Conference on Slavic Studies; Atlanta, Georgia; October 8, 1983. An abbreviated version of this paper, lacking the passage cited, appeared as "A Note on May Eve, Good Friday, and the Full Moon in Bulgakov's *The Master and Margarita,*" *Slavic and East European Journal* 28 (1984), pp. 533-37.

25. Piper, p. 134.

26. Bulgakov's self-description comes in a letter to Joseph Stalin himself. A readily available brief treatment of the letter may be found in Elena Levin, "Exuberant Works by a Russian Who Talked Back to Stalin," *Saturday Review* (April 29, 1972), 64.

27. Milne, p. 10.

28. Cited in Chudakova, p. 203.

29. Milne, p. 10.

30. Howe, p. 71.

31. Glenny, "Mikhail Bulgakov," p. 13.

32. Judy C. Ullman, "The Conflict between the Individual and Authority in the Works of Mixail Bulgakov," p. 141. Unpublished Ph.D. dissertation, University of Chicago, 1976.

33. Shirley Ann Gutry, "An Approach to *The Master and Margarita* through the Creative Prose and the Letters of M. A. Bulgakov," p. 125. Unpublished Ph.D. dissertation, Princeton University, 1976.

34. Michael Glenny, "Existential Thought in Bulgakov's *The Master and Margarita,*" *Canadian-American Slavic Studies* 15 (Summer-Fall 1981), 238.

35. Bethea, p. 193.

36. Haber, p. 382.

37. Oleg Ivsky, *Library Journal* (October 15, 1967), 3658. Untitled review.

38. Fanger, p. 118.

39. E.g., Howe, p. 71.

40. V. Lakshin, "M. Bulgakov's Novel *The Master and Margarita,*" *Soviet Studies in Literature* 5 (Winter 1968-69), 6. Tr. and rptd. from *Novy Mir*, 1968, no. 6.

41. Milne, p. 33.

42. Ellendea Proffer, "Bulgakov's *The Master and Margarita*: Genre and Motif," *Canadian Slavic Studies* 3 (Winter 1969), 628. Proffer learned this fact directly from Bulgakov's widow.

43. Beatie and Powell, "Bulgakov, Dante, and Relativity," p. 264.

44. Bolen, p. 427.

45. Chudakova, p. 203.

46. Chudakova, p. 207.

47. Chudakova, p. 207.

48. Ellendea Proffer, "Red-Bricked Moscow: 1921-23," *Canadian-American Slavic Studies* 15 (Summer-Fall 1981), 176.

49. Cited in Milne, p. 3. See her note 13 for further details.

50. Milne, p. 3.

NOTES TO CHAPTER TWO

1. Mikhail Bulgakov, *The Master and Margarita*, tr. Michael Glenny (New York: Harper & Row, 1976), pp. 5, 6, 7, 9. Further references to the novel are cited in the text.

2. See especially Ellendea Proffer, "On *The Master and Margarita*," *Russian Literature Triquarterly* 6 (Spring 1973), 533-64; Barbara Kejna-Sharratt, "Narrative Techniques in *The Master and Margarita*," *Canadian Slavonic Papers* 16 (Spring 1974), 1-12; Vida Taranovski Johnson, "The Thematic Function of the Narrator in *The Master and Margarita*," *Canadian-American Slavic Studies* 15 (Summer-Fall 1981), 271-86.

3. Cited in Marietta Chudakova, "*The Master and Margarita*: The Development of a Novel," *Russian Literature Triquarterly* 15 (1978), 195.

4. Mikhail Bulgakov, *The Early Plays of Mikhail Bulgakov*, ed. Ellendea Proffer (Bloomington: Indiana University Press, 1972), pp. 349-418.

5. V. Lakshin, "Mikhail Bulgakov's Novel *The Master and Margarita*," *Soviet Studies in Literature* 5 (Winter 1968-69), 11-12. Tr. and rptd. from *Novy Mir*, 1968, no. 6.

6. Saint Augustine, *The City of God, Books VIII-XVI*, tr. Gerald G. Walsh and Grace Monahan (Washington: Catholic University of America Press, 1952), pp. 201, 220. (Vol. 14 of *The Fathers of the Church*.)

7. Elisabeth Stenbock-Fermor, "Bulgakov's *The Master and Margarita* and Goethe's *Faust*," *Slavic and East European Journal* 13 (1969), 309-26.

8. Ellendea Proffer, *Bulgakov: Life and Work* (Ann Arbor: Ardis, 1984), p. 552.

9. Michael Glenny, "Existential Thought in Bulgakov's *The Master and Margarita*," *Canadian-American Slavic Studies* 15 (Summer-Fall 1981), 248.

10. T. R. N. Edwards, *Three Russian Writers and the Irrational: Zamyatin, Pil'nyak, and Bulgakov* (Cambridge: Cambridge University Press, 1982), p. 176. Edwards sees Manichaeism as only one influence of Persian ideas on Bulgakov. He also espies Manichaeism elsewhere in Russian literature, including Tolstoy and Dostoevsky.

11. Laszlo Tikos, "Some Notes on the Significance of Gerbert Aurillac in Bulgakov's *The Master and Margarita*," *Canadian-American Slavic Studies* 15 (Summer-Fall 1981), 321-29.

12. Proffer, *Bulgakov*, p. 637.

13. Tikos, pp. 322, 325. Besides the Tikos article, for information on Aurilachs see Henry Charles Lea, *Materials toward a History of Witchcraft* (New York: Thomas Yoseloff, 1957), Vol. I, p. 150.

14. Sergius Bulgakov, *A Bulgakov Anthology*, ed. James Pain and Nicolas Zernov (Philadelphia: Westminster Press, 1976), p. 150.

15. A. Colin Wright, "Mikhail Bulgakov's Developing World View," *Canadian-American Slavic Studies* 15 (Summer-Fall 1981), 163. As gratuitous and speculative as I consider this statement to be, at least it avoids the error of making Woland into a sentimentally good fellow.

16. A. Colin Wright, *Mikhail Bulgakov: Life and Interpretations* (Toronto: University of Toronto Press, 1978), p. 270.

17. Wright, *Mikhail Bulgakov*, p. 262.

18. Wright, *Mikhail Bulgakov*, p. 253.

19. Wright, "Mikhail Bulgakov's Developing World View," p. 161.

20. Wright, "Mikhail Bulgakov's Developing World View," p. 162.

21. Wright, "Mikhail Bulgakov's Developing World View," p. 161.

22. Wright, "Mikhail Bulgakov's Developing World View," p. 161.

23. Bruce A. Beatie and Phyllis W. Powell, "Story and Symbol: Notes toward a Structural Analysis of Bulgakov's *The Master and Margarita,*" *Russian Literature Triquarterly* 15 (1978), 250.

24. D. G. B. Piper, "An Approach to Bulgakov's *The Master and Margarita,*" *Forum for Modern Language Studies* 7 (April 1971), 143.

25. Raymond Rosenthal, "Bulgakov's Sentimental Devil," *New Leader* (November 20, 1967), 18-19.

26. Ewa Thompson, "The Artistic World of Michail Bulgakov," *Russian Literature* 5 (1973), 57. 59.

27. Chudakova, p. 178. See also Proffer, *Bulgakov,* p. 525.

28. Judy C. Ullman, "The Conflict between the Individual and Authority in the Works of Mixail Bulgakov." Unpublished Ph.D. dissertation, University of Chicago, 1976, p. 163.

29. Ellendea Proffer, with her encyclopedic knowledge of Bulgakov's life and works, is very helpful on this subject, especially in the chapter on *The Master and Margarita* in her book *Bulgakov.* Shirley Gutry has written a full dissertation on these parallels: "An Approach to *The Master and Margarita* through the Creative Prose and the Letters of M. A. Bulgakov." Unpublished Ph.D. dissertation, Princeton University, 1976.

30. *The Early Plays of Mikhail Bulgakov,* pp. 356-57.

31. *The Early Plays of Mikhail Bulgakov,* pp. 357.

32. Mikhail Bulgakov, *The Life of Monsieur de Moliere,* tr. Mirra Ginsburg (New York: Funk and Wagnalls, 1970), p. 115.

NOTES TO CHAPTER THREE

1. Ellendea Proffer is the only scholar whom I have read who questions this family relationship. *Bulgakov: Life and Work* (Ann Arbor: Ardis, 1984), p. 1. In any case, these two had many ideas in common, as this chapter will show.

2. Nicolas Zernov, *Eastern Christendom* (New York: G. P. Putnam's Sons, 1961), pp. 235-36.

3. Zernov, *Eastern Christendom*, p. 236.

4. Zernov, *Eastern Christendom*, p. 40.

5. Sergius Bulgakov, *The Orthodox Church* (London: Centenary Press, 1935; 2nd ed. New York: Morehouse Publishing Co., 1960), p. 119.

6. Sergius Bulgakov, *The Orthodox Church*, p. 99.

7. Sergius Bulgakov, *The Orthodox Church*, p. 119.

8. R. M. French, *The Eastern Orthodox Church* (London: Hutchinson's University Library, 1951). p. 150.

9. Nicolas Zernov, *The Russians and Their Church* (London: S. P. C. K., 1945), p. 181.

10. Quoted in Irenee Henri Dalmais, *Eastern Liturgies* (New York: Hawthorn Books, 1961), p. 141.

11. Zernov, *Eastern Christendom*, p. 260.

12. Sergius Bulgakov, *A Bulgakov Anthology*, ed. James Pain and Nicolas Zernov (Philadelphia: Westminster Press, 1976), pp. 151-52.

13. Sergius Bulgakov, *The Orthodox Church*, p. 16.

14. Sergius Bulgakov, *The Orthodox Church*, p. 130.

15. Sergius Bulgakov, *The Orthodox Church*, p. 168.

16. Sergius Bulgakov, *The Orthodox Church*, p. 168.

17. Sergius Bulgakov, *The Orthodox Church*, p. 168.

18. Sergius Bulgakov, *The Orthodox Church*, p. 74.

19. Sergius Bulgakov, *The Orthodox Church*, p. 74.

20. Sergius Bulgakov, *A Bulgakov Anthology*, p. 15.

21. Sergius Bulgakov, *The Orthodox Church*, p. 164.

22. Sergius Bulgakov, *The Orthodox Church*, p. 165.

23. Sergius Bulgakov, *The Orthodox Church*, p. 165.

24. Sergius Bulgakov, *The Orthodox Church*, p. 165.

25. Sergius Bulgakov, *The Orthodox Church*, p. 166.

26. Ernst Benz, *The Eastern Orthodox Church* (Chicago: Aldine Publishing Co., 1963), p. 51.

27. John Meyendorff, *The Orthodox Church* (London: Darton, Longman and Todd, 1960), p. 198.

28. Zernov, *Eastern Christendom*, p. 266.

29. See, for example, Sergius Bulgakov, *The Orthodox Church*, pp. 128-29.

30. Sergius Bulgakov, *The Wisdom of God* (New York: Paisley Press, 1937), pp. 215-16.

31. Zernov, *Eastern Christendom*, pp. 276, 297-98.

32. Carnegie S. Calian, *Icon and Pulpit* (Philadelphia: Westminster Press, 1968), p. 111.

33. M. J. Le Guillou, *The Spirit of Eastern Orthodoxy* (New York: Hawthorn Books, 1962), p. 51.

34. Benz, p. 17.

35. I am indebted for this lead to Elisabeth Stenbock-Fermor, "Bulgakov's *The Master and Margarita* and Goethe's *Faust*," *Slavic and East European Journal* 13 (Fall 1969), 319.

36. "The Descent of the Virgin into Hell," in *Medieval Russia's Epics, Chronicles, and Tales*, ed. Serge A. Zenkovsky (New York: E. P. Dutton and Co., 1974), pp. 153-60.

37. Zernov, *Eastern Christendom*, p. 297.

38. Sergius Bulgakov, *The Orthodox Church*, p. 129.

39. Sergius Bulgakov, *A Bulgakov Anthology*, p. 183.

40. Benz, p. 51.

41. Benz, p. 47.

42. Benz, p. 52.

43. Benz, p. 52.

44. Adrian Fortescue, *The Orthodox Eastern Church* (New York: Burt Franklin, 1969), pp. 388-89.

45. Sergius Bulgakov, *The Orthodox Church*, p. 209.

46. Sergius Bulgakov, *The Orthodox Church*, p. 211.

47. Zernov, *Eastern Christendom*, pp. 234-35.

48. Sergius Bulgakov, *The Orthodox Church*, p. 157.

49. Sergius Bulgakov, *The Orthodox Church*, pp. 208-209.

50. French, p. 150.

51. Sergius Bulgakov, *The Orthodox Church*, p. 154.

52. Sergius Bulgakov, *The Orthodox Church*, p. 154.

53. Sergius Bulgakov, *The Orthodox Church*, pp. 147-48.

54. Calian, p. 159.

55. Sergius Bulgakov, *The Orthodox Church*, p. 203.

56. Sergius Bulgakov, *A Bulgakov Anthology*, p. 158.

57. Alexander Schmemann, *Introduction to Liturgical Theology* (Portland, Maine: American Orthodox Press, 1966), p. 57.

58. T. F. Glasson, *The Revelation of John* (Cambridge: Cambridge University Press, 1965), p. 2.

59. Sergius Bulgakov, *The Orthodox Church*, p. 219. A similar sentiment is found in Zernov, *The Russians and Their Church*, p. 167.

60. Introduction to *A Bulgakov Anthology*, p. xvi.

61. Sergius Bulgakov, *A Bulgakov Anthology*, p. 20.

62. Sergius Bulgakov, *A Bulgakov Anthology*, p. 160.

63. Mikhail Bulgakov, *The White Guard*, tr. Michael Glenny (New York: McGraw-Hill Book Co., 1971), p. 13.

64. Mikhail Bulgakov, *The White Guard*, p. 282.

65. Mikhail Bulgakov, *The White Guard*, p. 283.

66. Mikhail Bulgakov, *The White Guard*, p. 285.

67. Mikhail Bulgakov, *The White Guard*, p. 283.

68. Mikhail Bulgakov, *The Master and Margarita*, tr. Michael Glenny (New York: Harper & Row, 1967), p. 364.

69. Mikhail Bulgakov, *The White Guard*, p. 284.

70. Mikhail Bulgakov, *The White Guard*, pp. 9, 289.

71. Mikhail Bulgakov, *The White Guard*, p. 297.

72. Mikhail Bulgakov, *The Master and Margarita*, p. 369.

73. In Chapter Nine, "The Apocalypse," we shall return to the subject of the Four Horsemen.

74. Mikhail Bulgakov, *Early Plays of Mikhail Bulgakov*, ed. Ellendea Proffer (Bloomington: Indiana University Press, 1972), p. 380-81.

75. Mikhail Bulgakov, *Black Snow: A Theatrical Novel*, tr. Michael Glenny (New York: Simon and Schuster, 1967), p. 31.

76. Ronald H. Preston and Anthony T. Hanson, *The Revelation of St. John the Divine* (London: SCM Press, 1965), p. 28.

77. D. S. Russell, *The Method and Message of Jewish Apocalyptic, 200 B.C.-A.D. 100* (Philadelphia: Westminster Press, 1964), p. 106.

78. Russell, p. 122.

79. Sergius Bulgakov, *The Orthodox Church*, p. 31.

80. Sergius Bulgakov, *The Orthodox Church*, p. 31.

NOTES TO CHAPTER FOUR

1. Marietta Chudakova, *"The Master and Margarita*: The Development of a Novel," *Russian Literature Triquarterly* 15 (1978), 182.

2. Ellendea Proffer, *Bulgakov: Life and Work* (Ann Arbor: Ardis, 1984), p. 525.

3. Proffer, *Bulgakov*, p. 558.

4. Chudakova, p. 177.

5. Chudakova, p. 181.

6. Chudakova, p. 178.

7. Mikhail Bulgakov, *The Master and Margarita*, tr. Michael Glenny (New York: Harper & Row, 1967), p. 131. Further references to the novel are cited in the text.

8. V. Lakshin, "Mikhail Bulgakov's Novel *The Master and Margarita*," *Soviet Studies in Literature* 5 (Winter 1968-69), p. 20. Tr. and rptd. from *Novy Mir*, 1968, no. 6.

9. Elisabeth Stenbock-Fermor, "Bulgakov's *The Master and Margarita* and Goethe's *Faust*," *Slavic and East European Journal* 13 (Fall 1969), 311.

10. Proffer, *Bulgakov*, p. 556.

11. Priscilla Conwell Deck, "Thematic Coherence in Bulgakov's *The Master and Margarita*." Unpublished Ph.D. dissertation, Brandeis University, 1976, p. 125.

12. Proffer, *Bulgakov*, p. 556.

13. Lakshin, p. 24.

14. Proffer, *Bulgakov*, p. 536.

15. Lakshin, p. 24.

16. Lakshin, p. 28.

17. Proffer, *Bulgakov*, pp. 559-60.

18. G. V. Shann, *Euchology: A Manual of the Holy Orthodox Church* (New York: AMS Press, 1969), p. 95. Rpt. of 1891 edition.

19. Lesley Milne, *The Master and Margarita: A Comedy of Victory* (Birmingham, England: Birmingham Slavonic Monographs, 1977), p. 31.

20. Milne, p. 31.

21. Milne, pp. 31-32.

22. R. H. Charles, *The Apocrypha and Pseudepigrapha of the Old Testament in English.* (London: Oxford University Press, 1963), Vol. II, p. 193.

23. Charles, p. 193.

24. Henry Charles Lea, *Materials Toward a History of Witchcraft* (New York: Thomas Yoseloff, 1957), Vol. I, p. 22.

25. I Enoch 86:1ff., as cited by D. S. Russell, *The Method and Message of Jewish Apocalyptic, 200 B.C.-A.D. 100* (Philadelphia: Westminster Press, 1964), p. 251.

26. Louis Ginzberg, *The Legends of the Jews* (Philadelphia: The Jewish Publication Society of America, 1912), Vol. I, p. 149.

27. R. Campbell Thompson, *Semitic Magic: Its Origins and Development* (London: Luzac & Co., 1908), p. 75.

28. Russell, p. 256.

29. Russell, pp. 243, 256-57.

30. Ginzberg, Vol. I, p. 149.

31. Proffer, *Bulgakov*, p. 643.

32. Charles, p. 192.

33. See, *e.g.*, Charles, pp. 192-94.

34. Russell, p. 372.

35. Russell, pp. 365-233.

36. Russell, p. 382.

37. Austin M. Farrer, *The Revelation of St. John the Divine* (Oxford: Clarendon Press, 1964), p. 143.

38. Lea, Vol. I, p. 10.

39. Lea, Vol. I, p. 9.

40. Ginzberg, Vol. I, p. 30.

41. Charles, p. 224.

42. Ginzberg, Vol. I, p. 30.

43. Ginzberg, Vol. I, p. 30.

44. Charles, p. 224.

45. Ginzberg, Vol. V, p. 44.

46. Lea, Vol. I, p. 285.

47. Ginzberg, Vol. I, p. 30.

48. Lea, Vol. I, p. 59.

49. Russell, p. 294. The same passage is cited in Charles, p. 497.

50. Farrer, pp. 143-44.

51. Proffer, *Bulgakov*, p. 643.

52. Milne, p. 21.

53. Deck, p. 131.

54. D. G. B. Piper, "An Approach to Bulgakov's *The Master and Margarita*," *Forum for Modern Language Studies* 7 (April 1971), 144.

55. Stenbock-Fermor, p. 312.

56. Stenbock-Fermor, p. 312.

57. Stenbock-Fermor, p. 312.

58. Proffer, *Bulgakov*, p. 643.

59. Bruce A. Beatie and Phyllis W. Powell, "Story and Symbol: Notes toward a Structural Analysis of Bulgakov's *The Master and Margarita*," *Russian Literature Triquarterly* 15 (1978), 247.

60. Milne, p. 28.

61. Milne, p. 28.

62. Milne, p. 28.

63. Milne, p. 29.

64. Lea, Vol. I, p. 147.

65. I am indebted for this lead to an undergraduate student paper by David Landegent. Landegent had other suggestions about possible borrowings by Bulgakov from Norse mythology, including references to the stories of Weland the smith and Woden the god as they might apply to Woland.

66. Milne, p. 32.

67. Laura D. Weeks, "Hebraic Antecedents in *The Master and Margarita*: Woland and Company Revisited," *Slavic Review* 43 (Summer 1984), 238-39.

68. Weeks, p. 240.

69. G. B. Caird, *A Commentary on the Revelation of St. John the Divine* (New York: Harper & Row, 1966), p. 120.

70. Lea, Vol. I, p. 292.

71. Ellendea Proffer, "Red-Bricked Moscow: 1921-23," *Canadian-American Slavic Studies* 15 (Summer-Fall 1981), 175.

72. Beatie and Powell, p. 229.

73. Donald M. Fiene, "Further Elucidation of the Pilate Theme in Bulgakov's *The Master and Margarita*, with a Note on May Eve, Good Friday, and the Full Moon," pp. 11-13. Unpublished paper presented at Southern Conference on Slavic Studies; Atlanta, Georgia; October 8, 1983.

74. Proffer, *Bulgakov*, p. 562.

75. Proffer, *Bulgakov*, p. 537.

76. See, *e.g.*, Edwards, pp. 151-52.

77. Stenbock-Fermor, p. 309.

78. Stenbock-Fermor, pp. 312-13.

79. Stenbock-Fermor, p. 314.

80. Proffer, *Bulgakov*, p. 537.

81. Ellendea Proffer, "On *The Master and Margarita*," *Russian Literature Triquarterly* 6 (Spring 1973), 544-45.

82. Helen Muchnic, "Laughter in the Dark," *New York Review of Books* (July 11, 1968), 28.

83. "Diabolical Experiment," *London Times Literary Supplement* (December 7, 1967), 1181.

84. Shann, p. 95.

85. Proffer, "Red-Bricked Moscow," pp. 170, 175.

86. Proffer, *Bulgakov*, p. 561.

87. Edwards, p. 155.

88. Proffer, *Bulgakov*, p. 563.

89. Edythe C. Haber, "The Mythic Structure of Bulgakov's *The Master and Margarita*," *Russian Review* 34 (October 1975), 388.

90. Judy C. Ullman, "The Conflict between the Individual and Authority in the Works of Mixail Bulgakov," p. 157. Unpublished Ph.D. dissertation, University of Chicago, 1976.

91. A. Colin Wright, *Mikhail Bulgakov: Life and Interpretations* (Toronto: University of Toronto Press, 1978), p. 266.

92. Proffer, *Bulgakov*, p. 562.

NOTES TO CHAPTER FIVE

1. D. G. B. Piper, "An Approach to Bulgakov's *The Master and Margarita*," *Forum for Modern Language Studies* 7 (April 1971), 139.

2. Shirley Gutry, "An Approach to *The Master and Margarita* through the Creative Prose and the Letter of M. A. Bulgakov." Unpublished Ph.D. dissertation, Princeton University, 1976, pp. 178-79.

3. Barbara Kejna-Sharratt, "Narrative Techniques in *The Master and Margarita*," *Canadian Slavonic Papers* 16 (Spring 1974), 3.

4. Ellendea Proffer, "Bulgakov's *The Master and Margarita*: Genre and Motif," *Canadian Slavic Studies* 3 (Winter 1969), 618.

5. Proffer, "Bulgakov's *The Master and Margarita*: Genre and Motif," 619.

6. Gutry, p. 95.

7. Mikhail Bulgakov, *The Master and Margarita*, tr. Michael Glenny (New York: Harper & Row, 1967), p. 291. Further references to the novel are cited in the text.

8. Lesley Milne, *The Master and Margarita: A Comedy of Victory* (Birmingham, England: Birmingham Slavonic Monographs, 1977), p. 7.

9. Judy C. Ullman, "The Conflict between the Individual and Authority in the Works of Mixail Bulgakov." Unpublished Ph.D. dissertation, University of Chicago, 1976, p. 155. Vida Taranovski Johnson, "The Thematic Function of the Narrator in *The Master and Margarita*," *Canadian-American Slavic Studies* 15 (Summer-Fall 1981), 276. Ellendea Proffer, *Bulgakov: Life and Work* (Ann Arbor: Ardis, 1984), p. 548.

10. Johnson, p. 275.

11. Proffer, *Bulgakov*, p. 527.

12. Milne, p. 10.

13. Johnson, pp. 274-75.

14. Johnson, p. 275.

15. Proffer, *Bulgakov*, p. 540.

16. Proffer, *Bulgakov*, pp. 540-41.

17. Irving Howe, "The Continuity of Russian Voices," *Harper's* (January 1968), 71.

18. Mikhail Bulgakov, *The Master and Margarita*, tr. Mirra Ginsburg (New York: Grove Press, 1967), p. 24.

19. Priscilla Conwell Deck, "Thematic Coherence in Bulgakov's *The Master and Margarita*." Unpublished Ph.D. dissertation, Brandeis University, 1976, p. 161.

20. Sergius Bulgakov, "Meditations on the Joy of the Resurrection," in *Ultimate Questions: An Anthology of Modern Russian Religious Thought*, ed. Alexander Schmemann (New York: Holt, Rinehart, Winston, 1965), pp. 305-306.

21. Ellendea Proffer, "On *The Master and Margarita*," *Russian Literature Triquarterly* 6 (Spring 1973), 546-47.

22. Mikhail Bulgakov, *The White Guard*, tr. Michael Glenny (New York: McGraw-Hill Book Co., 1971), p. 12.

23. V. Lakshin, "Mikhail Bulgakov's Novel *The Master and Margarita*," *Soviet Studies in Literature* 5 (Winter 1968-69), 37. Tr. and rptd. from *Novy Mir*, 1968, no. 6.

24. Margot K. Frank, "The Mystery of the Master's Final Destination," *Canadian-American Slavic Studies* 15 (Summer-Fall 1981), 293.

25. T. R. N. Edwards, *Three Russian Writers and the Irrational: Zamyatin, Pil'nyak, and Bulgakov* (Cambridge: Cambridge University Press, 1982), p. 166.

26. Nicolas Zernov, *Eastern Christendom* (New York: G. P. Putnam's Sons, 1961), p. 233.

27. Ernst Benz, *The Eastern Orthodox Church* (Chicago: Aldine Publishing Co., 1963), p. 150.

28. Michael Glenny, "Existential Thought in Bulgakov's *The Master and Margarita,*" *Canadian-American Slavic Studies* 15 (Summer-Fall 1981), 238.

29. Donald B. Pruitt, "St. John and Bulgakov: The Model of a Parody of Christ," *Canadian-American Slavic Studies* 15 (Summer-Fall 1981), 313 ff.

30. Deck, pp. 184-85.

31. Milne, p. 8.

32. Milne, p. 17.

33. Raymond Rosenthal, "Bulgakov's Sentimental Devil," *New Leader* (November 20, 1967), 18.

34. Deck, p. 193.

35. Gutry, p. 168.

36. Gutry, p. 168.

37. Deck, p. 188.

38. Milne, p. 12.

39. Elena N. Mahlow, *Bulgakov's The Master and Margarita: The Text as a Cipher* (New York: Vantage Press, 1975), p. 5.

40. Gutry, p. 166; see also p. 96.

41. *The Apocryphal Books of the New Testament* (Philadelphia: Gebbie & Co., 1890), pp. 272-73.

42. *Apocryphal Books of the New Testament*, p. 271.

43. James DeQuincey Donehoo, *The Apocryphal and Legendary Life of Christ* (New York: Hodder & Stoughton, 1903), p. 490.

44. Donehoo, pp. 467-69.

45. Donehoo, p. 471.

46. Donehoo, p. 490.

47. Donehoo, p. 490; see also p. 502.

48. Donehoo, p. 490.

49. Donehoo, p. 504.

50. Frank Morison, *And Pilate Said—: A New Study of the Roman Procurator* (London: Rich & Cowan, Ltd., 1939), p. 237.

51. Morison, P. 238.

52. Morison, pp. 238-39.

53. Bruce A. Beatie and Phyllis W. Powell, "Story and Symbol: Notes Toward a Structural Analysis of Bulgakov's *The Master and Margarita,*" *Russian Literature Triquarterly* 15 (1978), 236. Deck, pp. 204-205. Pruitt, pp. 314-15.

54. Pruitt, p. 315.

NOTES TO CHAPTER SIX

1. Mikhail Bulgakov, *The Master and Margarita*, tr. Michael Glenny (New York: Harper & Row, 1967), p. 131. Further references to the novel are cited in the text.

2. Margot K. Frank, "The Mystery of the Master's Final Destination," *Canadian-American Slavic Studies* 15 (Summer-Fall 1981), 287.

3. Priscilla Conwell Deck, "Thematic Coherence in Bulgakov's *The Master and Margarita.*" Unpublished Ph.D. dissertation, Brandeis University, 1976, pp. 106-107.

4. Ellendea Proffer, *Bulgakov: Life and Work* (Ann Arbor: Ardis, 1984), p. 560.

5. Proffer, *Bulgakov*, p. 560.

6. Deck, p. 116.

7. Shirley Gutry, "An Approach to *The Master and Margarita* through the Creative Prose and the Letters of M. A. Bulgakov." Unpublished Ph.D. dissertation, Princeton University, 1976, p. 165.

8. Frank, p. 294.

9. V. Lakshin, "Mikhail Bulgakov's Novel *The Master and Margarita*," *Soviet Studies in Literature* 5 (Winter 1968-69), 45. Tr. and rptd. from *Novy Mir*, 1968, no. 6.

10. Mikhail Bulgakov, *Diaboliad and Other Stories*, ed. Ellendea and Carl R. Proffer (Bloomington: Indiana University Press, 1972), pp. 3-47.

11. Ernst Benz, *The Eastern Orthodox Church* (Chicago: Aldine Publishing Co., 1963), pp. 18-19.

12. Benz, p. 4.

13. A. Colin Wright, *Mikhail Bulgakov: Life and Interpretations* (Toronto: University of Toronto Press, 1978), p. 267.

14. T. R. N. Edwards, *Three Russian Writers and the Irrational: Zamyatin, Pil'nyak, and Bulgakov* (Cambridge: Cambridge University Press, 1982), p. 156.

15. Proffer, *Bulgakov*, p. 561.

16. Elisabeth Stenbock-Fermor, "Bulgakov's *The Master and Margarita* and Goethe's *Faust*," *Slavic and East European Journal* 13 (1969), 311.

17. Edythe C. Haber, "The Mythic Structure of Bulgakov's *The Master and Margarita*," *Russian Review* 34 (October 1975), 391.

18. Joan Delaney, "*The Master and Margarita*: The Reach Exceeds the Grasp," *Slavic Review* 31 (March 1972), 99.

19. Delaney, p. 91.

20. Proffer, *Bulgakov*, p. 528.

21. Lakshin, p. 47.

22. Lesley Milne, *The Master and Margarita: A Comedy of Victory* (Birmingham, England: Birmingham Slavonic Monographs, 1977), p. 15.

23. Milne, p. 16.

24. Gutry, p. 191.

25. Delaney, p. 99.

26. Gutry, p. 205.

27. Proffer, *Bulgakov*, p. 528.

28. Lakshin, p. 43.

29. Gutry, p. 191.

30. Marietta Chudakova, *"The Master and Margarita*: The Development of a Novel," *Russian Literature Triquarterly* 15 (1978), 178.

31. Wright, *Mikhail Bulgakov*, p. 144.

32. Chudakova, p. 178.

33. Wright, *Mikhail Bulgakov*, p. 150.

34. Proffer, *Bulgakov*, p. 538.

35. Wright, *Mikhail Bulgakov*, p. 252.

36. Wright, *Mikhail Bulgakov*, p. 253.

37. Cited in Ellendea Proffer, "Red-Bricked Moscow: 1921-23," *Canadian-American Slavic Studies* 15 (Summer-Fall 1981), 176.

38. A. Colin Wright, "Mikhail Bulgakov's Developing World View," *Canadian-American Slavic Studies* 15 (Summer-Fall 1981), 157.

39. Proffer, *Bulgakov*, p. 560.

40. Milne, p. 11.

41. Sergius Bulgakov, *The Wisdom of God* (New York: Paisley Press, 1937), p. 119.

42. L. Skorino, "Characters without Carnival Masks," *Soviet Studies in Literature* 5 (Spring 1969), 32. Tr. and rptd. from *Voprosy Literatury*, 1968, no. 6.

43. Lakshin, p. 46.

44. Bruce A. Beatie and Phyllis W. Powell, "Story and Symbol: Notes Toward a Structural Analysis of Bulgakov's *The Master and Margarita*," *Russian Literature Triquarterly* 15 (1978), 229-38.

45. Austin M. Farrer, *The Revelation of St. John the Divine* (Oxford: Clarendon Press, 1964), p. 66.

46. R. M. French, *The Eastern Orthodox Church* (London: Hutchinson's University Library, 1951), p. 152.

47. French, p. 153.

48. G. V. Shann, *Euchology: A Manual of Prayers of the Holy Orthodox Church* (New York: AMS Press, 1969), p. 191.

49. Wright, "Mikhail Bulgakov's Developing World View," p. 164.

50. Proffer, *Bulgakov*, p. 581.

51. Deck, p. 152.

52. Edwards, p. 171.

53. Milne, p. 25.

54. Milne, p. 25.

55. Milne, p. 26.

56. Frank, p. 288.

57. Frank, p. 288.

58. Frank, p. 292.

59. Wright, "Mikhail Bulgakov's Developing World View," p. 165.

60. Bruce A. Beatie and Phyllis W. Powell, "Bulgakov, Dante, and Relativity," *Canadian-American Slavic Studies* 15 (Summer-Fall 1981), 261.

61. Beatie and Powell, "Bulgakov, Dante, and Relativity," p. 262.

62. Beatie and Powell, "Bulgakov, Dante, and Relativity," p. 264.

63. Beatie and Powell, "Bulgakov, Dante, and Relativity," p. 267.

64. Chudakova, p. 197.

65. Chudakova, p. 197.

66. Chudakova, p. 197.

67. Chudakova, p. 198.

68. Beatie and Powell, "Bulgakov, Dante, and Relativity," p. 265.

69. Sergius Bulgakov, *The Orthodox Church* (London: Centenary Press, 1935; 2nd ed. New York: Morehouse Publishing Co., 1960), pp. 208-209.

70. Sergius Bulgakov, *The Orthodox Church*, p. 209.

71. French, p. 160.

72. Donald B. Pruitt, "St. John and Bulgakov: The Model of a Parody of Christ," *Canadian-American Slavic Studies* 15 (Summer-Fall 1981), 318-19.

NOTES TO CHAPTER SEVEN

1. Bruce A. Beatie and Phyllis W. Powell, "Bulgakov, Dante, and Relativity," *Canadian-American Slavic Studies* 15 (Summer-Fall 1981), 261.

2. Lesley Milne, *The Master and Margarita: A Comedy of Victory* (Birmingham, England: Birmingham Slavonic Monographs, 1977). p. 22.

3. Mikhail Bulgakov, *The Master and Margarita*, tr. Michael Glenny (New York: Harper & Row, 1967), p. 215. Further references to the novel are cited in the text.

4. Priscilla Conwell Deck, "Thematic Coherence in Bulgakov's *The Master and Margarita*." Unpublished Ph.D dissertation, Brandeis University, 1976, p. 139.

5. Michael Glenny, "Existential Thought in Bulgakov's *The Master and Margarita*," *Canadian-American Slavic Studies* 15 (Summer-Fall 1981), 239.

6. Deck, p. 134.

7. Deck, pp. 136-37.

8. Deck, p. 142.

9. Bruce A. Beatie and Phyllis W. Powell, "Story and Symbol: Notes Toward a Structural Analysis of Bulgakov's *The Master and Margarita*," *Russian Literature Triquarterly* 15 (1978), 225.

10. Beatie and Powell, "Bulgakov, Dante, and Relativity," p. 268.

11. See, *e.g.*, Beatie and Powell, "Story and Symbol," pp. 233-34; Deck, p. 140; Milne, p. 13; D. G. B. Piper, "An Approach to Bulgakov's *The Master and Margarita*," *Forum for Modern Language Studies* 7 (April 1971), 153.

12. Milne, p. 13.

13. Piper, p. 153.

14. Deck, p. 109.

15. Milne, p. 12.

16. V. Lakshin, "Mikhail Bulgakov's *The Master and Margarita*," *Soviet Studies in Literature* 5 (Winter 1968-69), 57. Tr. and rptd. from *Novy Mir*, 1968, no. 6.

17. Sergius Bulgakov, *The Wisdom of God* (New York: Paisley Press, 1937), p. 150.

18. Sergius Bulgakov, *The Wisdom of God*, pp. 150-51.

19. Sergius Bulgakov, *The Wisdom of God*, p. 204.

20. Nicolas Zernov, *The Church of the Eastern Christians* (London: S.P.C.K., 1946), p. 49.

21. Ellendea Proffer, "On *The Master and Margarita*," *Russian Literature Triquarterly* 6 (Spring 1973), 533.

22. Piper, p. 135.

23. Piper, p. 135.

24. Marietta Chudakova, "*The Master and Margarita*: The Development of a Novel," *Russian Literature Triquarterly* 15 (1978), 186.

25. Proffer, "On *The Master and Margarita*," p. 533.

26. Ellendea Proffer, "The Major Works of Mikhail Bulgakov." Unpublished Ph.D. dissertation, Indiana University, 1970, p. 331.

27. Vida Taranovski Johnson, "The Thematic Function of the Narrator in *The Master and Margarita*," *Canadian-American Slavic Studies* 15 (Summer-Fall 1981), 286.

28. A. Colin Wright, "Mikhail Bulgakov's Developing World View," *Canadian-American Slavic Studies* 15 (Summer-Fall 1981), 156.

29. Milne, p. 12.

30. M. J. Le Guillou, *The Spirit of Eastern Orthodoxy* (New York: Hawthorn Books, 1962), p. 54.

31. Adrian Fortescue, *The Orthodox Eastern Church* (New York: Burt Franklin, 1969), p. 421.

32. Irenee Henri Dalmais, *Eastern Liturgies* (New York: Hawthorn Books, 1961), p. 63.

33. Fortescue, pp. 425-26.

34. Deck, p. 129.

35. Jeffrey Burton Russell, *Lucifer: The Devil in the Middle Ages* (Ithaca, N.Y.: Cornell University Press, 1984), p. 296.

36. Montague Summers, *The History of Witchcraft and Demonology* (New York: University Books, 1956), pp. 121-22.

37. Donald Attwater, *The Christian Churches of the East* (Milwaukee: Bruce Publishing Co., 1961), Vol. I, p. 48.

38. Zernov, *The Church of the Eastern Christians*, p. 42.

39. Ellendea Proffer, *Bulgakov: Life and Work* (Ann Arbor: Ardis, 1984), p. 558.

40. Beatie and Powell, "Story and Symbol," pp. 220-22; Beatie and Powell, "Bulgakov, Dante, and Relativity," p. 259.

41. Nicolas Zernov, *Eastern Christendom* (New York: G. P. Putnam's Sons, 1961), p. 258.

42. Russell Hope Robbins, *The Encyclopedia of Witchcraft and Demonology* (New York: Crown Publishers, 1959), p. 418.

43. Harry E. Wedeck, *Treasury of Witchcraft* (New York: Philosophical Library, 1961), p. 126.

44. John Meyendorff, "The Time of Holy Saturday," in *Orthodox Synthesis: The Unity of Theological Thought*, ed. Joseph J. Allen (Crestwood, N.Y.: St. Vladimir's Seminary Press, 1981), p. 52.

45. Donald M. Fiene, "Further Elucidation of the Pilate Theme in Bulgakov's *The Master and Margarita*, with a Note on May Eve, Good Friday, and the Full Moon," p. 6. Unpublished paper presented at Southern Conference on Slavic Studies; Atlanta, Georgia; October 8, 1983. In the abbreviated published version of this paper, Fiene revises this line to assert that "the novel almost forces us to recognize Good Friday as falling on 30 April, with Easter occurring on 2 May." "A Note on May Eve, Good Friday, and the Full Moon in Bulgakov's *The Master and Margarita*," *Slavic and East European Journal* 28 (1984), p. 535.

46. Fiene, "A Note," p. 536.

47. Fiene, "Further Elucidation," p. 6.

48. A. Colin Wright, *Mikhail Bulgakov: Life and Interpretations* (Toronto: University of Toronto Press, 1978), p. 266.

49. Milne, p. 14.

50. Deck, p. 144.

51. G. V. Shann, *Euchology: A Manual of Prayers of the Holy Orthodox Church* (New York: AMS Press, 1969), pp. xv-xvi.

52. Sergius Bulgakov, *The Orthodox Church* (London: Centenary Press, 1935; 2nd ed. New York: Morehouse Publishing Co., 1960), p. 152.

53. Sergius Bulgakov, *The Orthodox Church*, p. 159.

54. Wedeck, p. 160.

55. Arthur Lyons, *The Second Coming: Satanism in America* (New York: Dodd, Mead & Co., 1970), p. 50.

56. Henry Hatfield, "The Walpurgis Night: Themes and Variations," *Journal of European Studies* 13 (1983), 71.

57. Wedeck, p. 126.

58. Henry Charles Lea, *Materials Toward a History of Witchcraft* (New York: Thomas Yoseloff, 1957), Vol. I, p. 170; see also Wedeck, p. 121.

59. Robbins, p. 461.

60. Summers, p. 69.

61. Lyons, p. 52.

62. Robbins, p. 374.

63. Robbins, p. 461.

64. Sergius Bulgakov, "Meditations on the Joy of the Resurrection," in *Ultimate Questions: An Anthology of Modern Russian Religious Thought*, ed. Alexander Schmemann (New York: Holt, Rinehart, Winston, 1965), p. 303.

65. Zernov, *Eastern Christendom*, p. 245.

66. Shann, p. 392.

67. Ernst Benz, *The Eastern Orthodox Church* (Chicago: Aldine Publishing Co., 1963), p. 21.

68. Benz, p. 151.

69. Sergius Bulgakov, *The Wisdom of God*, p. 204.

70. Sergius Bulgakov, *The Wisdom of God*, p. 151.

71. Sergius Bulgakov, *A Bulgakov Anthology*, ed. James Pain and Nicolas Zernov (Philadelphia: Westminster Press, 1976), p. 93.

72. Sergius Bulgakov, *A Bulgakov Anthology*, p. 95.

73. Sergius Bulgakov, *A Bulgakov Anthology*, p. 96.

74. John Meyendorff, *The Orthodox Church* (London: Darton, Longman and Todd, 1960), p. 200.

75. Nicolas Zernov, *The Russian Religious Renaissance of the Twentieth Century* (New York: Harper & Row, 1963), p. 286.

76. George H. Demetrakopoulos, *Dictionary of Orthodox Theology* (New York: Philosophical Library, 1964), p. 11.

77. Zernov, *Eastern Christendom*, p. 281.

78. Milne, p. 13.

79. Sergius Bulgakov, *The Wisdom of God*, p. 177.

80. "The Descent of the Virgin into Hell," in *Medieval Russia's Epics, Chronicles, and Tales*, ed. Serge A. Zenkovsky (New York: E. P. Dutton & Co., 1974), pp. 153-60.

81. "The Descent of the Virgin into Hell," p. 158.

82. Sergius Bulgakov, *The Orthodoxy Church*, pp. 137, 139-40.

83. Leonide Ouspensky, *Theology of the Icon* (Crestwood, N.Y.: St. Vladimir's Seminary Press, 1978), p. 32.

84. Sergius Bulgakov, *A Bulgakov Anthology*, p. 182.

85. Wedeck, p. 104.

86. Sergius Bulgakov, *The Wisdom of God*, p. 182.

87. Abram Tertz, "Thought Unaware," *New Leader* 48 (July 19, 1965), 9-15. (Abram Tertz is Andrei Sinyavsky's pseudonym.)

88. Johnson, p. 271.

89. *Larousse Encyclopedia of Mythology* (London: Paul Hamlyn, 1959), p. 286. I am indebted for this lead to David Landegent, an undergraduate student of mine in 1977 at Northwestern College (Iowa).

90. *Larousse Encyclopedia of Mythology*, p. 287.

91. Demetrakopoulos, p. 1.

92. Benz, pp. 52-53.

93. Zernov, *Eastern Christendom*, pp. 234-35.

NOTES TO CHAPTER EIGHT

1. Mikhail Bulgakov, *The Master and Margarita*, tr. Michael Glenny (New York: Harper & Row, 1976), p. 371. Further references to the novel are cited in the text.

2. Ellendea Proffer, *Bulgakov: Life and Work* (Ann Arbor: Ardis, 1984), p. 539.

3. Carol Avins, "Reaching a Reader: The Master's Audience in *The Master and Margarita*," *Slavic Review* 45 (Summer 1986), 281.

4. Val Bolen, "Theme and Coherence in Bulgakov's *The Master and Margarita*," *Slavic and East European Journal* 16 (Winter 1972), 434.

5. Judy C. Ullman, "The Conflict between the Individual and Authority in the Works of Mixail Bulgakov." Unpublished Ph.D. dissertation, University of Chicago, 1976, pp. 150-51.

6. Carol Arenberg, "Mythic and Daimonic Paradigms in Bulgakov's *Master I Margarita, Essays in Literature* 9 (Spring 1972), 434.

7. Lewis Bagby, "Eternal Themes in Mixail Bulgakov's *The Master and Margarita*," *International Fiction Review* 1 (January 1974), 29.

8. Pierre R. Hart, "*The Master and Margarita* as Creative Process," *Modern Fiction Studies* 19 (1973), 170, 172.

9. Barbara Kejna-Sharratt, "Narrative Techniques in *The Master and Margarita*," *Canadian Slavonic Papers* 16 (Spring 1974), 11; C. E. Pearce, "A Closer Look at Narrative Structure in Bulgakov's *The Master and Margarita*," *Canadian Slavonic Papers* 22 (1980), 370-71.

10. Richard W. F. Pope, "Ambiguity and Meaning in *The Master and Margarita*: The Role of Afranius," *Slavic Review* 36 (March 1977), 23.

11. Laura D. Weeks, "In Defense of the Homeless: On the Uses of History and the Role of Bezdomnyi in *The Master and Margarita*," *Russian Review* 48 (1989), 46, 45.

12. Weeks, p. 46.

13. Weeks, pp. 47-48.

14. Weeks, p. 54.

15. Weeks, p. 54.

16. Weeks, p. 59.

17. Weeks, p. 58.

18. Weeks, pp. 55, 58.

19. Weeks, p. 58.

20. Weeks, pp. 59, 60.

21. Weeks, pp. 60, 61.

22. Weeks, pp. 61-65.

23. A. Colin Wright, *Mikhail Bulgakov: Life and Interpretations* (Toronto: University of Toronto Press, 1978), pp. 268-69.

24. Ullman, p. 149.

25. Ullman, p. 149.

26. Hart, p. 173.

27. Weeks, p. 56.

28. Weeks, p. 58.

29. Weeks, pp. 58-59.

30. Barbara Kejna-Sharratt, "The Tale of Two Cities: The Unifying Function of the Setting in Mikhail Bulgakov's *The Master and Margarita*," *Forum for Modern Language Studies* 16 (1980), 334.

NOTES TO CHAPTER NINE

1. David M. Bethea, "History as Hippodrome: The Apocalyptic Horse and Rider in *The Master and Margarita*," *Russian Review* 41 (October 1982), 376.

2. Edward E. Ericson, Jr., "The Satanic Incarnation: Parody in Bulgakov's *The Master and Margarita*," *Russian Review* 33 (January 1974), 20-36.

3. Bethea, p. 383.

4. Bethea, p. 375.

5. Bethea, p. 393.

6. Bethea, p. 376.

7. Bethea, p. 397.

8. Laura D. Weeks, "Hebraic Antecedents in *The Master and Margarita*: Woland and Company Revisited," *Slavic Review* 43 (Summer 1984), 236.

9. Nicolas Zernov, *The Russians and Their Church* (London: S.P.C.K., 1945), p. 180.

10. Austin M. Farrer, *The Revelation of St. John the Divine* (Oxford: Clarendon Press, 1964), p. 19.

11. Farrer, p. 52.

12. Ronald H. Preston and Anthony T. Hanson, *The Revelation of Saint John the Divine* (London: SCM Press, 1955), p. 43.

13. Preston and Hanson, p. 71.

14. Farrer, p. 56.

15. D. S. Russell, *The Method and Message of Jewish Apocalyptic, 200 B.C.-A.D. 100* (Philadelphia: Westminster Press, 1964), p. 105.

16. G. B. Caird, *A Commentary on the Revelation of St. John the Divine* (New York: Harper & Row, 1966), pp. 9-10.

17. Sergius Bulgakov, *The Wisdom of God* (New York: Paisley Press, 1937), p. 215.

18. Farrer, p. 8.

19. Mikhail Bulgakov, *The Master and Margarita*, tr. Michael Glenny (New York: Harper & Row, 1967), p. 364. Further references to the novel are cited in the text.

20. Farrer, p. 47.

21. Mikhail Bulgakov, *The Master and Margarita*, tr. Mirra Ginsburg (New York: Grove Press, 1967), p. 371.

22. Weeks, p. 236.

23. Caird, p. 88.

24. Bethea, p. 394.

25. Robert H. Mounce, *The Book of Revelation* (Grand Rapids: Wm. B. Eerdmans Publishing Co., 1977), p. 142.

26. George Eldon Ladd, *A Commentary on the Revelation of John* (Grand Rapids: Wm. B. Eerdmans Publishing Co., 1972), p. 81.

27. R. H. Charles, *A Critical and Exegetical Commentary on the Revelation of St. John* (Edinburgh: T. & T. Clark, 1920), Vol. I, p. 138.

28. Mounce, p. 152.

29. T. F. Glasson, *The Revelation of John* (Cambridge: Cambridge University Press, 1965), p. 48.

30. Mounce, p. 152.

31. Preston and Hanson, p. 79.

32. See Caird, p. 97.

33. Preston and Hanson, pp. 86-87.

34. Glasson, pp. 59-60.

35. Sergius Bulgakov, *The Orthodox Church* (London: Centenary Press, 1935; 2nd ed. New York: Morehouse Publishing Co., 1960), p. 203.

36. Sergius Bulgakov, *The Orthodox Church*, p. 210.

37. Mikhail Bulgakov, *The White Guard*, tr. Michael Glenny (McGraw-Hill Book Co., 1971), pp. 294-95.

WORKS CITED

The Apocryphal Books of the New Testament. Philadelphia: Gebbie & Co., 1890.

Arenberg, Carol. "Mythic and Daimonic Paradigms in Bulgakov's *Master I Margarita*." *Essays in Literature*, 9 (Spring 1972), 107-25.

Attwater, Donald. *The Christian Churches of the East*. Milwaukee: Bruce Publishing Co., 1961. Vol. I.

Saint Augustine, *The City of God, Books VIII-XVI*. Trans. Gerald G. Walsh and Grace Monaghan. Washington: Catholic University of America Press, 1952. Vol. 14 of *The Fathers of the Church*.

Avins, Carol. "Reaching a Reader: The Master's Audience in *The Master and Margarita*." *Slavic Review*, 45 (Summer 1986), 272-85.

Bagby, Lewis. "Eternal Themes in Mixail Bulgakov's *The Master and Margarita*." *International Fiction Review*, 1 (January 1974), 27-31.

Beatie, Bruce A., and Phyllis W. Powell. "Bulgakov, Dante, and Relativity." *Canadian-American Slavic Studies*, 15 (Summer-Fall 1981), 250-70.

——————. "Story and Symbol: Notes toward a Structural Analysis of Bulgakov's *The Master and Margarita*." *Russian Literature Triquarterly*, 15 (1978), 219-51.

Benz, Ernst. *The Eastern Orthodox Church*. Chicago: Aldine Publishing Co., 1963.

Bethea, David M. "History as Hippodrome: The Apocalyptic Horse and Rider in *The Master and Margarita*." *Russian Review*, 41 (October 1982), 373-99.

——————. *The Shape of Apocalypse in Modern Russian Fiction*. Princeton: Princeton University Press, 1989.

Blake, Patricia. "A Bargain with the Devil." *New York Times Book Review*, October 27, 1967, 1, 71.

Bolen, Val. "Theme and Coherence in Bulgakov's *The Master and Margarita*." *Slavic and East European Journal*, 16 (Winter 1972), 427-37.

Bulgakov, Mikhail. *Black Snow: A Theatrical Novel*. Trans. Michael Glenny. New York: Simon and Schuster, 1967.

——————. *Diaboliad and Other Stories*. Eds. Ellendea and Carl R. Proffer. Bloomington: Indiana University Press, 1972.

——————. *The Early Plays of Mikhail Bulgakov*. Ed. Ellendea Proffer. Bloomington: Indiana University Press, 1972.

——————. *The Life of Monsieur de Moliere*. Trans. Mirra Ginsburg. New York: Funk and Wagnalls, 1970.

——————. *The Master and Margarita*. Trans. Michael Glenny. New York: Harper & Row, 1967.

——————. *The Master and Margarita*. Trans. Mirra Ginsburg. New York: Grove Press, 1967.

——————. *The White Guard*. Trans. Michael Glenny. New York: McGraw-Hill Book Co., 1971.

Bulgakov, Sergius. *A Bulgakov Anthology*. Eds. James Pain and Nicolas Zernov. Philadelphia: Westminster Press, 1976.

——————. "Meditations on the Joy of the Resurrection." In *Ultimate Questions: An Anthology of Modern Russian Religious Thought*. Ed. Alexander Schmemann. New York: Holt, Rinehart, Winston, 1965.

————. *The Orthodox Church*. London: Centenary Press, 1935. 2nd ed. New York: Morehouse Publishing Co., 1960.

————. *The Wisdom of God*. New York: Paisley Press, 1937.

Caird, G. B. *A Commentary on the Revelation of St. John the Divine*. New York: Harper & Row, 1966.

Calian, Carnegie S. *Icon and Pulpit*. Philadelphia: Westminster Press, 1968.

Charles, R. H. *The Apocrypha and Pseudepigrapha of the Old Testament*. London: Oxford University Press, 1963. Vol. II.

————. *A Critical and Exegetical Commentary on the Revelation of St. John*. Edinburgh: T. & T. Clark, 1920. Vol. I.

Chudakova, Marietta. "*The Master and Margarita*: The Development of a Novel." *Russian Literature Triquarterly*, 15 (1978), 177-209.

Dalmais, Irenee Henri. *Eastern Liturgies*. New York: Hawthorn Books, 1961.

Davenport, Guy. "With a Long Spoon." *National Review*, January 30, 1968, 92-94.

Deck, Priscilla Conwell. "Thematic Coherence in Bulgakov's *The Master and Margarita*." Unpublished Ph.D. dissertation, Brandeis University, 1976.

Delany, Joan. "*The Master and Margarita*: The Reach Exceeds the Grasp." *Slavic Review*, 31 (March 1972), 89-100.

Demetrakopoulos, George H. *Dictionary of Orthodox Theology*. New York: Philosophical Library, 1964.

"The Descent of the Virgin into Hell." In *Medieval Russia's Epics, Chronicles, and Tales*. Ed. Serge A. Zenkovsky. New York: E. P. Dutton and Co., 1974.

"The Devil in Moscow." *Time*, October 27, 1967, 105-106.

"Diabolical Experiment." *London Times Literary Supplement*, December 7, 1967, 1181.

Donehoo, James DeQuincey. *The Apocryphal and Legendary Life of Christ*. New York: Hodder & Stoughton, 1903.

Edwards, T. R. N. *Three Russian Writers and the Irrational: Zamyatin, Pil'nyak, and Bulgakov*. Cambridge: Cambridge University Press, 1982.

Ericson, Edward E., Jr. "The Satanic Incarnation: Parody in Bulgakov's *The Master and Margarita*." *Russian Review*, 33 (January 1974), 20-36.

Fanger, Donald. "Rehabilitated Experimentalist." *Nation*, January 22, 1968, 117-18.

Farrer, Austin M. *The Revelation of St. John the Divine*. Oxford: Clarendon Press, 1964.

Fiene, Donald M. "A Comparison of the Soviet and Possev Editions of *The Master and Margarita*, with a Note on Interpretation of the Novel." *Canadian-American Slavic Studies*, 15 (Summer-Fall 1981), 330-54.

————. "Further Elucidation of the Pilate Theme in Bulgakov's *The Master and Margarita*, with a Note on May Eve, Good Friday, and the Full Moon." Unpublished paper presented at Southern Conference on Slavic Studies. Atlanta, Georgia. October 8, 1983.

————. "A Note on May Eve, Good Friday, and the Full Moon in Bulgakov's *The Master and Margarita*." *Slavic and East European Journal*, 28 (1984), 533-37.

Fortescue, Adrian. *The Orthodox Eastern Church*. New York: Burt Franklin, 1969.

Frank, Margot K. "The Mystery of the Master's Final Destination." *Canadian-American Slavic Studies*, 15 (Summer-Fall 1981), 287-94.

French, R. M. *The Eastern Orthodox Church*. London: Hutchinson's University Library, 1951.

Ginzberg, Louis. *The Legends of the Jews*. Philadelphia: The Jewish Publication Society of America, 1912, Vols. I, V.

Glasson, T. F. *The Revelation of John*. Cambridge: Cambridge University Press, 1965.

Glenny, Michael. "Existential Thought in Bulgakov's *The Master and Margarita*." *Canadian-American Slavic Studies*, 15 (Summer-Fall 1981), 238-49.

—————. "Mikhail Bulgakov." *Survey*, October 1967, 3-14.

Gutry, Shirley Ann. "An Approach to *The Master and Margarita* through the Creative Prose and the Letters of M. A. Bulgakov." Unpublished Ph.D. dissertation, Princeton University, 1976.

Haber, Edythe C. "The Mythic Structure of Bulgakov's *The Master and Margarita*." *Russian Review*, 34 (October 1975), 382-409.

Hamilton, Ian. "Revenger." *Listener*, November 30, 1967, 727.

Hart, Pierre R. "*The Master and Margarita* as Creative Process." *Modern Fiction Studies*, 19 (1973), 169-78.

Hatfield, Henry. "The Walpurgis Night: Themes and Variations." *Journal of European Studies*, 13 (1983), 56-74.

Howe, Irving. "The Continuity of Russian Voices." *Harper's*, January 1968, 69-74.

Ivsky, Oleg. Untitled Review. *Library Journal*, October 15, 1967, 3658.

Johnson, Vida Taranovski. "The Thematic Function of the Narrator in *The Master and Margarita*." *Canadian-American Slavic Studies*, 15 (Summer-Fall 1981), 271-86.

Kejna-Sharratt, Barbara. "Narrative Techniques in *The Master and Margarita*." *Canadian Slavonic Papers*, 16 (Spring 1974), 1-12.

—————. "The Tale of Two Cities: The Unifying Function of the Setting in Mikhail Bulgakov's *The Master and Margarita*." *Forum for Modern Language Studies*, 16 (1980), 331-40.

Ladd, George Eldon. *A Commentary on the Revelation of John*. Grand Rapids: Wm. B. Eerdmans Publishing Co., 1972.

Lakshin, V. "M. Bulgakov's Novel *The Master and Margarita*." *Soviet Studies in Literature*, 5 (Winter 1968-69), 3-65. Trans. and rptd. from *Novy Mir*, 1968, no. 6.

Larousse Encyclopedia of Mythology. London: Paul Hamlyn, 1959.

Lea, Henry Charles. *Materials toward a History of Witchcraft*. New York: Thomas Yoseloff, 1957. Vol. I.

Le Guillou, M. J. *The Spirit of Eastern Orthodoxy*. New York: Hawthorn Books, 1962.

Levin, Elena. "Exuberant Works by a Russian Who Talked Back to Stalin." *Saturday Review*, April 29, 1972, 59-61, 64, 66.

Lyons, Arthur. *The Second Coming: Satanism in America*. New York: Dodd, Mead & Co., 1970.

Mahlow, Elena N. *Bulgakov's The Master and Margarita: The Text as a Cipher*. New York: Vantage Press, 1975.

Meyendorff, John. *The Orthodox Church*. London: Darton, Longman and Todd, 1960.

—————. "The Time of Holy Saturday." In *Orthodox Synthesis: The Unity of Theological Thought*. Ed. Jospeh J. Allen. Crestwood, N.Y.: St. Vladimir's Seminary Press, 1981.

Milne, Lesley. *The Master and Margarita: A Comedy of Victory*. Birmingham, England: Birmingham Slavonic Monographs, 1977.

Morison, Frank. *And Pilate Said—: A New Study of the Roman Procurator*. London: Rich & Cowan, Ltd., 1939.

Mounce, Robert H. *The Book of Revelation.* Grand Rapids: Wm. B. Eerdmans Publishing Co., 1977.

Muchnic, Helen. "Laughter in the Dark." *New York Review of Books,* July 11, 1968, 26-28.

Natov, Nadine. "Mikhail Bulgakov 1891-1981: Preface." *Canadian-American Slavic Studies,* 15 (Summer-Fall 1981), 149-50.

Ouspensky, Leonide. *Theology of the Icon.* Crestwood, N.Y.: St. Vladimir's Seminary Press, 1978.

Pawel, Ernst. "The Devil in Moscow." *Commentary,* March 1968, 90-93.

Pearce, C. E. "A Closer Look at Narrative Structure in Bulgakov's *The Master and Margarita.*" *Canadian Slavonic Papers,* 22 (1980), 358-71.

Piper, D. G. B. "An Approach to Bulgakov's *The Master and Margarita.*" *Forum for Modern Language Studies,* 7 (April 1971), 134-57.

Pope, Richard W. F. "Ambiguity and Meaning in *The Master and Margarita*: The Role of Afranius." *Slavic Review,* 36 (March 1977), 1-24.

Preston, Ronald H., and Anthony T. Hanson. *The Revelation of St. John the Divine.* London: SCM Press, 1965.

Proffer, Ellendea. *Bulgakov: Life and Work.* Ann Arbor: Ardis, 1984.

————. "Bulgakov's *The Master and Margarita*: Genre and Motif." *Canadian Slavic Studies,* 3 (Winter 1969), 615-28.

————. "The Major Works of Mikhail Bulgakov." Unpublished Ph.D. dissertation, Indiana University, 1970.

————. "On *The Master and Margarita.*" *Russian Literature Triquarterly,* 6 (Spring 1973), 533-64.

————. "Red-Bricked Moscow: 1921-23." *Canadian-American Slavic Studies,* 15 (Summer-Fall 1981), 167-91.

Pruitt, Donald B. "St. John and Bulgakov: The Model of a Parody of Christ." *Canadian-American Slavic Studies,* 15 (Summer-Fall 1981), 312-20.

Robbins, Russell Hope. *The Encyclopedia of Witchcraft and Demonology.* New York: Crown Publishers, 1959.

Rosenthal, Raymond. "Bulgakov's Sentimental Devil." *New Leader,* November 20, 1967, 18-19.

Russell, D. S. *The Method and Message of Jewish Apocalyptic, 200 B.C.-A.D. 100.* Philadelphia: Westminster Press, 1964.

Russell, Jeffrey Burton. *Lucifer: The Devil in the Middle Ages.* Ithaca, N.Y.: Cornell University Press, 1984.

Schmemann, Alexander. *Introduction to Liturgical Theology.* Portland, Maine: American Orthodox Press, 1966.

Shann, G. V. *Euchology: A Manual of the Holy Orthodox Church.* New York: AMS Press, 1969. Rpt. of 1891 edition.

Simmons, Ernest J. "Out of the Drawer, Into the Light." *Saturday Review,* November 11, 1967, 35-36, 56.

Skorino, L. "Characters without Carnival Masks." *Soviet Studies in Literature,* 5 (Spring 1969), 20-45. Trans. and rptd. from *Voprosy Literatury,* 1968, no. 6.

Solotaroff, Theodore. "Christ and the Commissars." *New Republic,* December 2, 1967, 26-29.

Stenbock-Fermor, Elisabeth. "Bulgakov's *The Master and Margarita* and Goethe's *Faust.*" *Slavic and East European Journal,* 13 (1969), 309-26.

Summers, Montague. *The History of Witchcraft and Demonology*. New York: University Books, 1956.

Tertz, Abram (Andrei Sinyavsky). "Thought Unaware." *New Leader*, July 19, 1965, 9-15.

Thompson, Ewa. "The Artistic World of Michael Bulgakov." *Russian Literature*, 5 (1973), 54-64.

Thompson, R. Campbell. *Semitic Magic: Its Origins and Development*. London: Luzac & Co., 1908.

Tikos, Laszlo. "Some Notes on the Significance of Gerbert Aurillac in Bulgakov's *The Master and Margarita*." *Canadian-American Slavic Studies*, 15 (Summer-Fall 1981), 321-29.

Ullman, Judy C. "The Conflict between the Individual and Authority in the Works of Mixail Bulgakov." Unpublished Ph.D. dissertation, University of Chicago, 1976.

Wedeck, Harry E. *Treasury of Witchcraft*. New York: Philosophical Library, 1961.

Weeks, Laura D. "Hebraic Antecedents in *The Master and Margarita*: Woland and Company Revisited." *Slavic Review*, 43 (Summer 1984), 224-41.

————. "In Defense of the Homeless: On the Uses of History and the Role of Bezdomnyi in *The Master and Margarita*." *Russian Review*, 48 (1989), 45-65.

Williams, David. "New Novels." *Punch*, December 20, 1967, 950.

Wright, A. Colin. *Mikhail Bulgakov: Life and Interpretations*. Toronto: University of Toronto Press, 1978.

————. "Mikhail Bulgakov's Developing World View." *Canadian-American Slavic Studies*, 15 (Summer-Fall 1981), 151-66.

Zernov, Nicolas. *Eastern Christendom*. New York: G. P. Putnam's Sons, 1961.

————. *The Russian Religious Renaissance of the Twentieth Century*. New York: Harper & Row, 1963.

————. *The Russians and Their Church*. London: S. P. C. K., 1945.

INDEX

STUDIES IN SLAVIC LANGUAGE AND LITERATURE